A TALE OF
Two Lives

A TALE OF
Two Lives

CARIN RENTON

PARTRIDGE

To order additional copies of this book, contact
Toll Free 800 101 2657 (Singapore)
Toll Free 1 800 81 7340 (Malaysia)
orders.singapore@partridgepublishing.com

www.partridgepublishing.com/singapore

Based on a True Story

This book is dedicated to my three wonderful
children, who I love with all my heart.

My Childhood

As I try to remember my childhood, it is truly a mixture of churning memories and feelings experienced.

We lived in an old, converted three level house in Lambeth, London, England. We lived on the top floor, with my father's aunt, Auntie Doll and her husband Charlie (who was a miserable old coot) on the second floor and Nellie and Charlie on the ground floor. We all had old, black grates that burned coal, and the rooms had gas lighting and one of the worst experiences of my young life, was having to go downstairs to the cellar and bring up a bucket of coal for the fire. There was no light in the cellar, it was dirty and worst of all there were spiders in it, and we had to go and get the coal by the light of a torch. There were no lights on the stairs either, so my child's imagination knew all about the boogie men, etc., who lurked on the landings on the way back upstairs to our living room. "Jack Frost" was another danger on those stairs. He was always a threat to nipping at my toes when I went out on to the landing between our living room and my bedroom. He was especially active during the Winter months!

Initially I was in a cot, then bed in my parents' bedroom but ultimately they moved into the big front bedroom (which was really cold in Winter) and their original bedroom became mine. I had a stimulating view of a brick wall from my bedroom window so consequently from a very young age I was always changing round my room and putting my bed in different places to get a different perspective. It was always so exciting to go to bed that night, when I had spent most of the preceding day changing my room around, each corner of the room felt totally different.

Up to the age of 10, I think I had a fairly "normal" upbringing in London, in a loving home with a not so loving, older brother - Peter! Fleeting memories pass through my mind of sitting in my pram outside our front door on a warm, sunny day and another of being in my cot, one night, crying because I wanted my mother

1

and this large lady, who would have been my grandmother, coming in and telling me my parents had gone out for a short while and to "hush ma weesht". We must have gone to visit her in Scotland.

At the age of 3 I began dancing classes and our dance school gave an annual concert for parents and friends. I was blessed with a fairly tuneful voice as a child so was often singled out to sing solos or do small dance sequences. I have vivid memories of singing my heart out on stage with not a vestige of nerves (probably not a lot of tune either). The weeks running up to these performances were a whirl of rehearsals, costume fittings and excitement! Many years later when I watched my own child on stage, the memories returned of how it felt being up there, and the terror of knowing that you could not remember the next move in the dance routine, but also the fun of performing.

When I was 5 Peter and I went on a day trip being run by the church Sunday school where our downstairs neighbours went to church. I know my mother had misgivings about my going and told me afterwards she was worried about me all day. We went to the boating pond in Hyde Park. At one time my brother got hold of a boat and told me to get in, however when I had one foot in the boat and the other on dry land the boat pulled away (whether by accident or design I will never know) from the side of the pond and inevitably I fell into the water. I don't remember how deep it was, only that it was cold! I was, of course, soaked through and as it was a cool, autumn day, the ladies in charge were frantically trying to find towels and blankets to wrap me in. We had gone to the park in a coach and no one thought to get me sent home by taxi, so I spent the rest of the day looking like a third world refugee. The rest of the day is a blur, but as we arrived back to all the parents waiting for us that evening, my mother was frantically looking for me as she had heard one of the alighting children tell their parents that a little girl had fallen into the water and she knew instinctively that the "little girl" was me. She was furious with our neighbour because no one had arranged to get me home and she threatened physical violence if I suffered any ill effects from the day out! (Mum had an awesome temper when it came to protecting "her young"). A further dominant memory of that day, however, is that Mum had bought me some new flannelette pyjamas and after warming me in front of the fire in the big black grate, she dressed me in these and I felt warm, cosy and loved.

Mum would pay into a Christmas Club at the toy shop at the top of our street for the year preceding each Christmas. We always got a main toy, a secondary toy, the latest annual (book) and they had the most tremendous lolly novelties. They were works of art. One year my lolly novelty was a castle! It was beautiful; pink and silver with little doors that opened to reveal incredible (lolly) goodies! They were played with as much as our main toys. In my early years we would go downstairs to Auntie Nellie and Uncle Charlie's living room for a Christmas party sometime over the Christmas break and there would be singsongs around the piano and as I grew and learned more dance steps I would be called upon to "do a little dance" for everyone. Christmas really was a fun time when I was young.

My mother had a cat called "Dinkie" of whom I was very jealous because she was older than me and she would jump on to my mother's lap and stand with her paws around mum's neck, for all the world like a child. Mum thought the world of Dinkie. As we lived in the top flat of our house, Dinkie could not go out at ground floor level so she used to jump from our living room window out on to the roof every day. I have no idea where she went from there but she never "dirtied" inside the house ever! I remember when Dinkie died. Mum was heartbroken. Apparently Dinkie had jumped through the window in her normal way, then seemed to suffer a stroke, dying the following day. Mum cried so hard, and it is only now, after losing several much loved cats of my own through the years that I understand the extent of her grief at losing an old friend in Dinkie.

Following Dinkie's demise Peter and I were allowed to get a kitten each. As we were upstairs we had to provide a litter tray for their use. This came in the form of an old bath at the back of our scullery (kitchen). Kitty litter was not heard of then, we used sawdust which I used to go and collect, a bag at a time, from the saw mill which backed on to the back of our house. It was my job to clean the litter tray – as usual my brother never did anything to help. Peter's cat was a beautiful black and white female, he named "Whiskey". My cat was a tortoiseshell Manx cat which we called "Gill" (sounded better than Gin). The first night we got our kittens home we took them to bed with us, (or rather I put Gill in my doll's pram, just like a baby) and tended to their needs all night. Peter was found in the morning lying on his bedding on the floor next to Whiskey and when asked why he said "Well, she wouldn't come up to my bed so I went down to sleep with her". Sounded logical to me!

Whiskey and Gill were true character cats. Gill would jump on to my shoulder and drape herself around my neck like a scarf. She followed me everywhere and I loved her very much. When she "spoke" her little stump of a tail would move up and down in time with her little noises. Whiskey was such a beautiful cat and terribly vain. The pair of them reminded me of sisters, one the beauty of the family and the other the "tomboy". They would sit, side by side, at the end of the dresser each evening, to "welcome" each family member home. We always knew when someone was coming upstairs because they would both move from where they were sitting and go (as a pair of bookends) and sit looking at the door until our "visitor" arrived.

Peter was five years older than me so we didn't interact very much. It appeared he was always in trouble though, judging by the number of times my mum would "belt" him. She had an old army belt (I think belonging to my father) that used to send Peter scurrying to his room. He also had fights with some of the boys in the neighbourhood, one in particular, Johnny, was his mortal enemy and conversely my mother was often on the Baker doorstep threatening blood and violence to Johnny's mother if she didn't keep her "bully-boy son" away from my brother! Peter was most often out playing and I was kept pretty busy with my dancing lessons and when not going to those, I enjoyed reading. I had a voracious appetite for books, and still enjoy a good book.

Mum and Dad appeared to my young eyes to be a devoted couple and up until the age of 10/11, I do not remember them having a cross-word. Dad was a very quiet man and admittedly let my mother do what she wanted. As it was in those days, he did not interact much with us children; he was the man who woke me in the morning for school then disappeared "to the city" to work, then would appear again at night.

When I was 5 years old the Princess Elizabeth was crowned Queen following the death of her father George VI. The whole of London was treated to street parties, with all the local councils funding drinks and cakes spread out on trestle tables adorned with red, white and blue tablecloths, for the enjoyment of their ratepayers. Television was not particularly widespread at that time, so the few neighbours who had these wonderful inventions opened their living rooms to welcome as many of their neighbours as the room would hold, to view the spectacle of the young princess being crowned. The sun felt warm on my head as I twirled around in my beautiful new white dress, with red, white and blue sash, bought especially for the occasion, impatiently waiting to go and join the street party in progress.

Not far away from where I lived there was a market – Wandsworth Road Markets – where mum used to find a wide variety of (pre-loved) dresses and clothes for me. She loved buying me pretty dresses; I was indeed the envy of quite a few of my friends because of the number of dresses I owned. There was also a copious supply of baby clothes for my dolls, rendering my dolls better dressed than a lot of babies in my district!

When I was about eight years old I was happily out riding on my new roller skates when I lost my footing and fell very heavily on the base of my spine. There I sat on the kerbing incapable of either speech or movement for several seconds (I cannot recall just how long), before cautiously heaving myself up and making my way slowly and painfully, home. I believe I told mum "I had a fall today" but nothing else was said. However, in retrospect I realise that I badly damaged my spine on that day, the upshot of which was not entirely evident until some 20 years on! From that time onwards, however, I did experience an excruciating headache after performing acrobatics, etc., at dancing and could not understand why other children could enjoy handstands, cartwheels, etc., when it caused such pain. I did not know, of course, that they did not experience pain, only I did and it was not "normal" as I thought it was.

Every year my mum and dad would take us for a holiday to the seaside. The place we most seemed to frequent was Folkstone where we normally booked a caravan for the two weeks we were there. It was always so exciting the night before. Mum would pack our clothes into two huge suitcases, which my poor father had to heft down the three flights of stairs into a waiting taxi. The night before it was always difficult to sleep, we were so excited. Mum would make egg or egg and tomato sandwiches for the train trip and there would be the inevitable flask of tea for them and a bottle of Tizer or Lemonade for us children to drink on the train. There would be the mad, exciting ride to the railway station – usually Euston – in the taxi then all of us carrying our various bags of precious belongings, (buckets and spades, favourite dolls, cars, etc) on to the train. We would then watch as the dreary environs of London flashed by to be replaced by the green of fields of the country, dotted here and there with black and white cattle grazing lazily on the grass. Then we would eventually arrive at Folkstone, and get another taxi to our caravan site. Even now I can hear the sound of the seagulls as they circled around our caravan site, and smell the ozone of the sea, so alien to us, living as we did in the heart of London.

My brother would be up at the crack of dawn everyday we were away, and take himself down to the local fishing wharves and spend most of his day with the fishermen down there, returning in the evening with a fish one of them had given him or he had caught. Mum, dad and I would spend hours on the beach, with me building sandcastles and paddling in the water. Then we would wander into the townsite and get some afternoon tea and cakes. In the evening mum and dad would go down to the local pub and under the fairy lights outside sit and listen to the music playing and sometimes dance to it, while Peter and I would watch, happily munching on our packets of crisps and drinking our lemonade. Wonderful, wonderful memories.

Near where we lived there was a "green belt" full of bushes, shrubs and small trees with a carpet of soft grass. The small trees and shrubs formed various natural cubbies and hidey holes just meant for children to play "witches and fairies", "victims and kidnappers", "cops and robbers", etc. Many a weekend hour and early evening during the Summer months were spent playing around there. One day, however, we were playing and we noticed a "funny looking woman" coming out of a house nearby. I went home and told my parents this woman looked like a man but was dressed as a woman. They told me not to worry about it, but "she" intrigued us kids, so we started to watch for "her". I have to admit we made life hell for that person, as of course kids being kids we followed and heckled and generally were awful to what was, of course, a cross-dressing man. There was also a young man who intrigued me as he had a swathe of grey hair all across one side of his head. I could not understand why a "young man" would have grey hair and I would find myself staring unashamedly at him whenever he came into sight.

When I reflect on my early childhood I see how simple life was when I was growing up. Dad worked and "kept us" and Mum mainly stayed home but sometimes had a "little job" such as cleaning or worked in a café, etc. Food was the real thing, by that I mean we ate butter, brown or white bread, drank full cream milk, tea, coffee and the staple was a roast – with vegies, sometimes grown from your own vegie patch but mostly bought from your friendly local greengrocer.

Shopping consisted of taking a list round to your local grocer, handing it to him and he collected the items, put them in a brown paper bag or a box, you either paid cash or had credit – which was usually in place from pay day to pay day and sometimes – if he was a friendly grocer – he would pop in a free lollipop for the courier – me.

On the corner near my home was a baker and one of my fondest memories is taking my threepence or sixpence to this shop and even before I made my choice from the delicious array of cakes, buns, doughnuts and tarts, I could savour the anticipated taste by experiencing the aroma of freshly baked bread and cakes pouring out of the front door and reaching me 20 yards away. School holidays, particularly, were the best because Mum would leave me a few pence when she left for her early morning cleaning job and I would go to the baker and get a freshly made iced bun packed with dried fruit, so fresh it collapsed in your fingers on its way to your mouth. Or there were the fresh cream doughnuts, which left a moustache of sugar long after the last delectable bite had been taken.

There was also a fish and chip shop not far from my home and sometimes I would go there and get sixpen'orth of chips and go and sit in the park to eat them and drink from my bottle of Tizer or Lemonade and contemplate in my childish way, the simple joys of life.

I loved books and in the early days of television there was plenty of time to read a good book because TV transmission was limited so there were long periods when we actually had to amuse ourselves. Living in London the long Summery evenings were filled with playing at the park, riding a bike or simply sitting in the fading light and warmth reading a book. Occasionally, after tea, all the children in the street would get together and play a game of "rounders" – a kind of neighbourhood baseball, or "run-outs" where we would form teams – one to run and hide, the other to seek out. The idea was that the team hiding had to get back to a designated base camp before the seeking team could tag us. We would get so engrossed in our game, our parents would have to come and get us to go inside for bed.

Mum was usually home when I got home from school, ready for me to spill out the day's trials and tribulations. There was usually a food treat to go with the cup of tea we would enjoy together, then I either had dancing class to prepare for, which I went to on my own – we did not have a car – or I would play out with friends or read until it was time to wash for "tea" as we called it. Evenings were spent colouring in, playing a card game or two with my brother and later, watching the early TV programmes, before we were packed off to bed at about 8.00/8.30.

Picnics were another joyous occupation of my childhood. Our little group of girls would all agree to go home and make up something to bring back for a communal picnic, i.e. jam sandwiches, biscuits, and lollies! a bottle of drink, etc., then we would all meet up again and go round to the local park for a play and eat our picnic. Sometimes we would all take a doll and pram, and at other times we would concentrate on the swings and roundabouts. Food never tasted so good as when we ate it together at the park.

When we had a caller to our house, they would ring the bell three times, to signify they wanted the occupants on the third floor. We would look out of the top window and call "who is it" and whoever was on our doorstep would step out, look up and announce themselves. Every so often that caller would be my mother's sister, Auntie Mina, from Coventry – who would arrive totally unannounced for a visit. She was always a source of excitement to us children as she always brought with her some little gift for each of us and the evenings would be spent in the three of them sitting talking about old times and current happenings. Her son, also named Peter – and my cousin, was in the navy. He was considerably older than me and we would love hearing about his current whereabouts and activities. He and a friend, Bill, would also come and stay when their ship was in port and I have to admit to having a "crush" on Bill when I was 8!

One year, around 1957, my mother's other sister, Auntie Cissy, wrote and asked if she and mum (and me) could go away for a holiday together instead of the usual holiday with mum and dad. I remember mum wanted to go but dad was a little hurt that his holiday this year was not going to happen, however, as with everything to do with mum, dad did not stop her. When Mum saw her she was horrified at the weight which Auntie Cissy had lost and remarked on it to her. It turned out that Auntie Cissy had been told she had throat cancer and did not have long to live, how short that time was, we just did not realise. The time with Auntie Cissy, on holiday, was fun in spite of the awful cough I remember her having and the shortness of breath she experienced. She died not long after returning from that holiday and I know my father was eternally grateful that he had not stood in the way of my mother spending that time with her sister – my mother, whilst being a loving person, was sometimes an unforgiving one!

With electricity now widespread (I feel so old knowing I actually lived in a house lit by gaslight!) the wonderful new invention of television began spreading through all homes. At first they were big and cumbersome and it was normal to rent them rather than own them. When they first transmitted they used to shut down between 6.00 and 7.30pm and of course were not on during the day as they are now. Saturday evenings were a crushing bore to me as dad's soccer pools results would go on and on for ages. He played the pools every week, always chasing that dream of winning the 8 draws games and amassing a fortune. Much like we play lotto these days. I hated the black and white minstrel show, which mum used to love watching! The Sunday afternoon movies, however, were a different story. We would all be replete from a delicious Sunday lunch and would settle down to watch the afternoon matinee until about 5.00pm breaking up the viewing with a cup of tea and cake about 3.30.

We did not have a bathroom in our flat – I always envied my friends in their modern flats, which had a bathroom! Our bathroom consisted of a tin bath filled up from the copper in the corner of the scullery on a Sunday evening, in which we would all take turns having a bath. Dad was usually last and would empty out some of the (by now) disgustingly grubby water and replace it with some fresh. Then, freshly scrubbed and cleaned we would settle down to a delicious tea, sometimes of beans on toast, or spaghetti or soup – as we had had a large (main) meal in the middle of the day. Happily anticipating the evening's entertainment on the television.

Sometimes mum and dad would decide that they wanted to go to see a film, so we would either walk down to the "local" cinema or jump on a bus and go to a cinema in the near vicinity. When we went to the local cinema we would stop at the local fish and chip shop on the way home, usually about 10.30/11.00pm and buy a bag of chips each, wrapped on the outside with newspaper and on a cold evening wander home munching our chips, thoroughly happy with our lot in life.

One evening my dad arrived home and was exceptionally quiet. He eventually told my mother that he had been laid off from his job because the company, was going into liquidation. Dad had worked there, man and boy for 20 years. He was a ship's estimator. He was handed a letter thanking him for his years' service and an ashtray! My mother was livid on his behalf. That was one of the reasons dad had not wanted to tell her but of course, had no choice when there was no job. She went down to his ex works and pushed her way into my father's former boss's office and was only just restrained by others present, from hitting him over the head with "his cursed ashtray" (spoken in the deepest Glaswegian accent!) She was escorted off the premises! Dad managed to get himself a job with another construction company and it turned out to be the best career move he could have made, unfortunately, it was not to be a long career move as he was dead 14 months later.

In the Christmas of 1958, New Year 1959, we all went to visit my Auntie Mina in Coventry. The Coventry Cathedral had been heavily bombed during the war and it had only recently been completely rebuilt complete with the 360-odd steps up to the top of the cathedral tower. We all decided to walk up the steps to the top. It was a heart bursting exercise, but the view was superb.

When we returned to London, however, dad's heart was beating so hard that if he stood on one side of the room you could see the beat of his heart against his shirt – something was not right! Mum, of course, marched him off to the doctor and he was informed that he had a leaking valve in the heart. They maintained he must have had Rheumatic Fever as a boy and this "leaking valve" problem was a direct result of this illness. He could not remember having Rheumatic Fever, but then he had been a fairly "sickly" boy he said so he most probably could have had it and not known. The news was bad, however, as in those days they did not have heart/lung machines to work on one's behalf whilst work is done on one's heart and he was not strong enough to undergo the operation. He was told to go home and rest and see if the condition improved. The doctors, of course, knew his condition was not going to improve, but there was nothing they could do.

Dad spent a couple of weeks in hospital on a salt free diet, on complete bed rest. He was then allowed home, again on the proviso that he rest. It was during this time that I heard my parents actually "argue" for the first time in my life. Mum had asked him if he wanted anything to eat and he had said "no" he was not hungry. However, after mum had started cooking he had decided he was hungry after all but when he told mum she was annoyed because she had not started cooking enough for him as well. I realised that they were both terribly, terribly worried and upset about dad being so gravely ill, and they were bickering. The impact on me then, however, was immense and unsettling.

Dad tried to go back to work but the effort to get to work and then get home again became harder and harder for him. One Friday mum insisted he go to the hospital to see his heart specialist. She took him in a taxi. When they got there his specialist was not on duty and there was no one prepared to see him. He was positively grey, he was so ill, but they told mum to take him home and make another appointment next week. Mum pleaded, yelled and begged someone to see him, all to no avail. So she took dad home again, this time by bus, as they did not have enough money for another taxi. The journey home was a nightmare for them both. Dad could hardly get his breath and he still had to walk the length of our street – and up our stairs – before he could rest. He walked so slowly it took them five hours to get him eventually home and into bed. That night he had his first heart attack. Mum rang the doctor but there was no one there. In those days you could not ring an ambulance without the permission of a doctor, so she could not ring for help. There followed three more heart attacks before the next day. She frantically, managed to contact our doctor on the Saturday morning who was livid when he heard that they had actually had my father in the hospital the previous day and had let him go home! He arranged for an ambulance to get him and I did not see Dad again, as he died the following morning, peacefully in his sleep, at 8.30am on 15 February 1959.

I GROW UP VERY FAST!

$\mathcal{F}$ollowing the death of my father, I grew up very fast. My mother was heartbroken and totally incapable of being a mother to me or my brother from then on. Indeed, all she wanted to do was die and join him.

The day of the funeral dawned grey and cold as my Auntie Nell took me separately to the cemetery so as to avoid the church service. I am not sure why I was not allowed to go to the service, presumably my mother felt it was too sad an occasion for me to experience, which was bizarre really because I was taken to the cemetery later for his burial. I was wearing a new pale blue coat which Mum had bought especially for the funeral and stood in stark contrast beside Mum who was dressed entirely in black as were most of the mourners at the graveside.

I had been to "see" dad at the funeral parlour, but hadn't touched him, so looking at him he appeared to be just asleep. Because I had not had a great deal of interaction with dad I could not really mourn him or miss him, I remember more being concerned about what was happening to my mother. She was my mainstay now and was decidedly unstable at that! I did not know what to feel. In fact on the Monday following my father's death I was at school and said in a very matter-of-fact voice, "My father died yesterday" and was acutely hurt as one of my friends said "well, you don't look very upset about it!"

My brother, who had been getting into trouble (with petty crime and theft) tried to be "the man" of the family but I think he was tied in knots of guilt because not long before dad's death he and dad had had an awful fight which nearly came to blows and I think he secretly, wrongly blamed himself for hastening dad's death. He did try to take an overdose of Aspirin but all he got for his trouble was very sick and was left permanently slightly deaf in the one ear.

I had always hated confrontation. I was very much my father's daughter in that way and found it difficult to say what was on my mind. One day my brother was standing in the kitchen talking about "being no good" to mum and me, that

11

"it would be better to bugger off and leave us be". I desperately wanted to say how much we needed – mum needed – him but the words would not come to my 10 year old lips. He continued to get into trouble and finished up being sent down to a borstal for a while.

Before he was sent down, however, he had an awful accident. Peter used to clean windows on a Saturday morning to earn some extra money. Prior to one Saturday morning he hurt his wrist and it was strapped up. Mum was not happy with him going out doing his window cleaning as he cleaned 4 and 5 storey flat windows. He insisted he was okay and off he went.

At about 11.00am that day there was a knock at the door and once again a policeman was standing there. This time the police were calling to let us know that my brother had had an accident. He had been cleaning the windows of a third floor flat when he had lost his grip on the side on which he had his weak wrist and had fallen the three storeys to the ground. The flats in London at that time were very often surrounded by spiked railings and this was the case here. He told us later he could see he would land on his head so somehow managed to twist in mid air and push himself away from the railing with his feet as he landed – full blast on his feet. He broke every bone in both his feet. They were such a mess!

He was taken to the nearest emergency hospital where my mother and I rushed off to straight away. The doctors at the hospital could do nothing for his feet at this point as they were so badly smashed up. They could only wait and see what healing took place by itself concerning the smaller bones of the foot and then try and work on the larger bones later. He was in hospital for weeks and had several operations and of course was in dreadful pain.

My mother was working on the day he was released from hospital so I had to go and escort him home, on crutches, that day. It was an horrendous journey. Peter was in desperate pain and having to get on and off buses, followed by the long walk down our avenue he was in agony by the time we got home and I just did not know what to do to help him. He had been given some painkillers by the hospital, but they barely touched the pain he was in. It was a terrible time.

If my brother could have directed his will power into positive activities he would have been a very rich man. He was determined to walk again, despite the fact that the doctors told him he would need to walk with crutches and would ultimately end up in a wheelchair because of the injuries to his feet. But walk he did and even managed to ride a motorbike a year or so later. He was and still is in constant pain from his ankles and through the years has had so many operations to put pins in his anklebones, etc., that when he travels he has to let the airport staff know about it before he goes through the detectors, because the metal sets off the alarms!

The ensuing 18 months to two years following my father's death were really awful for me. Mum was terribly depressed, to the point that I began to dread leaving her on her own because I did not know if she would be alive when I came home. She had several blackouts at work and to a certain extent, I think she had a nervous breakdown. Added to everything else, she had been through the ordeal of going to court over my brother and hearing him sentenced to two years in borstal – even with his injured ankles he had managed to break in to shops, etc., and ultimately been caught because he could not run away from the police! So then it was just the two of us.

Mum regularly ran out of money and began asking me to go and ask various neighbours and friends for "loans" which they and I knew they would never be repaid. I was very humiliated. It was at that time I grew to hate smoking with a vengeance! My mother would spend money on cigarettes when we did not have enough money to buy food! My child's mind could not understand it. We constantly owed rent money and existed from week to week!

In the April/May following my father's death I sat my "11-plus" exam. This exam was to separate primary school children into the respective groups to continue on to Grammar School, Central School or Secondary Modern. Children who went to Grammar school were those who ultimately went on to university or professional jobs. Central school children could go either way and children who only gained a pass to go to Secondary Modern schools (to all intents and purposes they had failed their exam), were usually the children who went on to be manual workers and work in the non-professional trades.

Apparently I just missed out on Grammar and was allocated Central. So was despatched to a local school for girls (VMSG). It was as if the move from primary school to senior school opened my academic eyes and from the moment I went to VMSG I excelled at everything I did, coming top of my form and top of each and every exam I took that following year. At school I was very happy, which was a blessing as things at home were not improving.

One day, as I was Form Captain at my school, I was asked to go and get a present for a teacher who was leaving VMSG, so duly left the school, caught a bus to Brixton markets to carry out my task. On the way I noticed my vision was rather strange and before long I was having difficulty seeing where I was going. I got off the bus and proceeded to be violently sick and developed an excruciating headache! I had no alternative but to turn around and try and get home. I can't remember how I did this but ultimately managed it. I was sick so many times and the pain in my head was the worst I had ever experienced in my short life. I was very afraid, not knowing what was wrong with me.

My brother was home when I got there and as I ran crying into my bedroom, he did the only thing he thought would comfort me and made a cup of tea. I tried to drink it but brought it straight back up again and tried to sink into the blessed oblivion of sleep until this dreadful headache subsided. I really thought I was going to die! My uncle had died of a cerebral haemorrhage and I was sure I was going to go the same way.

The headache subsided after about 10 hours but for the following couple of days I was very vague and tried to avoid sneezing as the jarring was excruciating to my head! This was the beginning of my experience with Migraine headaches, which I continued to suffer with for the rest of my life. I did not know for another three or four years, however, that this was the cause of the periodic terrible pain and nausea I suffered, usually on an annual basis.

At one stage my mother toyed with the idea of returning to her roots in Scotland and we travelled up to Glasgow to visit and stay with my Aunt Cissy's (widowed) husband. I remember very vividly his face when he opened the door to us (he was not expecting us as Mum wanted to surprise him and my cousin Angus), he thought my Aunt Cissy had come back to him because she and my mother were so similar in appearance. We stayed with him for a week, also catching up with my mother's older sister, Aunt Peggie, and my three cousins, Joan, Celia and Patricia who were considerably older than I was. It was in fact the last time I saw them, as after her stay in Scotland mum decided England was where she wanted to be – Scotland seemed very dour and forbidding to us both.

One of the worst aspects of living with someone with depression is the apparent total inability of the sufferer to care what is happening to anyone else around them. When the person suffering the depression happens to be a parent, the feelings engendered in a child are those of terrible insecurity and abandonment. This was the case with my mother and me. Mum just did not seem to be able to care what I was feeling or experiencing anymore, she was so caught up in her own sad, world there was no room for me. One such example was when I had a dreadful ear infection and was left to cope with it myself as best I could.

A group from my dancing school used to take a "show" round to old folks' homes from time to time and we travelled all over London with our little troupe. One evening we were performing at a venue, I had had to organise to get myself there because Mum was not home from work in time to take me (and in any case I had been taking myself everywhere for some time). I had had earache all day at school and as the evening wore on it became steadily worse. I believe the

Adrenalin from performing helped whilst I was on stage because I could dance and sing oblivious of the pain in my ear, but as soon as I got offstage it would come back with a vengeance. The other girls' mums were really sympathetic and gave me what painkillers they had so I managed to keep going through the performance. I cannot remember how I got home, but I do remember when I got there saying to my mum "I had a really bad earache tonight, mum and I wished you were with me." She replied in a very listless manner "did you dear?" and I felt totally abandoned by her at that point and miserably made myself a hot water bottle to take to bed, in the hope that it would help me cope with the pain. I now understand how devastating depression is, but I have never really been able to accept how self-orientated this disease is and have probably over compensated with my own children as a result.

We continued to live from hand to mouth in London but the time came when Mum decided she and I would have to move and she would go back into housekeeping work, which incorporated live in accommodation. This would, however, mean leaving London and all my hopes of a life in performance and theatre. If I thought the last year or so had been bad the next few months were even worse!

My sole companions were our cats, Whiskey and Gill. I loved Gill to distraction and she slept with me and when I was home was never really far away from my side. I had adopted Whiskey since my brother's departure so was also tremendously fond of her. After a few weeks my mother announced she had found a position in Somerset, in the west country of England (to my young mind, the end of the earth!) This would mean that we had to pack up everything, take a minimum with us and put the rest into storage. It also meant we had to get rid of our cats! I was devastated. Gill had been my sole comfort in these dark and sad days. They were only two years old and in perfect health and we had to send them off with the RSPCA, probably to be put down if they could not be found homes. Worst of all, I had to handle their pick up as Mum was still working and the RSPCA would only pick up during the day. That day is etched in my memory as being one of the saddest days of my life. I cried uncontrollably as my Gill and her sister were placed into cages. As Gill was taken from my arms she clung to me as if she knew what was about to happen. To think about it even now brings tears to my eyes, 42 years later! I think I cried solidly for the next two days and don't think I ever really forgave my mother, even though in hindsight I realise she felt it was the only thing to do for us at the time. It took me a very long time to care about another cat in the same way I loved my Gill, in fact I don't think I have ever loved a cat to quite the same extent since!

Our dancing school was putting on its annual performance just prior to my and mum's departure into the depths of the country, and it was after I performed my solo singing spot at this show that I was pushed back on stage and in front of an audience of 300 plus people I was presented with a farewell gift and wished good luck. It was a moving time for me also a sad one as I knew I would no longer be able to continue my dancing and singing career. I was too advanced in my levels to be teachable outside of the London area. I felt my world was really collapsing in on itself.

1960 – 1966

We arrived in a small village in Somerset called Wenton. Mum had been offered and accepted a position as house assistant, live-in, at a guest house situated a bus run from Weston-Super-Mare.

Mum was domestic help to a couple who ran a holiday guest house. It was a large sprawling manor house standing in the middle of several acres of wood and grassland and miles from anywhere. They had two children about my age and Mum and I shared a very large room above a garage. I had the chance to earn a little money too, as I helped in the kitchen, mainly loading and unloading the large dishwasher following meals.

I was given my first experience at horse riding, but unfortunately after only about 3 lessons, one day a car driving up the drive a little too fast spooked the horse I was on and the riding instructor (Catherine) who was leading my horse and riding a bicycle, was kicked in the head by the rearing horse's hooves and knocked unconscious. My horse bolted a little way. I was not hurt but was very, very shaken. I did go out on the horse again that afternoon, but from that time on I was not really happy in the saddle! Catherine was fortunately okay but had a very bad headache for the rest of the day. The same horse kicked me on the side of the knee later on, so I don't have a lot of interest in horse riding now!

I fitted in well to the household. Mum was a good worker and she and the owners got on well. She was also popular with the guests, so all seemed to go reasonably comfortably for a while.

Mum would have one day off in seven, which was normally Saturday, and we would catch the bus to Weston Super Mare, to see a movie or just to look around and spend a little money on trivia, etc. They were good outings, always ending in an ice-cream at the local ice-cream parlour, prior to catching the bus back home. It was there I got my first taste of the "Knickerbocker Glory" a wondrous concoction of vanilla icecream, bananas, strawberry syrup, chocolate sauce and nuts!

I really missed my dancing however, as we had made some enquiries only to find that the closest thing to a ballet teacher for me was a local lady who had not taken as many exams as I had, so I could have taught her! I also missed my school (VMSG) as I had been relegated to a secondary modern school in nearby Cheddar which necessitated a bus run to and from school each day. I hated the school and did not settle in there very well at all. The only excitement I experienced was the attentions of a red-haired, freckle-faced boy call Kevin Payne, who fell "madly in love" with me! (I don't fancy red-haired guys, even now).

Having lived in London all my life I was not used to the 'livestock' of the country, meaning the insects. I had never liked spiders but had not been afraid of them, as in London they had only been small little black things after all. In the country, however, it is an entirely different matter. The insects get a chance to grow big and strong as I found out one day in our room. I was lying on my bed late one afternoon, reading a book, when a slight movement from the corner of my eye took my attention. In front of my bed and slightly to the right there was a large piece of hardwood leaning against the wall. It was an old railway track, which used to be in use for the children's railway. In the fading light I noticed a slight movement again as I looked in that direction and realised, to my horror, that the movement was a very large brown spider walking across the board. It was the biggest spider I had ever seen and it quite literally terrified me. From the depths of my chest I let out a blood-curdling scream, which brought half a dozen people scurrying into the vicinity and all I could do was point, speechless, at this spider! They of course thought I was quite mad and derided such fear, but I could not help it and as they managed to remove the beast, I sat looking at nothing in particular, just shuddering for about 20 minutes. From that moment on I was phobic about spiders.

It was around this time that I discovered that boys found me attractive. This was a first for me as hitherto I was blissfully unaware that boys existed, being too busy with my dancing, etc., to bother with outside activities. I was quite well developed, having started my period early, and my personality seemed to be funny enough for them to consider me "one of the boys", so when guests came down to the house with their children, Cilla, the boss's daughter and I would play with them until they left. One night we were having an innocent game of Kiss Chase, when the boys all seemed to be making a beeline for me. We were having innocent fun, but somehow Cilla's father read more into our game than was there and labelled me "a little too free and easy with the boys". We did not get up to anything, they were just mates! But I was to discover the small mindedness of the inhabitants of country villages first hand from that time onwards.

He proceeded to ostracize me and leave me out of any outings with his children, which hitherto I had always been included in, and generally made things very uncomfortable. The whole situation culminated in my mother having a blazing row with him and her giving notice. So after just 4 months she was job hunting again and we were on the move.

Devon here we come

Mum answered an advertisement for a housekeeper to a widower and his son in Tiverton, Devon. The father, Fred, had nursed his wife through cancer until her death and he and his son, Leonard, now required a housekeeper.

I began making friends in Tiverton although, once again I did not like the secondary school I went to;. I just did not fit in. I found the work relatively easy but I did not like the children in my class.

At about this time my brother came down to visit us - he had got out of Borstal by this stage and seemed to be making good money at something – we never knew what, probably criminal. He was a dreadful show-off; the big London boy who would show the local country yokels a thing or two. I got to dread going out with him because someone just had to look twice at him and he would advance up to them, face to face and ask them if they "wanted bovver"! A good thing that did come out of his visit, however, was one day I came home from school and Mum and Peter told me to go and look in the shed. So I did and there, in all its glory, was a wonderful pink and white bicycle – called a "Pink Witch". I was so excited and proud as I madly pedalled up and down the street to show my friend, Susan. The other good thing was the discovery of his copy of the book "Lady Chatterley's Lover" which was the big "naughty book of the time" by D H Lawrence – quite an education!

I had turned 13 and in the country areas the school children seem to get a second chance at going to Grammar School. They have, what is known as the 13+. I was in the age group to sit the exam and passed the academic side.

About this time things began to sour with Mum and her employer again. He was a terribly mean man and Mum found it hard providing food from the meagre amount he would give to her for housekeeping. We stayed a total of about 8 months with them and although in the end it was not much fun, during the time we were there initially I enjoyed myself and early teenage years.

Our next port of call was a small village called High Chipperton! Mum was offered a position as housekeeper to an ex Squadron Leader and his wife. They were a lovely couple. I remember the lady of the house as being a tall, thin lady with an overlarge nose and who always played with her pearls when she was speaking to anyone. While we were there Mum re-discovered and I discovered the joys of the village dances. Mum could not drive so the local taxi driver made a fortune out of us as he would take us to the surrounding villages and then pick us up and bring us home again. I became renowned as the area Twist Champion and with a partner I picked up whilst on my sojourns to the dances, acquired a jive partner with whom I also won a lot of the local jive contests. It was about this time that I met a lovely Welsh boy called Len who was in the army, with whom I fell madly in love! He was a friend of two local lads who I was friendly with so I saw him for a few weeks whilst he was on leave. He asked me to marry him! I was 14 and he was 21! He went off to Benghazi for a 6 month sojourn and we wrote faithfully to each other the whole time he was away. Of course it became obvious when he returned that the gap in our ages and maturity was too wide and we split up, but it was a lovely "young love" experience for me.

Mum enjoyed working for the her new employers and we stayed there nearly a year. Unfortunately, the lady of the house died and the Squadron Leader decided he did not want to stay on in the house without her and sold up. We were on the move again!

We moved from High Chipperton to Exeter and Mum and I found a double bedsitter to live in. She got a job in a local bottling factory and I was sent to the another girls' school – it was so bad! Each school seemed worse than the one before. It was in Exeter I first started "finding" reasons why I could not go to school and would stay home all day reading magazines or going for walks, anything rather than to go that dreadful, overbearing school. I never got round to getting their uniform, which was a depressing shade of grey, because whilst we were in Exeter word came through that I had passed the educational side of the 13+ and was required to go for an interview in Tiverton. As I did not have a school uniform as such to wear, I just wore a red blouse and a flowered skirt, taking time to make sure I looked tidy and neat, and jumped on to the bus to Tiverton.

The interviews were being held at the secondary school and by the time I arrived I was feeling somewhat nervous at the thought of the upcoming interview. The headmaster and head mistress of the school were, to put it kindly, insensitives of the worst kind. They were overbearing and domineering and when I arrived at the school not wearing my school uniform, they told me off so viciously that I was reduced to tears. When they realised they had gone too far, to the point where they may have jeopardised my chances at passing the interview they panicked and immediately took steps to resurrect the situation by taking me to the kitchen to get me a drink and a biscuit "to calm me down". I managed to get myself under control enough to sit through the interview but my misery showed through as the interviewers recommended I be passed to go to the Grammar School but should undergo psychiatric counselling as I appeared "depressed"!! If they did but know what had happened just prior to my going into the interview the headmaster and headmistress would have got into a lot of trouble. Indeed, when I went back to Exeter I did not tell my Mother about what they had done as I would have been unable to stop her from getting physical with them both!

I found life in Exeter very lonely as I did not make any friends whilst there. I used to go for walks quite frequently and it was during one of these walks I was "picked up" by a guy, whose name I cannot even remember. I was sitting on a park bench reading a book when he sat down beside me. He was older than I was and I liked him quite well. He asked me if I would like to go to the "pictures" with him sometime and I arranged a "date". We saw each other a few times, but he was 17 and I was only 14, so was not really ready for a "boyfriend" as such. The problem was that he liked me and was not going to give up without a fight. It got to the point that I asked mum to tell him I was not home when he next came to take me out and whatever she said to him did the trick and I thankfully, never saw him again!

Mum was still trying for live-in jobs and around this time she obtained a position again in a small guest house in a small village in Bortheton just outside Tiverton, so once again I was to go to school in Tiverton but this time I would go to the Grammar School instead of the secondary school. I was indeed glad to leave Exeter and even to this day my time there was so unhappy that I cannot stand the place.

We moved to Bortherton and there began one of the few really settled times of our stay in the country. I became friends with another girl called Alida and we were inseparable. We went everywhere together and young life in the village of Bortherton was great. We had the local youth group, which was the highlight of our week and in between times, Alida and I got ourselves Saturday jobs working at the Woolworths in Exeter. It was great having a little money of our own, we felt very grown up.

It was sometime around this that my mother met John Gibson – through ballroom dancing, as he loved to dance also and like Mum, was a good dancer. He wanted to marry Mum and set about doing up a cottage he owned. It was an old farmhand cottage in the middle of nowhere. The water was not connected to a toilet so we had to have a "dry toilet" which had to be emptied once a week. Guess whose job it was to empty the toilet! I hated the place, and it was mid Winter when John wanted to move us into it and absolutely freezing! Mum gave notice to her boss in Bortherton, much to my dismay as I was really happy in Bortherton, and we moved into "the cottage"! It seemed that from that time on John just could not stop picking on me, calling me a "useless towny" and "needing a lesson in the important things in life". I never really knew what his problem was but suffice it to say that after a while my mother started taking exception to him picking on me and packed our bags and walked out. Leaving John to live in his 'done up" cottage all by himself. We were not popular!

Mum decided we would move up to Coventry to live with her sister, my Auntie Mina, so once again we were on the move. I was determined not to start yet another school, as my senior years at school had been interrupted no less than six times and I had had enough. I wanted to leave school and as I had turned 15 earlier in the year I was allowed to do so.

COVENTRY – 1964 -1966

We had not seen my Aunt Mina for three or four years and I certainly had no memory of visiting her much in Coventry apart from that last fateful trip. She lived by herself in a very small terrace house in the area of Coventry currently being systematically demolished. We were about four or five houses down from her local pub. The house was a dump with no inside water supply or sink and certainly no inside toilet. I was horrified when we arrived, to see that this was to be our future home! Mum and I shared a room at the back of the house, upstairs and Auntie Mina had her own room at the front. She was waiting to be moved into a new council flat but when this would be was totally unknown. There were only half a dozen houses still standing in their street so we were surrounded by ruins! I have to admit to a sense of shame and embarrassment at living there and knew I would never be able to ask any friends I may make back to "my home".

I had always been interested in office type activities so as I could not now follow my wish to be a Translator without further study, I decided to get a job in an office. Mum took me to the local Labour Exchange and they told me about a job with the a local car manufacturer. The position was as a junior mail girl and I would attend Secretarial School in the mornings to learn typing and shorthand. So, after passing the interview I duly started work at the princely sum of £1 13s 6d per week.

I really enjoyed the work and did very well at the Secretarial School. Learning shorthand was a matter of endurance in the first instance but I have never regretted persevering as the skill has put me in good stead throughout my working career. I quickly was promoted from the Mail Room to a junior secretarial position in the Service Department of the company, as secretary to the Workshop Supervisor. He was a lovely, fatherly man who was very patient with his new (young) secretary and from whom I learned a lot about professionalism.

The Service Department was a great meeting place for the young Pupils and Apprentices who were sent to the car makers from their district dealerships, to learn about the mechanics of the cars they sold. There was another young lass there, Jane, who worked in the Accounts Section and she and I became great friends and are still in touch to this day. We went on foursomes with a few of the young guys who came through but then one lad came through who I really liked! His name was Richard Payne and I had a real crush on him! He was very shy, however, and I had to make all the "moves" to get him to ask me out, which he eventually did, but I was mortified when he picked me up and in the car was "his friend" who he had asked along to go bowling with us! It was, however, the last time he brought him along on a date, thank goodness.

The Rootes Group ball was coming up and I was seeing Richard. I really liked him so the ball was a fairy tale evening for me. I managed to save my money and get a white lamé dress and my mother bought me a white, shimmery scarf to go with it. Richard picked me up and we had the most magical evening. He told me later he wanted to ask me to marry him that night, but as he was nearly 21 and I was barely 16, commonsense prevailed. The evening, however, was everything a young girl's first ball should be and a treasured memory.

His 21st birthday was coming up and he invited me down to meet his family who were throwing a 21st party for him. When we got to his very palatial detached house in the best area just outside London, I began to feel totally out of my depth. His parents were polite but were obviously not impressed with my "breeding" and did not think I was good enough for their son, and as I was introduced to his privately educated friends I was feeling very uncomfortable. I had had no idea he was from "money". The evening wasn't too bad, however, even though it started off a little slow to warm up, I eventually started to feel better with his friends, who were really rather nice to me (in a condescending way). The next day, I was up earlier than Richard and without giving it a second thought, after I was dressed and had had breakfast, I tapped on his door and asked if it was okay for me to come in. He said yes, and as I sat talking to him on his bed for a couple of minutes, there was a hammering on the door by his mother, demanding to know why I was in Richard's bedroom! I tried to tell her we were only talking but this went down very badly and the weekend went down hill from then on! I was really upset when we returned to Coventry and poor Richard did not know how to comfort me! I wrote a letter of apology to his mother, but I fear I was a "persona non-grata" as far as they were concerned from then on.

I continued to see Richard for several months but he was eventually transferred to another of our factories and we drifted apart. Probably much to his parents' relief! But I think he was my "first love".

Whilst staying with my aunt, my cousin, Peter, took me along to a rehearsal of his drama group. They were producing a play and yours truly obtained a part as a young girl with a kind heart but who is a bit of a tart. I thoroughly enjoyed the experience and watched with amusement as the various cast members formed their little relationships. One I remember was quite sad, another young lass in the cast really liked the leading man and was devastated when she learned he was married. That was my first taste of amateur dramatics, but I didn't get a lot of opportunity to pursue this interest for quite a few years after this initial blaze of glory.

My mother had been troubled with bad stomach pains for a few years now and she was told that she was suffering with a Gastric Ulcer. In retrospect I feel I was not particularly sympathetic to her, when she must have been in a lot of pain, but she ALWAYS seemed to have something wrong with her so I became rather a 'hard nut' when it came to mum having another session of weeping, etc. She and Auntie Mina were getting on okay but Auntie Mina was a drinker and Mum really was not – Auntie Mina nicknamed Mum her "lady sister" to the locals. Mum got so unwell, however, that she was advised to leave Coventry and move to the sea to get away from some of the stress of city living. At this stage though I was thoroughly enjoying my job and was determined not to move (yet again) to some more dead than alive hole near the sea. My alternatives were to continue living with Auntie Mina after Mum moved, which I did not relish, or to find a place of my own! At just 16!

A couple of weeks prior to this question having to be answered I had met a girl called Janet who was 15 and lived with her mother and her mother's de facto husband. The de facto was making life hell for Janet and she was going to have to move out. We had talked at the party where we met and the subject of accommodation came up. She contacted me later and asked me if I had been serious about moving out from home. I said that I was and she asked whether I would be prepared to share with her. We could afford to share somewhere but neither of us could afford to live on our own. So we agreed to look around for a flat or bed-sitter to lease.

We were lucky and found a terraced house, furnished, quite close to work, which we could just afford and duly moved in. We had very little in the way of linen, etc., to move in with but we managed. Janet and I had not been there long when I met a boy called Chris Kenton, to whom I was immediately attracted. Ours was an emotionally volatile relationship and it was to him I eventually lost my virginity! We went out for about three months then had a blazing row, one of many, and broke up. Not long after our break up Jane, Janet and I were at a party and Chris made a play for Jane, about which I was most upset. There happened to be there a guy called Keith, who I had met briefly when he had spent some time in the Service Department. I had quite liked him but he had never asked me out and then he was subsequently transferred to another factory with his Traineeship and had only recently returned. He gave me his shoulder to cry on (quite literally) and took me home. John came round – as he had not really wanted to split with me – to see if we could patch it up, which we did for a while but once again we rowed and broke up. Jane and I, meanwhile, mended our differences and we were all licking our wounds, as Janet had also had a problem relationship recently die on her.

One Friday evening the three of us decided we wanted to experience getting drunk! Jane still lived at home with her parents but spent a lot of time with us at our house. This particular night we bought ourselves some sherry and some beer and set out to get ourselves "pickled". We had decided to do this at home so we would not make fools of ourselves in public. The process was gradual and up to a point not unpleasant, as I sat in a chair contemplating this feeling of not being quite normal, and finding everything being said and done around me as funny and highly amusing. There comes a time, however, when there is a change over from "pleasant" to being drunk! I remember well going outside to the toilet and having the greatest difficulty finding my way back into the house, trying the shed several times and not understanding where the kitchen sink had gone. When I did eventually get back inside, I entered the kitchen and leant against the door for support and proceeded to slide down the door, in slow motion, totally unable to control my limbs or speech! The problem now was that I needed to go to the toilet again, this time to be violently sick but could not sort out my arms from my legs, so decided to crawl on all fours just to be on the safe side. Janet and Jane did not seem to be quite so bad, so when I had finished being ill they came and got me and decided I should go to bed. The pantomime that ensued trying to get me up the stairs to my bed, must have been a sight to behold as I would crawl, assisted by my partners in crime, up three steps and slide back down two. It was the best aversion therapy possible as I did not drink anything alcoholic for ten years after that experience!

Keith continued to call and see how I was, with the following eight weeks continuing with my romance with Chris being on again, off again, on again, off again and when it was "off" I was seeing Keith and when it was "on" I was not seeing Keith. I finally rang Keith and told him I could not see him again as I was definitely going out with Chris. He had had enough at this stage and took himself out of the arena on courses, etc., and when he was in town, managed to avoid me like the plague. I really hurt him, but I could not get Chris out of my system!

Janet, Jane and I were part of a big group of young people who worked at the car makers. We had to leave our house because it became too expensive there, so moved into a shared house with a couple of guys from work. There were two bedrooms upstairs where Janet and I were. We shared one and we needed someone to help with our costs for the house by utilising the spare bedroom. So we advertised for a couple of girls to join us. After seeing a few girls we settled on two friends who ultimately came to take up residence with us. Janet and I didn't interact with these two very much as they were slightly older and we were still worldly naïve. So much so that when they were busted for smoking pot it came as a bad shock to we innocents and we were lucky not to be implicated by the police in our housemates' sordid goings on. We think the policemen who came to arrest the girls took one look at Janet and me and decided we wouldn't know one end of a bong from the other and were the innocents in the whole sordid situation. So with stern warnings from them about being a bit more careful about the company we kept, we were left alone.

One night I came back from a particularly stormy date with Chris to find Keith and a couple of his housemates over visiting with Janet. I had arrived home early because we had yet again had a row. Keith was mortified to see me, as it was unexpected and Janet had assured him I would not be there. They beat a hasty retreat and I was once again hit by the fact that Keith really was a very nice person and I wished I could feel about him the way he felt about me, so I sat down and wrote to him – a letter in which I just intended to explain to him how I was sorry to have hurt him and how highly I regarded him, etc. I just wanted to let him know how I felt and really did not expect a reply. I was going on leave for a couple of weeks and the following day, I walked round to his house and dropped the note into the mailbox.

Two days later I received a call from Keith asking if we could go and "get a coffee" in town and talk. We met that night and talked for ages and as if by magic the emotional tie I had to Chris finally stopped and when I told Chris – again – that we were finished, he of course did not believe me and it was only after a few weeks where I had not made contact that he finally believed me. From then on I saw Keith on a regular basis.

Cooking and I have never been compatible, but one night I invited Keith over for dinner. The only meal I could think of to do was pie and chips, so I duly heated up our pies and proceeded to heat up the fat to cook the chips. They were sizzling merrily but after a while I became aware of the fact that the atmosphere was decidedly smokey. I checked in the kitchen and realised that the smoke was issuing from the pot in which the chips were cooking, as there was a small hole in the base of the pan and fat was leaking on to the burner, thus causing the smoke to billow out from the kitchen. As the hole was small however, I allowed the chips to continue to cook and Keith manfully ate my offering of soggy chips and overdone pie without a murmur of complaint – although I did notice he did all the cooking for us from then on!

The house Janet and I were sharing was sold and once again we had to find somewhere else to move to. Keith had been transferred back to Yorkshire with his work and I was seeing him probably most weekends – he made the 4 hour trip down every Friday night!

We were very lucky and looked at a bedsitter in a lovely area quite near to the car maker's factory (where we both worked) and were given the room. Neither of us could afford to live there on just our pay from our day jobs so we had to get extra jobs. We both managed to get evening jobs at the local Locarno Ballroom, so our routine would be to have a decent meal in the canteen at work at lunch time, rush home and have a snack of some cereal or a sandwich and then go to the ballroom for the evening to work in the snack bar there until about 10.00pm. Being young we could cope with this pace of life but neither of us was very old and worldly wise and housekeeping was not within our scope of experience! Add to this our lack of money and hence, lack of bed linen, etc., and we had problems.

I had subsequently become engaged to Keith and just two weeks following my engagement Janet announced her engagement to her current boyfriend, Manny. Our stay at our bedsitter came to a sudden end when our landlady realised that Keith and sometimes Manny was staying over with me or Janet and we were asked to find alternative accommodation because the landlady "did not condone that sort of thing". Keith had been urging me to come up to Yorkshire to live with his family and this seemed the ideal time to go, so Janet and I parted company. She moved in with Manny and I went up to Yorkshire, leaving my job at the car makers, to start a new life with Keith's family. I was just a month away from my 18th birthday.

1966 – 1968 – YORKSHIRE

*K*eith came down to collect me and my belongings, which over the years had accumulated quite dramatically, and drove me up to Yorkshire.

I realised that 18 was rather young to be getting married and did ask why we had to get married, rather than just "going out". Keith, however, was six years older than me and was ready to settle down so I asked myself "Why not?"

When I had been up to Yorkshire the previous Christmas his family, which consisted of his (widowed) mother, Martha, one of his two brothers, Sean, and his grandmother, Granny Loton, all lived at his grandmother's house, however in the interim four months they had sold the house and begun renting a house in Bingley. It was originally a doctor's house and surgery and covered three levels. Downstairs there was an entry hall at the side which had originally been the waiting room, this was connected to the L shaped kitchen which had an electric stove in addition to an AGA solid fuel cooker, which was a source of comfort and warmth on the cold Yorkshire nights. The first floor consisted of a large lounge, two bedrooms (mine and Granny's) and a large bathroom and toilet. The top floor held a further three bedrooms where Martha, Keith and Sean slept.

Martha was a very "private" lady and somewhat authoritative and for the first couple of weeks I was unsure how to address her. She was "Martha" to everyone, including the small grandchildren, Keith's older brother Martin's children. I felt a little uncomfortable calling her Martha but eventually made myself do so one day and when "the sky didn't fall in" I realised this was okay. If I had been older and a little more mature I would of course, have felt easier just asking her if I should call her Martha instead of Mrs Renton!

Keith was already working at the car dealership that had sent him down to Coventry in the first place and I had no difficulty finding a job initially with a chemical manufacturing company, and then with a firm of solicitors – both in Bradford.

We were originally going to get married the following year – 1967 – but living in close proximity to each other all the time began to tell, on Keith particularly, and so we brought the wedding forward to the October of 1966. We had no money so everything had to be done as cheaply as possible. Martha was invaluable in this, she had good contacts so all the catering could be done by friends, etc., and I had my very simple wedding dress made by another family friend for the cost of an invite to the wedding.

My mother was living in Skegness still, where she had gone when I moved out from home. She had subsequently met a man called Jim Linn and was talking "marriage" with him. As my wedding was going to be in Yorkshire all my relatives would have to travel up to us and bunk down as best they could. My brother was married by this time (although I found out later they were having difficulties and not long after my wedding they split up!) So a couple of days before the wedding the house was full of my relatives, my brother and his wife and Mum and Jim. I had asked Janet to be my bridesmaid, also Jane but as Janet had decided to get married to Manny at about the same time, she had asked Jane to be her bridesmaid and as Jane could not afford to get dresses for both weddings she said she wouldn't be a bridesmaid at either wedding – just to be fair – so I finished up with one bridesmaid and four groomsmen! Such was my ignorance of wedding protocol I did not realise they should have been equal in numbers! As it turned out it was just as well that Jane did not agree to be a bridesmaid at my wedding as earlier in the year, she had visited me and told me she thought she was pregnant! This proved to be so and at the time of my wedding she was busy organising her own!

My mother and Martha had not really hit it off and the days leading up to the wedding were very trying! My family did not do a great deal to help and I felt very embarrassed by this fact. It all came to a head on the morning of my wedding when I burst into tears and threatened to call off the whole thing. I had a very heavy cold and instead of it being the happiest day of my life I felt thoroughly wretched.

Prior to the ceremony, as I was so overwrought, Martha had given me a "Relaxatab" to calm me down, but my brother had also given me a small shot of whiskey! Consequently by the time I was walking down the aisle I was somewhat "high" and had to work very hard to control my fits of nervous giggling which threatened to overcome me throughout the service. Keith was so nervous I could feel him shaking beside me and was no doubt wondering why I was finding everything so hilarious.

The service itself went very well although my lingering memory is that of my face aching badly at the end of it because of all the photographs! The reception was being held at our house and Martha had recruited her friends to help in the serving, etc. She did a wonderful job. One of our wedding "presents" was the use of a caravan at Anglesea – Wales – for our honeymoon. We were driving to Manchester after the ceremony and then travelling on to Wales from there.

We got married at 3.00pm and left the reception at 6.00pm. It is unbelievable how low I felt. My cold had really taken off and I was really depressed – some bride! We drove to Manchester and in true Manchester tradition, when we got there it was pouring with rain! We had not booked an hotel, thinking there would be no problem finding accommodation, but unfortunately, there was a big convention in the city and all the bigger hotels in the city were full! We tried several hotels, getting colder and wetter with each attempt until eventually we found a "B class" hotel which had one room left. It was right next door to the kitchens. By this time, however, we were desperate so decided to take it!

Our room was a little unnerving because it had an emergency fire door in it and I had visions of hotel guests and staff running riot through our room to get to the exits in the event of an emergency! We were very close to the kitchens as well so we could hear the rumble of voices and the clanging of pots and pans until quite early in the morning. My cold worsened and all I wanted to do was go to sleep!

The following day we were due to go to Anglesea to take up residence in our caravan "gift"! We travelled all day and arrived in Wales in the early evening of the Sunday. Nothing was open – the place was as dead and cold as the grave! Not an auspicious start to our stay, as being October the weather was cold and dank. We decided to go straight to the caravan. When we eventually found it, however, because of its non-use for a few months, it was not in the best condition to eat or sleep in – the bed was rather cold and damp. We decided to go for a walk along the shore and to our delight found a lovely little hotel - which was open – called the "Min y don" "edge of the sea". We went inside to enquire about a meal and were told we could dine there but would have to eat by candlelight as they had lost their electricity supply! No great hardship – quite romantic in fact.

Our evening meal was lovely and we enjoyed the atmosphere of the place so much we decided to enquire as to whether they had any rooms available. There were none that night but the following few days were available so we decided to "hang the expense" and leave our cold caravan after staying there one night and stay at the hotel. It was a very good decision as we had a room which overlooked the sea so we could hear the waves and see the moonlight on the water as we drifted off to sleep. It was a magical place and we stayed at there for about 3 nights after which we were off up to London to catch up with friends at the London Motor Show.

Our honeymoon lasted for about a week then we had to return to Yorkshire and take up our normal routine again. I was working for the chemical company but the Managing Director of that company was not a particularly pleasant boss, so I left and started work with a firm of solicitors in Bradford. It was an okay job but I was restless. Keith was working for his car dealership in Bradford but we did not seem to be getting anywhere, so in essence we had a living room and bedroom "flat" and we shared the kitchen and bathroom facilities, but there was no prospect of our buying a place of our own anywhere in the near future.

We began spending time with a group of young people we had met through our respective jobs. One evening the talk turned to the supernatural, and ouija boards. Just for a laugh we decided to make a ouija board and see if we could contact "the other side". We were all excited as we sat around the table with our fingers on a glass asking "is there anyone there". We all gasped when the glass seemed to take on a life of its own and move through the letters Y-E-S. The questions asked had to be simple one word answers or answerable with a "yes" or "no". It was all very exciting and we found that whenever we got together we wanted to use the ouija board. After a while, Christine, one of our group, began picking up a pencil and writing. At first what she wrote did not make any sense but after a while it seemed she was getting a message from a "Reverend Tweed" (who we subsequently nicknamed "Tweedy"). At this point for various reasons we did not see the group for a couple of months, but one night we ran into one of our friends and asked him whether they were still using the ouija board. He said no they hadn't because they had had rather a scare. Apparently one night Christine had received what she thought was a message from Tweedy telling her he wanted them all to go to the local graveyard so they could meet. After much discussion on this some of the group decided they did not want to go any further, but four of them did go down to the local graveyard late that night. As they sat in the car waiting for a "message", one of the group asked if anyone could see the forms that were taking shape over the graves and Christine said she had been watching them for a while. The forms – misty and white – began moving towards the car. By now the group was thoroughly spooked and decided to get out of there. So started the car and screamed off back to Christine and her husband's house. When they got there Tweedy had told Christine he was glad they left when they did because "the others" (presumably the misty forms) wanted to take them over and it had become dangerous. After this bad experience Christine and her husband spoke to a local Anglican Minister and told him what they had been doing. He told them to burn everything they had been using, including a book they had got on contacting the dead, and to never, ever dabble in the supernatural again, that mental hospitals were full of people who had done just as they had been doing. Needless to say, Keith and I never played "ouija boards" again.

Keith and I had been married for approximately a year when the Australian Government embarked on an advertising campaign to attract migrants to Australia. If they stayed for a minimum of 2 years, their fares (by either plane or ship) would be paid for by the Australian Government. My interest was aroused by the advertisements depicting bronzed young people frolicking on golden beaches under the blue skies and sunshine of the Australian climate. The English are obsessed by the search for sun, sand and a tan because of their wretched, dull climate, so the prospect of blue skies and sunshine was very enticing indeed.

I did not say anything to Keith at first but just sent off for brochures and information and privately read them to find out more. I found myself becoming very excited by the prospect of life on the other side of the world and it was only for a period of two years then we could return home if that was what we wanted. The advertising lauded the low unemployment and Australia being the land of opportunity! I showed the brochures, etc to Keith and he, too, felt it could be the way to go for us, so we filled in the copious number of forms and sent them off.

We received a pretty prompt reply giving us further information and requesting that we undergo a medical examination and informing us that pending the satisfactory medical outcome we would be notified of a time and place to attend a personal interview. The process seemed to gain its own momentum and by Christmas 1967 we were summoned over to Leeds for our final interview.

From the start of my enquiries to the date of our interview in Leeds it had been approximately three months. I have to admit that we were having a few second thoughts about the idea of emigrating and leaving everything that is familiar, including family, so on our way to the interview we wondered how we were going to tell the person interviewing us that we had changed our mind. It was a typical Yorkshire Winter's day, grey sky, drizzling rain and a cold wind. We waited in a draughty corridor in the Leeds Town Hall and were eventually ushered into a small office, occupied by an Australian ex-patriot who was vertically challenged, full of cold and just hanging out to "go home" to Sydney after his two-year stint in the U.K. He did not like our weather! Somehow we did not get around to telling this man that we had changed our mind. We got caught up in the excitement of hearing about the very low unemployment levels throughout Australia but particularly in Perth, Western Australia. We had not heard much about Perth at that stage, whenever Australia had been mentioned at all it was generally regarding one of the eastern states cities i.e. Melbourne or Sydney. The clincher for me was when upon enquiring about the kind of salary I could expect as a secretary in

Perth, I was told I could expect to earn an amount which was practically triple my current salary at the solicitors in Bradford. Almost without realising it, we had chosen to migrate to Perth and walked out of the office in a daze, wondering how we were going to tell the family about our planned exodus!

Telling the family was indeed very hard. I was under the impression that my mother was going to marry her current beau, Jim Linn, and was therefore not going to be left on her own if I went away. Martha was very supportive and Keith's brothers and their families stated flatly that they would believe it when they saw us off at the station! What was really a shock was the speed with which we had our dates for departure notified to us – we received a letter just a week later telling us we were leaving on 14 February, just a couple of months away! One of the stipulations to our going was that we had to have £100 in the bank when we arrived in Australia, we also had to save some spending money as we had opted to travel by ship (which was a 28-day journey), so we embarked on a strict savings plan with Keith working at a second job to get some money together. By the time we were due to leave we needed a holiday!

The day we had been dreading finally arrived. I had to go over and see my mother for the last time as we were leaving to travel down to London the following day and leave for Southampton a couple of days after that. It was awful. I cried as though my heart would break. Mum was terrific she tried bravely to not cry by telling herself we were just going away for a holiday, not forever. I shall never forget the memory of her standing next to Jim waving goodbye as I stared out of the back window of our retreating car. We then went home to meet up with all the relatives, who had travelled over from Lancashire to say goodbye. We had had a farewell party a couple of weeks prior to our departure date where we had farewelled the wider family members, cousins, etc but Martha and the immediate family were seeing us off at the train station the following day. As the train pulled out of the station, Keith and I both stared resolutely out of the carriage window, unable to look at each other for fear that this would open the dam of misery we were both feeling!

We travelled down to London and were staying with my brother and his wife Marjorie, as they were still together at this stage. My Uncle Ted, who I had not seen for some four years, also came to visit and say farewell. It was also hard leaving my brother, surprisingly, as we had not spent much time together in the previous four years, and what time I had spent with him, had been fraught with stress, but he was my brother and it all added to our sense of apprehension and concern as to whether or not we were making the right decision by taking such a big step in our lives.

We arrived in Southampton and waited patiently to be cleared by Customs. Looking around me I saw the same concern and apprehension etched on the faces of our fellow travellers. To me, the families were the most courageous, in that they were uprooting their children and taking their belongings to an unknown world, whereas it was just the two of us. My insides churned as I stared up at the huge ship, the "Fairsky", that was to be our home for the next 28 days.

THE "FAIRSKY" – FEBRUARY 1968

As the "Fairsky" slowly edged its way out of Southampton Docks, it was difficult to choke down the lump which persistently pushed its way into my throat. People, friends and family on the quay, sadly waved goodbye to their loved-ones on board, keeping a brave smile in place despite the knowledge that their son, daughter or friend was leaving them to travel half way around the world to live for an indefinite period. We had avoided this last emotional drag by saying goodbye to everyone in Yorkshire and London then travelling to Southampton on our own. We wanted it that way.

It was at that moment, when the first deafening blast from the ship's funnel heralded our departure that I realized that I was saying goodbye to my native land for – how long? – perhaps forever! A feeling akin to panic and sheer misery overwhelmed me and I desperately bit my lip and breathed deeply in an effort to control the tears welling up inside, unlike the majority of passengers around me, as sobs and the sound of crying women and children (and in some cases, men) hitherto controlled, now broke out in a tirade of misery. The weather, as if feeling the sadness of the occasion, was dull and grey with a chill so deep it penetrated our very soul. This fact helped in a way, however, as it was a demonstration of a good reason to be leaving this rain-sodden country called England.

We stayed on deck for a while; unwilling to lose sight of our homeland, then decided to go back to our minute cabin on "C" deck, and begin the task of finding room for the mountain of clothes we had, in the mole-hill of storage space. Our first impression on reaching our cabin, the Steward, a gesturing and sullen looking Italian leading the way, was that it appeared to be of claustrophobic proportions! It consisted of a 12" wide wardrobe by the door, with a wash hand basin – complete with a mirror, next to it. There was a twin to the first wardrobe on the other side of the basin at right angles to it. Beside the far wardrobe was a fixed dressing table and four drawers (again with a mirror) and opposite this were the bunk beds, on which we were to spend the next twenty eight nights rolling around on the high seas. With both Keith and I in the cabin at the same time it was crowded. We could not get out of there quick enough then, but later it became a haven of rest!

Everywhere on the ship, in the maze of passages, doors, halls and decks, was absolutely full of people milling around, making their way, shakily, either to their cabins or, like us, to get their meal tickets. There were queues everywhere. We had to queue for two hours to book our sitting for all meals, also the table number. However, the serendipity of this was that we made our first shipboard friends. They, like us, were a young married couple, from Essex. Terri, for that was the wife's name, was still red-eyed from weeping earlier, but seemed pleasant enough, as was her husband, Rick. We finally got to book our meals and inevitably, we chose a table for four, sharing it with Rick and Terri. They were on "D" deck, just below us and though their cabin was similar to ours, we were fortunate in having a dressing table with drawers, as theirs consisted only of the wardrobes, the wash hand basin and the bunks. Their deck, however, was much quieter than ours, as judging by the noise we heard I am sure we had most of the 400 children on board on our deck!

After having obtained our meal tickets, we noted that our sitting, for there were two, was at 8.00pm for dinner. Time had flown on rather, what with one thing and another, so by the time we found the dining room, (for future reference), which, incidentally was dining room "B", it was time to begin dressing for the aforesaid meal.

I realized I had sent the case with my change of clothes down to the Baggage Room, which we located, after much enquiry and vacant head shaking from the Italian stewards, on "E" deck. We made our way down to the said deck as best we could, following the directions on the wall to the best of our ability. However, we still managed to get lost several times, but finally we were at the top of the steps leading down to this elusive deck. Then, it happened….a violent wave of dizzy nausea swept over me and reminded me that we were at sea! Having never spent a great deal of time on a ship before, I did not know whether I was a good sailor or not. This was the beginning of my painfully finding out that I was not. From that moment on I never felt quite right in the stomach until we set foot on dry land once more. If this was how I was going to be when the sea was comparatively calm and the weather was not rough how would I go if things got rougher? We found after staggering down the steps – set at a suicidal angle to the floor – that the Baggage Room did not open until 10.00am the following morning so it would seem we would have to dine in what we were wearing! Once again, we made our way uncertainly back to our "cubby hole" cabin to rest and wait for dinner-time to come round.

On arriving at dining room "B" later that evening we were pleasantly surprised to find that this resembled an impeccably kept restaurant, complete with white-jacketed waiters. Mario, our particular waiter, on first meeting was a most uncommunicative character, and we anticipated icy tolerance of us at mealtimes to come. He was a very good waiter, however, and served up the rather good meals in a very efficient manner, if unsmiling. The meals themselves were all four-course affairs and not of bad quality and ending with Italian ice cream. The exception was the coffee and tea. I can tolerate a mediocre cup of tea or coffee if I have to but from the moment I first tasted the tea and coffee on board I decided to find an alternative for the rest of the voyage. It tasted like dirty dishwater, made further unpalatable by the use of powdered milk! My dining companions struggled gamely on, however, and I think they eventually forgot what good tea and coffee tasted like!

After dinner, we found our way to the Grand Social Hall (GSH) on the boat deck, which was the main social hall on the ship. There were, in actual fact, three other bars on board. These were the Lido, Bavarian and Cocktail bar, the latter becoming our main haunt throughout the voyage. The ship had its own band, which wasn't bad, except that we were to find their programme did not vary much from week to week. Eventually, after staying for about an hour in the GSH we decided we would all retire and try and sleep. Surprisingly, it was not difficult to drift off to sleep that night, lulled by the distant throbbing of the vast engines and the emotional wear and tear of the day.

The crew of the "Fairsky" had a big task keeping nearly a 1000 passengers happy and occupied for almost a month. At the time Keith and I sailed, the Suez Canal had been closed due to political upheaval in those regions, so throughout our 28 day voyage we would only touch land twice!

For the first two days out of Southampton, I spent most of my time being horribly "ill" in our cabin. I don't remember much about it but Keith tells me he spent quite a bit of time trying to get soup or fluids smuggled into me from the kitchens. The cabin steward was very hot on policing foodstuffs/liquids being brought from the dining area into the sleeping area, and I think it was only the threat of having one dead passenger from the effects of dehydration, which eventually caused him to accede to Keith's entreaties.

I finally emerged, bleary eyed and weak legged, from my bunk and gradually began exploring alternative sources of beverage. I eventually discovered warm lemon juice, available from the cocktail bar and this became my main source of drink. No scurvy for me!! I did try once again to drink the coffee and tea but with each sip my already delicate stomach would heave in protest. I managed a few of the meals, but eventually began eating ham rolls – once again from the cocktail bar.

There were lots of activities on board – mainly sporting ones – with competitions and "mini Olympic games" to keep the minions occupied. There was also a selection of small shops on the ship, mainly beauty parlours, a book and gift shops, which I explored but did not utilize as we were on a strict daily budget. When we left the cold waters of Europe and hit the warmer climes they opened the "swimming pool" which was probably as big as four to six bathtubs pushed together – it was not large! It seems amazing to say, but being on board gave me my first opportunity to experience "a shower"! Living in the UK all my life showers weren't really the norm because it was usually too cold, so most people sank thankfully into a bath on a regular basis. It was also my first experience of real burning sun. Both Keith and I have a good skin for tanning and we were careful – the crew were always warning us to be aware of the damage extended sunbathing could do. One passenger I remember unfortunately fell asleep in the sun and woke up feeling and resembling a cooked lobster. She spent several days in sick bay with third degree burns.

It was also the first time I experienced jealousy! On board there were several unattached young people and one I remember vividly was a girl called Jennifer – and she was very attractive! She was the sort of girl that (unwittingly – to be fair) made any other female in her proximity fade into oblivion! All the men liked her, including my young husband! And she was "alone" so his caring instinct went rampant. I don't think to this day he ever realized the effect she had on him when she was around. It made my nails curl in bitchy anticipation of using them on her face! Jennifer "had" to be included in our group activities because she was "alone" yeah right!

About seven days into the journey, Rick was beginning to get on our nerves with his constant verbal innuendos about "other women" in front of Terri. Maybe she was used to his verbalizing about imagined liaisons with other women and let it go over her head as pure wishful thinking on his part, but to Keith and I it really rankled. Consequently, we began spending time with other groups of young people we had befriended on board, and Rick and Terri went their way, we went ours and we met amicably for meals to chat about our day's activities.

We had been at sea approximately 11 days when we hit our first land call. It was Las Palmas in the Canary Islands. We were all very excited, particularly Keith and I as we had never been abroad so it was a whole new experience for us, although our sightseeing and spending would be very limited by the restraints of our budget.

The day for landing arrived and I had a bowel upset – to put it politely. I had also lost a lot of weight because of my light eating habits. I had never been so slim and had to admit to liking this new svelte me. We only had a few hours in Las Palmas and we decided to go with Rick and Terri on a guided tour of the place. We did have some free time in the town itself and we met so many of the passengers throughout the day – in milk bars – devouring milk shakes and anything containing fresh milk. Never, did a coffee taste as good as when we bought our first one off the ship! The tour operators obviously had their haunts of touristy shops to help empty the pockets of the tourists and Keith and I indulged in buying decent sun glasses for ourselves, (now so necessary) as we delved into our budget of ten shillings a day! The proprietors of these rather dubious establishments would, however, have made a killing with others less strapped for cash.

All too soon it was time to leave solid land and return to the ship. It was a bit like going "home" I suppose and I must admit that being unwell had left me a little lacking in energy so I was very tired. Las Palmas remains in my memory as a poor looking place, obviously dependent upon the tourist industry for survival, with its buildings in rather bad repair and painted various shades of pastel pink, yellow and blue. It was certainly pleasant, however, to walk on solid ground without the swaying sensation we had been used to over the preceding days.

Back on board, and there were important things to consider like what to wear to the fancy dress party and competition! We had not really put a lot of thought into this but come the day of the ball decided we would have to take part, so we adjourned back to our cabin to consider our options. I thought about making Keith a "harem girl" and we set to work checking out my clothes to see what we could do. It was a hilarious experience and we laughed so much. Keith finished up wearing a shirt with his legs through the sleeves and the top tucked into a pair of my pink frilly knickers. He pushed his size 9 feet into my size 6 sandals, donned my frilliest bra and covered his head with a scarf, and donned a yashmak (another scarf). Because he was an harem girl of a princeling, he had to be draped in jewels, so every item of jewellery I had in my jewellery box was pinned or clipped on to him. The effect was very authentic, and the creation process was great fun. There were some brilliant costumes; the eventual winner was a guy who was dressed literally half as a man and half as a woman and called himself/herself "Indecision".

There was next a call for entrants in a "talent contest". I had always fancied myself as a bit of a singer so decided even though I was scared stiff, I would give it a go. But I did not tell Keith I was going to enter and his face when I took the stage was a study in surprise (or was it shame?) I was embarrassingly bad but at least I felt better about myself because I had tried. We ultimately found out this was a ploy to weed out who, on board, would be game to take part in an old time music hall which was planned. All of those people who entered the talent contest, whether good or bad, were asked to attend "a meeting" in one of the theatrettes. When we got there we were told "what part you are going to take in the old time music hall". I had been allocated the lead female singer with the guy who won the talent contest (he was a semiprofessional entertainer on his way to Australia), and somehow those people attached to the "exhibitionists" (us) were also involved. Keith was told he was "the waiter". This did not sound too bad, so my shy husband said he would do it. It was only after he had acquiesced they informed him he would have to learn a couple of songs – to sing solo – he nearly died!

We were each given the words to the songs we were singing and told to go away and learn them. Due to my activities in my childhood and taking part in a group at my dancing school that went around entertaining at old peoples' homes and hospitals, these songs were all part of the repertoire, and I knew all of mine. I had to teach Keith his, however, and I discovered that in actual fact he had a fairly tuneful voice!

When we asked how many rehearsals we would have and were told "one" we were very apprehensive. These people were experts, though, and they knew that one was enough for the show and that spontaneity and adrenalin rush would account for the rest. So we had our rehearsal – which was a hilarious shambles – and waited, terrified, for the evening to arrive.

Keith was so nervous that even half a dozen shots of whiskey did not calm him! We all lined up for the opening shuffle and song and did our stuff. I was supposed to be the "love object" of the "star" and he sang a couple of songs to me – not being used to this I felt acutely uncomfortable and embarrassed, but because I was by this time "into the swing of things" my singing this time was passably fair. Keith, despite his fear was good and it did wonders for his self-confidence. The whole experience was terrific fun and we made friends with the group with whom we would begin a nocturnal lifestyle for the rest of the voyage. We were the noisy group that could be heard on the games deck playing "human wheelbarrows" and deck quoits until 2 and 3 in the morning. Our cabin steward gave up in disgust, as every morning he would try to get into our cabin to change sheets and towels and we were still asleep. He took to leaving the clean linen outside our cabin so we could do it ourselves! A fair compromise I thought.

The next big event on the horizon was the "Miss Fairsky" contest and I once again decided to join in the proceedings. The contest consisted of two parts. In the afternoon the contestants would be interviewed, just in casual gear, then in the evening we were to wear something dressy for the "formal" part. Once again, I was incredibly nervous and no doubt came over as a complete twit during the interview segment. "Jennifer" was so composed it made me sick! In the evening we donned our glad rags (I had had my wedding dress made over into an evening dress, and wore that). We all had to parade around the dance floor one after another. I felt like a horse on show! Then we all stood, feeling acutely self-conscious, waiting for the verdict. The second and third place getters were announced, neither was me, and then "Miss Fairsky" yes, you guessed – Jennifer!! I can still remember that dreadful feeling of overwhelming embarrassment standing there, not even rating a mention. I resolved then never to put myself into such a position again, and with tears of shame stinging my eyes I searched for my husband as the band struck up a dance to end the proceedings.

Putting "Miss Fairsky" behind me, we continued on our nocturnal way. By this time we had met and befriended a few couples: Jeff and Aileen (Aileen was second in "Miss Fairsky"), Sue and (later to be her husband) Dave, and Andrew and Sheila. These three couples were to become our close friends over the next few years in Australia and to this day, I still have contact with some of them. Dave was leaving the ship at Fremantle but Sue was going on to the eastern states. (She came back a few weeks later and they subsequently married – Keith and I were at their wedding.)

About halfway through our voyage there was the traditional "Crossing the Equator Ceremony". This consisted of a Court of Neptune and various poor devils who had been purported to have "done wrong". Once again, Keith was roped into it. Each poor "victim" was brought before King Neptune for sentencing. These sentences usually consisted of placing the poor wretch on a chair covered with sometimes marmalade, sometimes honey then liberally dousing them in baked beans or spaghetti. They were then taken away to be "cleansed" of their sins. It was all good if very messy, fun. The ceremony was followed by the "Crossing the Line Dinner" that night. We were all required to dress for the occasion and were promised a feast truly fit for a King's Court. When we walked into the dining room that night we could hardly believe our eyes. We had never seen so much food and so wonderfully set out and displayed. I think my love of seafood began from that evening as I devoured plate after plate of prawns, crab, cray meat, mussels... just recalling it now makes my mouth water. There was dancing into the night and the whole evening is one I shall never forget.

We were approximately 10 days from our destination but before reaching Australia we were to call at Cape Town. The crew informed us that we would be pulling into Cape Town at approximately dawn the next morning and if we wanted a truly unforgettable sight we should get up just before dawn and see the spectacle of Table Mountain Bay at that time. So, we did make the effort and the sight was truly magical. It was still dark when we looked out over the water and saw the whole of the Bay landward lit up - it resembled a true fairyland. We watched in awe as the sun rose and revealed Table Mountain, complete with its "tablecloth" of white cloud cascading down from the top. It was a truly an unforgettable sight and well worth the early start to the day.

It was around this time in the voyage that I discovered there was a daily "chocolates and sweets" shop set up on one of the decks! I realized suddenly that I would love a piece of chocolate so swiftly made my way to the "kiosk" and bought several bars of chocolate. Never had a piece of chocolate tasted so good as I devoured it, as a thirsty man would slake his thirst on water, I savoured every morsel of that chocolate bar!

We had a day in port and this time decided just to wander around at leisure and look at the town. We probably missed a lot of the landmarks most tourists see, but we certainly soaked up the atmosphere of the place. I did find the "white only" and "no blacks" signs in the city rather disconcerting and encountered for the first time a beggar sitting on the ground, minus legs, begging for money. We had cause to go into the post office, as we had mail we wished to send home, and waiting in the segregated queues was not pleasant. Even seats were marked with "whites only". Apartheid is a dreadful way for people to live and I thank God it was eventually abolished. We did not buy much but just enjoyed looking at the town and watching the people – everything was so bright and colourful. All too soon it was time to return to the ship. We were commencing the home run to Australia.

The ensuing days and nights were spent in entertainment and the swapping of addresses, so that we would not lose touch with our newly found (and much needed) friends from on board the ship. Several of the group we had formed were alighting at Fremantle – Andrew and Sheila, Jeff and Aileen and Dave. We were particularly friendly with Andrew and Sheila and indeed, they proved to be friends indeed to me during the first few months of living in Perth.

WESTERN AUSTRALIA – MARCH 1968

*T*he day had arrived! We were due into Fremantle Passenger Terminal today. It was with a mixture of apprehension and excitement that we first caught a glimpse of land – Fremantle harbour. How would we find living in Perth? Would we get jobs, homes, make friends? We went below to pack up the rest of our things. As I surveyed this very small space in which we had slept for the past 28 days, I realized that it had become our haven from the albeit enjoyable activities on board and it was with mixed feelings of sadness and excitement I closed the door.

Before we had left Yorkshire (was it really just 28 days ago?) we had noticed an article published in the local paper, "The Yorkshire Post". It was a letter written to the paper requesting that they publish it and was from an organization called "The Roses Club", the membership of which was made up of people who had migrated to Perth from Yorkshire or Lancashire. The members of the club were offering to act as "sponsors" for people wishing to migrate to Perth. They were offering to meet people off the ship, give them hospitality in their homes, and assisting them to settle into their adopted country, all as a gesture of friendship. I had replied to the writer of the article and they had written back to say that there would be representatives from their club at the Fremantle terminal to meet us. This was a comfort to us as other passengers were literally being checked off the ship and sent to migrant hostels initially, from where they would then find their own accommodation, jobs, etc.

The customs clearing process took a while – hardly surprising as there were hundreds of us to clear – but at one stage I heard our names being called over the loudspeakers "Would Mr and Mrs Renton please make their way to the visitor information desk", so we did and there we found Wilf and Sylvia, from the Roses Club, waiting to meet us. They were an older couple, both of whom worked on the Perth bus service (the MTT in those days) and it was with them that we were to spend our initial stay in Perth.

As we drove along Stirling Highway from Fremantle to their home in a suburb called Dianella, we hungrily looked at what was to be our new home for at least the next two years. It appeared to us to be very "Americanized" with rather unsightly billboards lining the highway and overhead power lines. We had arrived in March, the latter end of WA's Summer and our overcoats were both unnecessary and uncomfortable in the heat!

Another article we read before leaving the UK was one on Australian snakes and spiders. It seemed that everyone we knew who was aware that we were emigrating to Australia was taking a delight in showing us articles written by disgruntled migrants who, in some cases, had stepped off the plane arriving here and immediately begun arrangements to go back home! "Whingeing Poms" they were christened! The other articles were about the hundreds of poisonous snakes and spiders invading the very land on which we would walk! With my fear of spiders, this was an aspect of Australia I did not relish.

When we got to Dianella, and Wilf and Sylvia's house, I was almost afraid to walk on the grass for fear of what would bite my pommy toes! I did recoil in horror as we passed one awesome spider lording it in his regal web...but was instantly reassured that it was not poisonous! Made no difference to me, a spider was a spider in my eyes and this one was BIG!

Wilf and Sylvia had been in Perth several years. They had no children, just their dog, on whom they doted. They were very kind and told us they wanted no "board" money from us but we could donate something towards food. This was a very helpful start to us, as we had literally the minimum amount of $100 in the bank on which to live until we got jobs.

I would have no problem getting a job, as secretarial work was plentiful and in those days you either applied from ads. in the paper or went to a secretarial agency. I opted to do both and within days had my first interview. It was a meat manufacturing company, as Personal Assistant to the Managing Director. His secretary of several years was leaving to have a baby. Unknown to me at the time, our friend from the ship, Sheila from the ship, had applied for the position also; in fact we were the final two applicants. In retrospect, she may have lasted longer in the position than I did.

I started working there – in an old building in William Street – all the buildings in Perth looked old to me at that time, in fact, Keith and I were not overly impressed by the central business district of Perth in 1968; we felt we had taken a step back in time – approximately 20 years! However, we were determined to make a go of our new life so ignored the shortcomings and got on with the job of earning a living. I was soon ensconced in a job; however, the story for Keith was not the same. His profession had been that of sales and service in the car industry in the UK but all the sales representative positions were going to people who had "local knowledge". A couple of weeks after we arrived in Perth, Jeff, with whom we had kept in touch, rang Keith and told him there were jobs going up at a place called Barrow Island, off the North West coast of WA. It was just as a roustabout but the money was quite good and the company, WAPET, was hiring now. When Keith told me about it I knew that was what he was going to do and when later that day he phoned me at work and told me he had got the job but that he was due to fly out on the following Monday, I was dismayed but not surprised. He, on the other hand, had thought it would be longer before he would have to leave. The terms were that he would be up on the island for seven consecutive weeks and then be down in Perth for one! Great!

We needed the money so there was nothing else that Keith could do. He hated waiting around trying unsuccessfully to get a job whilst our meager savings dwindled away to nothing. So the following Monday I tearfully waved off Keith at the airport and went home to Dianella in a very low frame of mind.

I had never learned to drive in the UK so my sole source of transport was by bus. Andrew and Sheila were very caring and often called round to pick me up from Wilf and Sylvia's place to go out with them, to ease my loneliness. The weekends in particular were very long and lonely and I was missing my mother and everything familiar. In fact the only way I could cope with homesickness for the first couple of months was to avoid thinking about my mother, home, friends, until I could do so without feeling sad.

During this time the Managing Director of the meat manufacturing company and I came to a parting of the ways. I had not felt secure in the position and I really did not like my boss very much. The final straw for him, I think, came when he asked me to book his brother into a Perth hotel – he was flying in from the eastern states. In 1968 there was only one decent hotel in the city and that was the Parmelia Hilton. I rang to make a booking for our visitor only to be told, to my dismay, that they were fully booked for the whole of the week I wanted a room. Panic! I had no knowledge of the local accommodation scene, so in desperation asked the staff if anyone could recommend a decent hotel for the MD's brother to stay at. I should, of course, have told my boss and asked what he wanted me to do now, but I wanted to present him with a fait accompli to show him how competent his new secretary was. To this day, I do not know whether or not the staff set me up but a couple of them recommended a hotel, just across the river. I did not know the hotel and so, on their recommendation, I booked our visitor into this hotel. I was sacked a couple of days later! It turned out that the place was rather a dive which played very loud heavy metal rock music most nights of the week. It was a shock to the system being sacked. It was something I had never experienced in the UK and it was quite a blow to my ego! I was not actually sorry to leave a meat manufacturing company but my pride had been wounded.

For my second job I went through an agency. In those days if an agency placed you in a position successfully, they kept your first week's wages and a week's wages from the employer – fortunately a year or so later they stopped slugging the poor old employee (who could hardly afford to lose their first week's wage) and just charged the employer.

I was a secretarial assistant with another organisation, based up in West Perth. All the primary schools in WA at that time had P and C Associations; they helped raise money for equipment, etc., for the schools. Once again, the office was old and my fellow colleagues even older! There wasn't a lot to do and really, I was not interested in the work. I did what was required of me, but as I was not inspired by the position, I did not look around for any further duties to do. Consequently, a fortnight after starting there I was told that perhaps the position was not quite what I wanted and promptly sacked – again! Strike two. My ego was seriously bruised now, not to mention my finances. Fortunately, Keith's money was regularly being paid into our bank account so I had something on which to live!

Irrespective of my erratic work history at this time, however, I still managed to save from our combined wages, enough money to set us up in a little flat, our first home on our own. Keith had been up on Barrow Island for roughly five weeks at this stage when I found a furnished flat in Mt Lawley with a weekly rent of $16.00, and bought the necessary little things we needed to set up on our own. I bade Wilf and Sylvia a fond and grateful farewell, vowing to keep in touch, and moved into our flat to await the return of my husband. I was, by now determined that he was not returning to Barrow island, I had had enough of being on my own so decided to try and get him an interview or two to attend whilst he was down in Perth on his week's leave.

When we had first arrived and prior to my getting the job at the meat manufacturing company, I had applied for a position with a private detective but had been unsuccessful then. I noticed it was advertised for a second time so I rang up the man and asked him for another go at the position, I rather fancied myself as a "Miss Moneypenny"! He told me to come for an interview that evening, and said he was busy during the day. So I arrived at his offices, in West Perth again, for my interview. He told me I had not got the job the first time round because he had felt we would not stay in Perth – well, we had stayed so he was interested in offering me the job.

He suggested we go for a drink to the local pub and discuss the position. I felt a little uncomfortable with this but as I only had a lonely flat to return to that night I saw no harm in using up some hours possibly discussing my new career position! It was during the "interview" over a drink that the alarm bells began to ring. Unfortunately, I had told him Keith was away (mistake number one) and that I had moved into a flat and was no longer with our sponsors (mistake number two). The "interview" was extending a bit and I felt was becoming a little too familiar so told him I thought I should leave now and he could let me know about the job the following day. He tried to persuade me to stay but I was adamant that I wished to leave. It was by now quite dark and he offered to give me a lift home. I naively accepted (mistake number three) and he drove me to my flat. It was then he made his move and suggested, coffee might be nice – in my flat! By this time I realized of course he was making a play for me and I could not get out of the car quick enough! I said no to coffee, whereupon he suggested a "kiss" might be good to seal the employment agreement. I once again told him no to both the "agreement" and the job and started to open the car door. He held on to my arm and told me not to be so hasty – whereupon I smacked him across the face with the back of my hand (ouch! that hurt) and bolted for the cover of the flats while he was still recovering from the shock! I ran up those stairs so fast and opened the door with shaking fingers, convinced he would follow me there, but fortunately he did not. After I had recovered from the shock of what had just happened I became so angry with Keith for "abandoning" me in this strange country and ranted and raged at him on paper for the next hour. I posted the letter the next day. Keith said later he could not believe that the letter he was reading, containing the rantings of an enraged and de-ranged woman was really from me, but he was suitably upset that I had been subjected to such an experience. Needless to say I did not fulfill my interest in becoming a "Miss Moneypenny"!

During the week before Keith was due to fly back from Barrow Island there was an advertisement in the paper for a "Service Assistant" at a well-known car dealership in Perth. Since this was the line of work Keith had been involved in, in the UK, I rang the contact in the advertisement and explained that my husband had all the qualifications he was looking for but would not be in Perth for another week. He, thankfully, said he would not finish interviewing before the end of the week and that Keith was to contact him when he flew down. Fingers crossed! The day before he was due to fly down there was a cyclone off the WA coast and all planes were grounded. Panic! As it happened, however, someone had a bad accident with some broken glass and had to be emergency air-lifted from the island and there were a couple of seats on the plane, Keith was lucky enough to get a seat, although he said there were a couple of moments on the flight when he thought it had been his destiny to die in a plane crash, as the flight was really rough due to the cyclone activity in the area.

After being separated for seven weeks, when I met him at the airport I felt incredibly shy and self-conscious. Keith told me later that he could not get over how young I appeared to him when he first saw me – which was not surprising since I was still only 20 – I had had my birthday whilst he was away. In his mind, however, he had built up this picture of me which was somewhat embellished by the lack of female company on the island over the past seven weeks. He in turn arrived with a full blown beard, which further heightened my sense of alienation from him.

When he first arrived in Australia, somehow the effort to emigrate had also given Keith the impetus to try "different" things to find where he wanted to make his career path. To keep me happy he did go for the interview at the car dealership and was offered the position. Before accepting it, however, he suggested a couple of things he was interested in trying – one was a correspondence photography course, another was male modeling (Keith?) and the other was a traineeship in New South Wales – as a pilot! All of these activities involved copious amounts of money, of course, and although I understood his frustration at not knowing what he wanted to do (this had always been a problem for him), we really did not have the money to do much and needed to consolidate a little first. I did not relish the idea of him flying off (and leaving me in Perth again) to New South Wales to do the pilot's course. We agreed he could get a portfolio of photographs together for a modeling career if he really wanted to do so and he could also try out the photography course. All of which he did, and all of which came to nothing – but at least he tried them!

It was whilst he was with the car dealership we met and were befriended by a couple called Bert and Eileen. (More pomms! This was something that had struck us about Perth, it was incredibly difficult to find Australians, born and bred. Everyone seemed to be an immigrant!) Keith had always loved VW beetle cars and Bert had an old VW beetle body into which he was intending to build an engine, etc. and on sell it. It was an interesting project and Keith said he would like to help build the car and would probably buy the vehicle when it was finished. Thus, after weeks and weeks of working on the car every weekend – around at Bert and Eileen's house – we eventually bought our first car in Australia for $150.00! They did a wonderful job on the car and we kept it for about 18 months before actually managing to sell it (at a profit) to buy our second VW beetle.

I, in the meantime, had managed to get myself a job with a home building company and after waiting with baited breath for about two months, wondering when they were going to sack me, one day the Sales Manager called me into his office and informed me not that I was being sacked, but being given a raise! At last, I had found myself somewhere to work, which I liked and where I was doing well.

WE MOVE TO THE SEA! 1968-69

We had been in the flat since May 1968. Keith was working at the car dealership and I was still enjoying my job in the building company.

One Sunday morning in October of that year, I was in the kitchen making a late (cooked) breakfast when I felt the area vibrating and saw a knife begin to "skip" off the work surface and on to the floor! My first reaction was that for some reason my husband was indulging in pretty active exercise and I made a comment to this effect. His reply was that he was still in bed and in no way exercising! We both realized at the same time that we were experiencing the effects of a fairly severe earthquake!

We immediately opened the door to our flat to see what was happening outside, only to be faced with several other occupants of our flats doing the same thing. It is amazing when something like this happens, you see "cracks" where you were sure there were none before! We were all standing in a kind of stunned horror, not quite knowing what to do! I vaguely remembered some long past advice about standing in a doorway, which was "reinforced" against possible collapse – or getting downstairs on to ground level for safety. However, none of us did any of those things; we all just stood in frightened disbelief at what we were experiencing. The very earth beneath our feet was shaking and unstable. It was really, really scary.

Eventually, the tremors stopped. To this day I do not remember for how long it went on. When we all eventually decided to go back into our flats, I heard on our radio, which had been on at the time, the shaky voice of the announcer saying that he had never got down two flights of stairs so fast in his life, and he confirmed that we had, indeed, experienced an earthquake.

Later that evening, of course, the news was full of the earthquake drama. It transpired that the centre of the quake was at a town in WA called Meckering and the whole town had been completely leveled! Everyone was talking about "the earthquake" for weeks afterwards and even today, many years later; most people can remember what they were doing when Perth experienced its first major earthquake in 1968.

We stayed in our flat for a further 4 or 5 months. We had continued our friendships from the ship, with Andrew and Sheila, friends of Andrew's, Don and Ann and Wayne and Gwynith. Each and every Sunday for months we all played tennis at a local tennis court in South Perth, returning each week, in turn, to one another's home to have a joint meal together. This continued for approximately two years altogether whether or not the temperature was 15 degs. or 39 degs. (The phrase from the song "Mad dogs and Englishmen go out in the midday sun", often came to mind as I would watch the four men play a doubles in scalding heat during the Summer, whilst I cowered in the shade trying to stay cool!) It was this Christmas I experienced my first "century" temperature. In those days the "bra-dress" was all the rage and I remember driving down William Street on our way to friends for Christmas dinner, wearing a white bra-dress and registering in my mind that it was extremely hot and very, very unlike Christmas Day!

In January of 1969 we began to think about trying to move into something a little bigger and closer to the sea. At about the same time Keith also applied for and got a position with a security company, as a trainee Sales Manager. The idea was that he would work in all the different areas of the company in turn, learning the ropes from the bottom up, so to speak. He began by doing some sales representative work, obtaining new accounts, as at that time in Perth business security was fairly new and ground-breaking, so it was an uphill battle to convince businesses that they needed night security. After a stint in sales he was put on to actually doing the night watching rounds of the businesses, which were covered by the company's security.

We had by this time – in February – found and moved into a small (old) house, north of Perth and near the beach in Marmion. We moved in our meager belongings – it was partially furnished – we practically lived in the huge (country) kitchen which had a wood stove and a two burner cooker/griller to augment it. The whole of the back wall was covered by a wide window, which overlooked the well-established and large back garden. I could look out of the window and watch the weather coming in over the sea towards land. There was a small granny flat attached to the house, in which there lived an elderly friend of our landlords. She was okay, but we did not have much to do with her – to begin with.

I had my 21st birthday whilst we lived in this house. We still were limited in our friendships to those people who we had befriended on the ship. Money was still a scarcity for us but I remember we bought a lovely teak coffee table, several cushions, which we scattered all over the floor of the lounge, lit candles and cooked goodies to feed our guests. There was an open fire in the lounge and as my birthday is in May it was beginning to get a little cool, so the fire in the lounge was cosy. We invited, all up, about five couples for a casserole tea, so with ourselves, our party numbered the grand total of 12! But it was fun. We ate and talked and danced and laughed, so although low key it was still a memorable 21st party for me.

Things were a little difficult and strained for Keith and me at this time. Keith's employers had sent him on night watching duty which, of course, was during the night. So he would come home in the morning at just about the time I was leaving to go to my job during the day. Because of his shift work, Keith was irritable and I was still somewhat homesick and lonely, so it was not the best time for our marriage. I had also lost interest in sex, due to the different sorts of birth pills I was taking, so all in all we were not at our happiest in May/June 1969.

One day as I was coming out of my office in the evening, Keith met me! This was really unusual as he should have been at home preparing to start work. In 1969 there was an afternoon paper called "The Daily News" and Keith had met me because he knew I usually bought the paper to read on the bus home. He wanted to warn me that the front page heading "Man Bashed!" was him!! During his watch the previous night he had disturbed a gang of thieves at one of his business sites, in the process of trying to break into the safe! One of the men had tried to grab Keith's arms and another had brandished a piece of wood around his head but Keith had managed to free his arm and in his hand was the huge bunch of keys to all the premises his company looked after. So he brought this around and hit one of the men. In the skirmish Keith was hit by the piece of wood brandished by one of the thieves, although the attack was half-hearted as the thief was in the process of running from the building! Obviously, Keith was very shaken by all of this and almost overnight sprouted grey hairs at his temples – at the tender age of 27! The owner of his company was not a very pleasant man; totally lacking in compassion, and when Keith went into the office the day after his experience, not one word was said to him to convey that anyone gave a damn about what had happened. It was at this time his interest in the company began to wane.

Following his experience with the thieves Keith decided to get a dog! So off we went to the Shenton Park Dogs' home to get a night watching mutt. He chose a black Labrador who we called "Bob" and took our new family member home. We had by this time acquired a stray kitten (who we called "Puss" – very original) and she was less than impressed when we arrived home with this black monster! The only problem with Bob being a night watchman's dog was that after 1.00am in the morning he would not budge out of the car! Keith spent so much time trying to get him out of the back of the car that in the end he gave up. So we were left with a dog who did not want to fulfill the duty for which we had got him and not only that, during the day when Keith had to sleep he would bark or howl mournfully, thus incurring the wrath of the elderly lady living next door – unfortunately, Bob had to be returned to the Dogs' Home or we would not have anywhere to live!

About this time we started to want a home of our own but thought this was a while away as we had not saved very much money, having to use what we saved to buy items of furniture, etc. One day, however, we noticed an advertisement in the paper for a duplex unit in a place called Kardinya, with a particularly low deposit. At that time people usually needed a 10% (of the purchase price) deposit to put down on a house – this was saying with a deposit of $500.00 we could get our own home! We enquired about the property and went off to see it. We loved it as soon as we saw it: White rendered and very modern looking, it nestled in the shelter of a vast pine plantation and we wanted it very much. We went inside and further fell in love with it, so decided we would see about trying to buy it. The purchase price was $13,500.00. We would need a loan for about $14,000 to cover stamp duty, etc. We signed up and awaited settlement. Whilst we waited, one evening a young couple called around to see us. It transpired that Eric and Tricia were the owners of the other unit to ours and they had brought round a deed, for us to sign. Apparently they had begun negotiations for their half before we did and had discovered that the property was on a Purple Title, which meant everything we did with the properties had to be doubly signed. During the course of the evening the conversation turned to the price of the units and it transpired that their unit, which was identical to ours, had had a price tag of $12,500 - $1,000 cheaper than we were paying. We wished we had negotiated the price now, but then, we were very inexperienced when it came to buying houses! We had had to take out a second mortgage to buy the house, so things were going to be very tight for a while. Still, I was going to work for a few more years, so we would soon get on our feet.

In July 1969 we moved into our new home, with the help of Andrew and Sheila It did not take long because we did not have much in the way of furniture, just clothing and odds and ends, etc. Our mattress was on the floor (the floors were concrete throughout, floor coverings were not in our budget for the moment) and we still had our coffee table and a couple of pouffees. We had no table and chairs, just the bare essentials – a roof over our head and a mattress on which to sleep, but it was ours.

Keith was not happy with the night watching company and really did not wish to stay there, but what could he do? We now had two mortgages to cover. I had changed my job too. I left the building company to try and earn more money elsewhere and was now working for a wholesale manufacturer of medical scientific equipment, again in West Perth. It was what they called then, a Girl Friday position. I was the only administrative help in the office and worked closely with the State Manager in our two-man office. One lunch time my boss obtained a particularly lucrative contract for the company and decided we would go out to lunch to celebrate.

It was at that lunch that I had my first taste of raw oysters! It was a long lunch and so John, my boss, suggested we should call it a day and go home at about 3.30. That night I re-lived the taste of raw oysters quite a bit as I lay feeling extremely queasy on our mattresses (aka settee) on the floor.

A local bank was at that time advertising for staff. Andrew suggested to Keith that maybe a career in banking might be the way to go. We had not considered this idea, but Keith sent off his application and received an invitation to go for an interview. He had had some accounting experience for a couple of years, after he left school. Martha, his mother, had been so desperate to get him into a stable career she had "pulled strings" to get him into an accountancy firm as an articled clerk. It was an unfortunate experience for him, however, as the atmosphere was positively "Dickensian". Nevertheless he had shown an aptitude for figures so it was worth a try with the bank.

By the time he had been turned down by the bank for "being too old without experience" I had discovered I was in fact pregnant! My nausea was not the on-going effect of raw oysters. Keith was now quite desperate to get himself settled into a career and he did something totally out of character for him. He telephoned the Human Resources Manager of the bank and told him he thought he should re-consider his application. They needed staff and Keith needed and wanted a job (preferably with the bank) and it worked. He told Keith to come in again and talk some more. The upshot of which was that Keith was offered a position with the Bank and began his banking career. We heaved a sigh of relief, but our finances were still going to be extremely tight when I gave up work in April the following year.

1970 - 1972

*K*eith and I always seemed to be on a "budget". It was my fault I suppose, I got careless with my birth control and instead of my working for, say, five years to help put furniture and floor coverings into our little home, I fell pregnant within three months of moving into our unit!

I continued to work (queasily) well into my 8th month. Although at the time I did not realize it was so close to the birth of our daughter, as I had intended to stop and rest a month before her due date. Samantha was born two weeks prematurely, resembling a rather bald monkey, in the early hours of the 11th May 1970. I had a dream 5 hour first time labour and produced this 5lb 11oz doll-like baby relatively easily. She was so small I could not get clothes small enough to fit her.

I had been plagued by high blood pressure throughout my pregnancy – no doubt caused by all the stress of wondering what on earth was going to happen when my salary stopped coming in! Prior to Samantha being born, I had spent two weeks in hospital. Typical of those days the medical fraternity treated the patients as unintelligent morons with no right to know anything about their condition. I was therefore, told by my doctor I was being put into hospital for bed rest because my blood pressure was a little high. I was *not* told that I was not to get out of bed under any circumstances and if I developed a headache, I should tell someone! Consequently, the nursing staff would take my blood pressure, ask how I was and being used to headaches and taking them as fairly normal, I would say "fine". One day, however, a sister caught me getting back into bed after having been to the toilet. She asked me why I was out of bed and had not called for a bedpan, as the doctor had left instructions that I was not to get out of bed for any reason. This was news to me! She then asked if I had had any headaches and when I told her I had had one constantly since entering the hospital, I thought the poor woman was going to have a fit! "Why haven't you told a staff member?" I was asked. "No one told me I had to" I replied. I was watched like a hawk after that and six days later they grudgingly said I could go home for the weekend but only if I stayed in bed. I went. It was my 22nd birthday on the Saturday – the 9th – and the prospect of spending it in hospital was not enticing.

Poor Keith had been taking home my washing; nighties, panties, etc., and washing them by hand, hanging them out and after rushing home from the bank at the end of the day, would collect what was clean and dry and bring it to me that night. I have no idea when he found time to eat! I had not had a chance to buy any nighties, or extra clothes because I was (wrongly) under the impression I had time to do that before the baby came. Consequently, when I got home from the "blood pressure" stay in hospital I had no clean nighties and a couple of sad looking panties to change into! Keith had been told I had to stay in bed and he had taken this order to heart and insisted I stay there. He did not get around to washing my stuff on the Saturday. Our friends from the ship, Sue and Dave, came over on the Sunday evening for a birthday tea (a day late), so no washing had been done on the Sunday either. I was now wearing whatever tee shirt I could find that would fit over my lump and clean panties I had clandestinely washed whilst in the shower – absolutely no spares. Thus when, at 7.30 I got up to go to the toilet and was leaking without pee-ing I realized my waters had broken and Samantha was on her way! Two weeks early.

We have all seen the scenes in plays, etc., where the husband rushes around madly, achieving nothing in particular, and making panicky noises about getting the wife to hospital. In my case it was not the husband but the visiting friend, Dave, who fulfilled the panicky role! He was quietly reading the paper and fully immersed in what he was reading. I had called Keith to give him the good news, and asked for a towel. Keith told Sue who asked if she could pack anything for me, but as I had no clean clothes there was nothing to pack. At this stage I got a fit of the excited giggles and as things hotted up, Dave glanced up from his reading to ask what was happening about dinner. Keith said, "Sorry, Dave it's off. Carin's gone into labour". Dave blinked uncomprehendingly and for a full five seconds digested this information. Then he was up. "What do we do?" He asked running round in circles. "Don't we boil water or something?" he enquired picking up the teapot. "How far is the hospital, do you know the way?" I wish video cameras had been as prevalent then as they are now, his performance would have been priceless. Sue told me later that driving behind us to the hospital was nothing less than a "keystone cops" skit. He was in such a state of panic you would have thought it was *his* wife in labour and *his* baby on the way!

Keith rang the hospital and told them my water had broken and the sister reluctantly told him he had better bring me in as the water had broken, but being a first baby it would be hours yet before the baby was born. We got to the hospital at about 9.30pm and all was quiet and dark. There were very few nurses on duty, but we were shown to the pre-delivery area and left to our own devices for a while. My contractions weren't at this stage particularly uncomfortable and their regularity was difficult to gauge. About half an hour later a nurse came in to check my blood pressure, as a matter of course. She went very quiet and excused herself. She was off to call the doctor as I learned later that my BP was dangerously high. Two nurses came back with the biggest syringe I had ever seen, and with apprehension I enquired whether it was for me – it was! The sister proceeded to give me one of the most painful injections in my bottom I have ever had, and the other nurse, who was on the other side of the table to catch me if I rolled off, said "won't be long now Mrs Renton" but the first sister said quietly, "She has to have another on the other side".

The injection I had received was some sort of sedative designed to bring down my BP very quickly, so balancing on the table on top of a bedpan was great fun! Unfortunately, it was a little dodgy for the baby as it tended to send it to sleep as well. It was very fortuitous, therefore, that my labour proceeded at a fair rate of knots from about 11.00pm onwards. It was also fortuitous that Keith decided not to believe the sister when she said it would be *hours* yet, as there was no spare staff and by this time my labour was really being felt in my lower back and Keith would rub it for me whilst timing the contractions.

When Samantha was born at 12.40am she was "tired" from the effects of the drug mainly and because she was so small, only 5lb 12oz. Consequently, we did not have a cuddle as she was whisked away immediately. "Bonding" was not a word used in those days. After the doctor had done his repair work on me, Keith and I settled down to a well-earned cup of tea then parted company. I always say that cup of tea was the best I had tasted for a full nine months, as one of the things I had no longer enjoyed whilst pregnant was tea and coffee.

Samantha was in a humidicrib for three days, so she was three days old before we got to hold her. She was so small, and with her dark wispy hair, really did resemble a little monkey. We thought we were so clever as we stood with our noses pressed up against the window of the special nursery – "we did that" we thought as we looked at her!

When she was first wheeled into my hospital room I eagerly collected my baby from her crib. I was now going to fulfill the maternal role and breastfeed. However, Samantha had other ideas and would not come anywhere near me! She screamed and screamed! I felt so rejected. No one can understand the fear of being a first time mother, (particularly if heretofore one has had no contact with small babies whatsoever), unless they have gone through the experience. I really did not know what to do with this screaming scrap and eventually, in tears, I handed her back to the sister and retreated behind the curtains of my area. My milk filled breasts throbbed abominably, my *three day blues* were inexorably descending upon me and to cap it off I had not managed a bowel movement yet and feared the pain from my stitches when it did eventually arrive. In short I was **so** depressed. This was a true low point in the proceedings.

I did eventually manage to feed my baby and I did eventually manage to go to the loo, but the experience of one's first baby is not all it is cracked up to be in a lot of ways, especially if you have no more experienced friends or relatives upon whom you can draw and oh those hormones! How they play havoc with your moods.

The time came, however, when I was due to go home. Keith could not have the whole day off from the bank, but picked us up and we went home with our bundle of joy. I look back on that time, and I really believe I went through postnatal depression but again, as I knew no different, thought the sadness, tiredness and fear were all *normal* for a first time mother so did not receive any help. Never was the reality of our monetary predicament as obvious as it was when I stepped through the door of our duplex onto the concrete floor. There were chairs (one each), a coffee table and two pouffees. We were using a card table and folding chairs, borrowed from next door, from which to eat. Our mattress had only recently been lifted from the floor onto a base and we had a wardrobe. However, not for Samantha the lovely nursery with all the attendant brightly coloured furniture. Her wardrobe was an upturned crate with a curtain across it. Her minute clothes were stored in a suitcase (no drawers) and we had a borrowed bassinet. I washed her nappies in a secondhand (wringer model) washing machine we had bought. Disposable nappies were not in use at that time.

Keith had tried to take away the starkness of our surroundings by buying some flowers for the lounge, which was sweet, but when he left to return to work I felt very, very alone and afraid of the responsibility I now had.

Because of her size, Samantha suffered badly from colic right from the beginning. I was desperate to breastfeed because in all honesty we really could not afford bought baby food! This in itself caused me acute anxiety and I think conveyed itself to Samantha as she was an uptight baby who cried a lot. It is the old, old story of wishing one had the knowledge later acquired, at the time when it was really needed. I would have cuddled her much more. Enjoyed her much more and no doubt would have not had as much trauma in her early weeks, if I had known then what I know now. Dr Spock's book was our *bible* when it came to trying to work out what to do with our screaming infant. I tried very hard to be a good wife as well as mother and at 5.00pm would ensure I was made up and tidy for my husband coming home, sometimes at the expense of attending to a screaming baby who was hungry. Consequently, by the time Keith got home I was an emotional mess because Samantha could not feed, as she had a stomach full of wind from crying so much. Ah, such ignorance!

The day after I got home, Keith experienced firsthand how to bath and handle a small baby because I developed a dreadful migraine and was unable to do anything but suffer and vomit! So he bathed Samantha and would bring her to me to feed, which I did in a blur of nauseous pain, then look after her as best he could until the next feed – which was about 2-3 hourly. A true baptism of fire, but as always, he took it in his stride.

When Samantha was about two weeks old I began to feel unwell and my right breast became very sore. I got progressively worse until Keith had to bundle me and our baby (in her bassinet), into our ancient old VW beetle and go to the closest doctor, which was in Applecross. By the time I got to the surgery I was almost unconscious and the doctor then dispatched my distraught husband to the nearest 24-hour chemist to obtain an anti-biotic prescription, initially as an injection and thereafter in pill form. I had developed a breast abscess, an extremely high temperature and was rather ill. The doctor then helped Keith carry me back out to the car, together with bassinet and baby. He called at our home later that night to see how I was, for which I was very grateful. I was pretty unaware of anything for a few days, except the excruciating pain whenever I tried to feed my poor little baby – not a good time in her short life.

At about three to four months, Samantha and I at last began to "bond". She was a little bigger and less colicky and demanding and I at last felt "human" again. She was beginning to eat some solid food (not much) but some. Samantha never did develop a liking for food and gained the distinction of being the only baby one of our friends had ever looked after "who chewed custard" before swallowing it! I sometimes despaired of her ever growing up! She seemed to live on Milo (and when I could get away with it a beaten egg mixed in) and custards.

When she was about 14 months old I decided I would have to return to work part time at least, to help with our finances. We found a good daycare center for her in Claremont and then Keith and I would commute into the city to our respective positions. I had managed to obtain a part time position with a small firm of real estate agents and for a while we began to make progress. That is until the day we were called by the daycare center and told that Samantha was not very well and we had better collect her. When I got there I was horrified to see her very red little face and eyes – she had caught Measles.

Samantha was a very sick little girl for about three weeks. Even to this day she gets prolonged coughs following any kind of cold. Seeing my daughter so sick with this "child's disease" has made me very pro – vaccine. For days on end all I could do was cuddle her and get as much fluid into her as she would take. It is the most miserable disease to have.

In March of 1972 I was convinced I was pregnant again, only this time we had planned it. What is more I was sure I was having a boy. Everyone laughed at me as I gaily went out and bought a new maternity dress at 2½ weeks pregnant, but I was right, our son would be born at the end of November/early December 1972.

MOORA

*K*eith had been promoted to Accountant at the Moora branch of the bank and we were being transferred up there and would have a bank house. This was the beginning of the turn in our economic struggles, as the bank house was a low rent and we could rent out our duplex – thus paying its mortgage. In a way it was sad to leave it, as we had not long put floor coverings throughout the house, after living on concrete floors for eighteen months, and bought various items of furniture, but we were ready to move on. We organized with an agent to manage and let our home.

It did not take long to pack up our goods and chattels and at last it was moving day! We dutifully dosed our cat up with sleeping pills for the (2-hour) journey to Moora. The weekend before – seems unbelievably stupid now – we had also acquired a Labrador/boxer cross puppy who we called Max. He was about 8 weeks old and very cute – he would not grow too big, the breeder assured us - of course!

Our furniture had been loaded up and all that remained was to load the family into our car, which by this time was a VW station wagon (still old but not quite as ancient as the beetle)! We were ready to leave but could not find the cat. After searching everywhere for her we found her feeling very sorry for herself at the bottom of a basket of linen. She still looked awake but not happy! We piled toddler, queasy wife, young pup and disorientated cat into the car. It was a very warm day in March and we began to worry about the puppy getting dehydrated so we fed it choc-milk all the way! (Yes, we really did that). The cat had not settled at all and was climbing all over us meowing pitifully. At this point I was reminded of my dreadful allergy to cat fur and began sneezing non-stop. Samantha was also not a very happy little ankle-biter and the whole trip, which started out with such promise, was deteriorating rapidly!

After what seemed like absolute hours – although it was really only two – we arrived in Moora and drove round to the address we had been given for the

Manager's house. By this time I had been sneezing so much I looked as though I had been crying for a month non-stop, rendering my eyes swollen slits above an equally swollen, beetroot coloured nose, and was not a pretty sight! The cat was still wailing and so was Samantha. The pup, however, had gone really quiet and we were convinced we had poisoned him, and given that I now know that chocolate is very bad for dogs, we probably had! When we reached the Manager's house we introduced ourselves to the Manager's wife. What an impression she must have formed of the new town bank 2IC and his family.

Whenever you are moved to a country town, the bank pays for the family to stay in a motel for a few days until the house has been sorted out and some unpacking done. So, following Maree's directions we went to the Moora Motel to check in. Whilst waiting for the keys, Keith noticed a very large sign stating "No pets" were allowed in the motel rooms. Great! Our first hour in the town and we already have to sneak our pets into a forbidden area.

The room was clean and cool and we immediately set up Samantha's cot and smuggled in the, by now drugged out of its brain cat, and a sad looking pooch. I had been told by someone that the water in Moora contained a higher than normal amount of salt, so the more you drank, the thirstier you got! By now, I was the one totally dehydrated from all the sneezing I had been doing, but try as I may I could not quench my thirst – oh the power of the suggestion! We were informed that the house did not have electricity because the previous occupants had been gone for more than six weeks, so as this was the weekend (Friday afternoon) there was no one around (they said) to switch on the power to the house. So we had no alternative but to stay in the motel, with our menagerie.

That night, Samantha slept very badly, the cat would from time to time emit the most mournful of wails, and I got thirstier and thirstier. During the night I got out of bed to answer a call of nature and stepped in something unspeakably disgusting that the puppy had deposited on the floor. The poor thing had diarrhea from all the choc milk we had fed it and we had not locked him in the shower recess. The mess in the morning was unbelievable – as was the smell – and I guiltily found the local grocery store and bought a large bottle of disinfectant which I proceeded to empty all over the offending patches, in an effort to conceal the fact that we had harboured a canine in the motel room!! We could not spend another night in the motel under these circumstances so we begged our Manager, to pull whatever strings he had to get the electricity switched on at our house so we could take our illegal charges away from the motel.

We managed to get into the house on Sunday. We had dispatched the cat and dog into the empty house for the Saturday night. Our neighbours later informed us that they set up a pathetic duet of miaowing, whining and barking for a large part of the night, no doubt endearing us to our neighbours straight away!

My pregnancy with Samantha had caused me considerable nausea and this pregnancy was not much better, plus I was extremely tired as is usually the case in early pregnancy. The house had been empty for the better part of eight weeks and in the country the dust can settle almost as you move your duster from area to area. The cleaning up was, therefore, quite horrendous and I was less than physically able to cope too well. However, over the next week I managed to clean up reasonably well, utilizing will power and good old fashioned elbow grease. It was not a pleasant week. Keith had to start at the bank straight away and I was left to tend the upset toddler, the unforgiving cat and puppy and try to clean up and feed us all.

Once things had settled down a little bit I decided to take Samantha for a walk in the pram to have a look around. After all the stress, I was feeling a little better and I should have been expecting it but I wasn't, I developed a migraine headache. In a desperate bid to stop it before the headache became totally unbearable, I called into the chemist and told them I was getting a migraine and they gave me an over the counter remedy to see if it would help. My migraines have always been very severe and in actual fact if I take a pill to try and counteract the headache, my digestive system has by this stage already shut down and with my first vomit, up will come the pill. This instance was no exception, but as it turned out it was advantageous because I subsequently found out there was a substance in the pill which could have brought about a miscarriage! The staff in the chemist shop should have enquired whether or not I was pregnant before giving me the remedy!

We had been in Moora approximately 8 days when, whilst washing some dishes I happened to glance out of the window and noticed an odd orange colour where the sky used to be! I was watching this in a rather bemused way when Margaret, our next door neighbour, came rushing in and said "Quick, close up all your windows, there is a dust storm approaching". Being a townie I had never experienced such a phenomenon but nevertheless proceeded to try and close all 150 louvre glass windows along the sleepout whilst Margaret closed the windows of the rest of the house. The storm hit us very quickly and was unbelievably noisy, but lasted only about a minute. I had no idea so much sand could be deposited into a house through closed windows in such a short time. I stared in speechless horror at the mess before me. That was it! "I am leaving this God-forsaken town and returning to Perth straight away," I sobbed. Margaret, however, ignored me apart from the "there, there" bit and proceeded to wipe the sand off the kettle and make a cup of tea. I stayed.

Another interesting aspect of living in the country is the septic tank situation. All of our water waste, washing water, toilet flushings, etc., disappeared into an underground septic tank. I had noticed that towards the end of the week the toilet had taken a long time to flush away, to the point where we could not use it! We found out, upon enquiring about this from the all-knowing Margaret, that this was because the septic tank needed emptying and was full. "Bullsie" the operator of the tank which did this task, was called and he arrived sometime in the afternoon. We had utilized Margaret's toilet when necessary and all water in the sink had painstakingly been bailed out on to the back lawn. We put up with a six day toilet for a month, whilst waiting for the bank to organize to have a leach drain put into our garden.

The bulldozers duly arrived at our back gate and began clearing a deep trench down one side of the back garden. The finished trench, by the end of the first day was approximately 2 metres deep and 25 metres long. Wonderful! A real play area for a 2 year old toddler! I was a bag of nerves all of the following day, keeping an eye on Samantha to ensure she did not utilize her new playground. Eventually, the drain was put in – about a week later – and the trench covered up. There was a metre high mound the whole length of our back garden when they had finished it which leant an interesting aspect to the landscape of the area, but at least we could use the toilet for the full seven days per week. Later, when the grass had grown over it the children had a great time running over and rolling down their very own hill.

Bank staff in small towns generally get involved in the local clubs; actually playing whatever sport it may be and holding an office on the various committees. Our interest was tennis, and Keith being a good tennis player became very involved in the Moora Tennis Club. Every Saturday we would walk up to the tennis club with an assortment of toys to keep Samantha occupied (hopefully) whilst I stole a game of tennis here and there. I was and am not a particularly great tennis player so one or two sets were enough for me. The Easter Tournament was a big occasion every year and that whole weekend would generally be taken up entirely with tennis, either (Keith) playing or our helping out with the catering etc. When I got a little further on with my pregnancy I accepted (sometimes rather ungraciously) that I would be a *tennis widow* at the weekends. However on the whole it was very much a family club and mostly we enjoyed our membership.

The same could not be said for the golf club. Keith had not played golf before and discovered this *disease* in Moora. I say disease because once the bug has been caught it is insatiable and lasts forever! Golf was the Winter game and I remember one Saturday afternoon there was a terrific hail storm in Moora. I stood at the back door of our house, watching in awe as first the rain then the hail pelted the ground and I naively thought to myself, "No, he would not be playing in this....

would he?" I realized that evening when my very damp husband returned home, how fatally this man was infected by the golf disease. We had a few arguments because of his new-found love of golf. Every weekend would run into my week for me. Keith was okay he went to work Monday to Friday and the weekends were a change for him. For me, who had never really settled into homely domesticity, I craved some outings, time with husband, family times, but golf always had to take precedence on a Saturday and I grew to hate the game. Even to this day I cannot stand to watch or play golf.

Our *little* Labrador pup took after his boxer father and grew to be the size of a small horse! In spite of this, however, he was a gentle giant and Samantha would climb all over him and ride him without him flinching. Though I am sure there were times when he looked at me with a pleading "get her off me, please" look on his face. We lived on the route into town for the local indigenous people as they came in from their camp area. I never actually saw any of the children baiting Max but we noticed an increasing agitation on Max's part as he frenziedly barked at the various groups walking past our gate. We feel he must have been poked with sticks or something similar, judging by his reaction, but we never actually saw anything. He was at least our own home security as only we knew he was as soft as a kitten. When he ran at you and barked he could really look awesomely vicious, even though he would probably lick most people to death rather than bite!

It was about this time that I noticed the bottoms of my sheets and towels were coming in from the line with holes in them. I scoured the clothesline to find the offending sharp edge or nail, which was causing this to happen. It wasn't until one day I happened to be going out the back door I discovered the cause of the holes – Max! He was having a wonderful time hanging on to the edge of my sheet and being dragged around when the wind blew the line! I can still hear my neighbour's loud laughter as she glanced over the fence to find out at whom I was swearing and cursing, only to see me chasing our dog with a stick vowing disembowelment!

My Mother had arrived in Australia when Samantha was just 2 years old and I was 4 months pregnant. I had not seen her for three years, although of course we had kept in touch during this time.

When I had left England in 1968, Mum was going to marry Jim Linn. I had met him a couple of times and although I was not over fond of him, he seemed to make Mum happy. Apparently, though after I left their romance petered out. Mum became very ill with her gastric ulcers and indeed had a lifesaving operation in 1970 in which two thirds of her stomach was removed due to the damage done by these ulcers (there were two). She had always wanted to come to Australia. In fact she and my father had enquired about emigrating over here before he died. So it was natural that she should come over here to me. Mum arrived off the plane with a sore looking burn on her chin. It transpired that she had burned herself with a cigarette by falling asleep in mid smoke! We drove her back to Moora and she spent time with her only grandchild, Samantha, who she had never seen apart from photographs. Keith and my mother had never really enjoyed spending time together so he made himself scarce whilst she visited.

Mum had not been with us very long before we noticed cigarette burns starting to appear in our chairs and sheets of her bed. She was scalding herself quite a bit at night when she woke and would sometimes make herself a midnight drink. She was speaking with a slurred speech, although we knew she had not had anything to drink! I was in a highly emotional state in my pregnancy and my annoyance at the burn marks appearing in our (hard earned) furniture erupted one night and we had a terrible row, because I wanted her to go to the local hospital and get checked out. Particularly, there was an awful burn between her fingers which indicated that once again she had fallen asleep with a lighted cigarette between her fingers and they had burned through the skin layers, before she woke up. She wouldn't go, but eventually after I had hysterics she grudgingly capitulated.

We subsequently found out that Mum took sleeping pills to enable her to sleep. Since my departure she had been so depressed that she had taken to needing pills in order to sleep. The problem was that she had grown so used to them that she would take a pill, fall asleep, wake up a couple of hours later and would assume that she must have forgotten to take her pill, and would take another. The situation was further made dangerous because she would insist on smoking in bed whilst reading (she was a copious reader), would fall asleep with a cigarette in her hand, hence the burning accidents. The sleeping pills were rather strong and accumulating in her system which would account for the slurred speech and her dopey frame of mind when brewing a cup of tea. One of the sisters at the hospital (to whom my mother took an immediate and intense dislike) explained what was happening. She told me that I would have to dole out mum's pills to her and hide the rest because she could not handle them, as they were addictive. As you can imagine, mum did not like this state of affairs at all and she became as devious as any drug addict about obtaining pills under false pretenses, *viz*: saying her pill had rolled under the bed could she have another, finding where I was hiding them and taking an additional couple, etc.

The stress of all this was beginning to show on me, mum and our marriage and fortunately mum found herself a live-in position in Perth and eventually left by train for the metropolis of Perth. We heaved a sigh of relief tinged with concern because of the pill problem.

BRADLEY KEITH RENTON

*B*rad was born after a 2½ hour labour on the 1st December 1972. Half the time it took me to have Samantha. The doctor joked that if I continued to half my labour times, when I fell pregnant again I had better book myself into hospital the week before! Actually, he was quite right as I found out many years later when I had my third baby.

By the time Brad was born I was feeling a lot more confident in my "baby experience" and also our finances had settled down considerably. All of this was just as well because Brad was a baby who did not believe in waiting for anything! He weighed in at 8lbs 2ozs at 9.00pm on Friday 1st December 1972.

He was actually due on the 29th November, so was a couple of days late. The only memorable things about his birth were the sister-in-charge at the hospital being horribly sick with food poisoning at the time, begging me to hurry up and have this baby so she could go home and "die" in peace! The other was the (old) doctor who attended me who insisted he keep his thumb in the place my emerging baby's nose should have been (to stop the baby slipping back he said, all I know is that it hurt like hell) which resulted in my baby's nose being crooked. So for the first 13 days of Brad's life he only had one nostril to breathe through. This did not, however, curtail in any way the strength of his cry, as my next door neighbour remarked when she visited the hospital later that night with a cut hand. She could not believe the baby crying in the "new born" nursery was my 1 hour old son, she said he had a cry strong enough for a 12 month old child and she should know, she had had five of her own!

Mum, of course, came up to "help" and see her new grandson. I was not well and was lying down one day whilst mum was staying. It was towards teatime and I heard an enormous "boom" from the kitchen. Keith came in a few minutes later unable to contain his mirth. He said mum had decided she was going to be helpful and make us all some dinner and in her endeavours to light our gas grill had left the gas on for too long before igniting it and it had exploded out at her. I was horrified he could find this funny, but he assured me she was okay but her eyebrows were singed and she had hastily told Keith not to tell me what had happened. How could I miss it? Poor mum.

Mum eventually returned to Perth and Keith and I spent the next couple of months getting ourselves back on to an even keel.

When Brad was 13 days' old we came down to Perth to see an ear, nose and throat specialist who, in 20 seconds, straightened my baby's nose and charged us an arm and a leg for the privilege. I had to gently push his nose into position each time I changed his nappy or whenever I thought about it over the next two to three weeks and so by the time he was about six weeks' old his nose was relatively straight.

For all his very loud cry, which waited for nothing and no one, Brad was a happy baby; always ready to have a hearty chuckle. I could always tell when he was putting on a growing spurt though because my ears would "crackle" when he cried which meant it had gone up a few decibels again!

I have always said the second baby is always a difficult time in a mother's life, because even though she may be more confident when handling the child, there is another demanding toddler to handle as well and somehow the two children never seem to be able to have a sleep at the same time! So you are on the go all the time. My two were no exception and add to this a toddler with recurring tonsillitis and you have constant demands on your time. My mother came up a couple of times "to help", but unfortunately despite her good intentions, all that seemed to happen when she stayed was a wedge being driven between Keith and me and disruptions to the shaky routine.

Mum had a live-in position as housekeeper/carer of the wife of a prominent politician in Perth, who unfortunately had cancer. She loved her position and was heartbroken when after about six months the lady died. I remember she came up to Moora to see us after the funeral and when Keith met her at the station, he was horrified to see mum stagger off the train, highly intoxicated – she had been drowning her sorrows in the dining car. She eventually recovered from her imbibing and a couple of days later she decided she would take Brad for a walk in his pram to the town. It was mid-Summer and mum was going to go for a walk at midday. We told her to wait for a while until things cooled down a little but she wouldn't listen. Mum returned an hour later, walked into the kitchen and promptly fainted clean away with sunstroke!

Brad was a pretty healthy baby up until about 10 months, however, one night just about the change of season from Summer to Autumn we were awoken around midnight by a terrible noise coming from Brad's bedroom, next door. When we rushed in there to see what was wrong we were horrified to hear and see our boy gasping for breath and making a dreadful noise in the process! We were so frightened and as is the way in the country in an emergency you don't call the doctor you just go straight to the local hospital. So grabbing Samantha and wrapping them both in a blanket we rushed off to the hospital with our son. Such was his condition that I was terrified we would not make it in time! When we got to the emergency section, however, his breathing was marginally easier but still very, very noisy. After careful examination by the doctor we were informed that our son was suffering his first bout of croup, brought about by the dusty winds that night. He had to stay in hospital overnight, which he did not like, and we were able to take him home the next day, with instructions on what to do when the next bout hit, as it inevitably would.

This was the beginning of frequent nights spent sitting in the bathroom running the hot water to ease his breathing. In all Brad had three stays in hospital, each one a little longer than the last, as they invariably turned into respiratory infections. The last stay was rather traumatic for our boy, however, as he was attacked and bitten by a fellow patient at the hospital and this was the insult added to the fact that he had to stay in there for 3 or 4 days.

We were advised that "Friars Balsam" was a great way to keep therapeutic fumes wafting around the house, so every night during the colder months (when croup seemed to prevail) we would have a pan of hot water on the boil with "Friar's Balsam" in it. It certainly seemed to work and at least it gave me something I could do in the event of a further attack.

Whilst in Moora we formed quite a few friendships with couples in similar circumstances to our own. Fred and Leslie Kyle had a small holding on the outskirts of the town. Fred was a sheep contractor and Leslie had been a nurse but was now a full time mum. Their daughter, Jane, was born just a couple of weeks before Brad. Another couple we spent some time with was Linda and John Burl. John and Linda arrived in the town around the same time as we did. Their children kind of slotted between ours, Samantha was the oldest of the four. Linda, Leslie and I formed what was known as the Young Wives Club in Moora. There were numerous activities which we organized, I think in a desperate attempt to stay sane in a country town, as a few of us had been placed there because of our husband's work positions and not by choice. Another couple we befriended was Peter and Ruth. Ruth wasn't as involved in the Young Wives Club but both she and Peter hit a mean tennis ball so a lot of our socializing was spent after the Saturday tennis games.

There was one time when we all went water skiing on a local "lake". One of the young farming couples in our group owned a small runaround boat. We all went out to the lake one weekend, Brad was about 4 months old I think and it was a really hot day. I noticed the flies were all congregating around my baby son – one look revealed the reason was the unmistakable aroma of a full nappy attracting them! It is not easy to change a smelly nappy on a sandy beach, whilst batting away determined flies! It was also towards the end of the tennis season and Moora Tennis Club had got into the finals of the local Tennis Pennants competition. Both Keith and Peter were in the team but wanted to try their hand at water skiing, as did I. None of us realized just how difficult it is to get up on skis for the first time but we all kind of managed, however, the next day we were all in diabolical pain, hobbling along on muscles we never knew existed, and Peter and Keith had a finals match to play in a couple of days! They did win but not without pain!

One of the highlights of my "amateur dramatics" career happened in Moora. The local newspaper reporter was very into drama and the musical arts and decided to produce a musical. The choice was "The Pyjama Game" and somehow I managed to get the lead role. When were just sitting around in the initial stages practising the songs I didn't put a lot of gusto into my singing, but when we got into the hall for the final rehearsals I really let rip; so much so that people backstage who could not see who was singing thought it was someone else when I launched into my songs! It was a huge success and I remember to this day my "glowing reviews" in the local paper. It had to last me a long time, as I did not take up my "singing career" again for another 16 years!

1974 – 1980

$\mathcal{W}$e stayed in Moora for approximately two years. Then came the call from head office to say that Keith had been promoted to a bigger branch. We had been hoping that we would have another country stint whilst the children were small so it did not interfere with their schooling. This was not to be, however, and we were posted back to the metropolitan area, with Keith now Accountant at the Gosnells branch of the R & I.

We moved back into our duplex, which was now somewhat crowded with four to share the house (plus a huge dog), instead of two. Brad and Samantha had long since been in beds, however, so we bought some bunk beds and squashed them into the bedroom which had housed our minute baby four years before.

Brad was a lively little boy, with no sense of danger, like all little toddlers. One Sunday morning Keith was getting ready to go to golf. At this point we still did not have a second car so when he left for golf I would have to stay put. We could hear the children playing in their bedroom then it went very quiet and subsequently, Brad came into our bedroom and very quietly climbed up on to my knee (I was still in bed). I noticed he looked rather pale and he felt clammy to the touch. I asked Samantha if she knew what was wrong with Brad and she told me he had fallen off the top bunk of their beds! At this point, as if to push the point, Brad proceeded to be sick. He must have hit his head.

I told Keith he would have to arrange to get a lift with someone because I was taking our son to Princess Margaret Hospital as I suspected he had concussion. He of course would not let me go by myself with the two children, so we organized for Samantha to stay with a neighbour and we placed Brad in his car seat and began to make our way, in quiet panic, to the hospital. By this time Brad was crying and said his head was sore. We hit the Freeway and Keith was speeding in his anxiety to get our son to hospital. We were pulled over by an unmarked police car and when we stopped I got into the back with Brad as he was saying he felt sick again.

Just as the policeman came to the driver's window to enquire as to the reason for our speed, Brad was sick again and I said very irritably, "If you are going to fine us, please hurry as our son needs to get to hospital". With that the policeman said "Don't worry M'am, just pull in behind and follow us". Thus began the hairiest car drive we had ever experienced. With the police car's blue light flashing and siren blasting we followed behind them trying to keep up as they skidded through intersections and stopped the traffic to let us pass without stopping. Keith said later he could not stop his leg from shaking because of the adrenalin rush!

We were rushed through emergency/admittance by the policemen letting them know there was a "head injury" on its way and true to form, just as we hit the desk, Brad was sick again.

We were seen straight away by an admitting doctor, who after a cursory check, told us to take Brad to X-ray. I shall never forget that experience! Imagine if you can, a very little boy, feeling very unwell and scared being placed unceremoniously underneath a huge machine with lights and gadgets everywhere and being told to "stop crying and keep still". He was scared to death and I was very pleased when we were finished with the procedure.

There was no apparent fracture of the skull, which was of course what they were searching for, however, he did have concussion. So after a few hours of observation, Brad was allowed to come home with us, with strict instructions to us to keep a close eye on him for the next 48 hours and if we noticed any of the symptoms listed on a sheet of paper they gave us, we were to bring him straight in again. It was a relief to be able to take him home, as after three separate stays in Moora hospital because of very bad croup, Brad was very unhappy away from home. Brad recovered, none the worse for wear, but he didn't get on to the top bunk again for quite some time.

After we had been back in the duplex for approximately 18 months, we decided we would have to move into a larger house. We had grown used to Kardinya and it was at last becoming civilized with real buses and a shopping center! However, we also wanted to see what was available closer to Gosnells, and Keith's bank branch.

Thornlie

We looked around and eventually found ourselves in an area of Thornlie which was comparatively new and had several partially built homes available. We found a house with the layout we liked, which was only half built. We liked it and proceeded to finish the tiles and floor coverings, etc to our specification. This was at the tail end of 1975 and Samantha was due to start school the following year.

Our home was ready early in January of 1976 and we moved in just in time for Samantha to start school at Primary School, which was a new school, just opening that year.

Like a good and dutiful parent, I became involved in the P and C Association, which was where I met Michael and subsequently his family. This family was to become very dear to us through the years. Michael and I would be amongst the movers and shakers to get activities going for the P & C Association over the next couple of years.

About this time the on-going problem we had experienced with Samantha's tonsillitis became acute and the day I took her to see a (referred) ENT Specialist he said she had a bad throat infection currently in progress, and I had not noticed any change in her – so frequent were her infections they had become the "norm"! So Samantha was duly booked into Bentley Hospital to have her tonsils out.

In our efforts to make things as easy for her as possible in hospital, once we had dropped her there we felt it would be best to wait until the following day to visit again. Oh to have the knowledge then that we have now! Samantha told me many years later that she had sat in the visiting room that night, which had windows which looked up the approach road to the hospital, waiting for us to come and see her. Oh, how I wanted to cry when she told me that. At home, I was aching to be with her and hold her close and I thought this would only unsettle her so stayed away, miserably sitting on her bed cuddling one of her soft toys. She never was one to tell us what she wanted in the way of contact with us when she was young. Fortunately, she did express herself later, but I wish so much that I had done lots of things differently with her, but then, don't we all think back to times when we could have done something so much better by following our heart and not our head.

We picked her up later the next day. She of course had a very sore throat and did not feel particularly well. We took her home and fortunately watched her like a hawk. I say fortunately, because we were not given a list of things that *might* happen – one of which was hemorrhaging! On the third day home I was with her in the morning when she suddenly started coughing and spluttering and thankfully managed to cough up an enormous blood clot. My heart stopped when I thought what might have happened had she been lying down. She could have choked to death. After this point, however, Samantha started to recover rapidly and her appetite at last began to improve.

Up until Brad was approximately 3½ years old I had ridden around everywhere with him on the back of my bike. It was getting to the point, however, that he was too heavy and my bike was dangerously out of balance. About this time Keith's boss asked if anyone was interested in buying an old Vauxhall Viva car, which had belonged to his late wife. It was in very good condition and he only wanted $400.00 for it. We bought it. I had my first, very own, car. It was dark red with grey vinyl upholstery and went like a colt, once it started! I felt a million dollars at the wheel of *my* car, it could have been a Ferrari I was so proud. The engine itself was really great it was the starter motor which was a little cantankerous. When we first got it, we would not have to physically rock it very often! Just now and then the engine would be turned off at just the wrong spot on the starter motor and we would have to rock the car from side to side until we felt the "clunk" which told us it was once again okay! I coped with this very well but Samantha and Brad were becoming very aware of their image amongst their peers and if they were in the car, say, going to school, they would slide down in their seats in the vain hope that their friends would not see their mother madly rocking her car at an intersection, in an effort to re-start it!

We kept my car for about a year. Towards the end, however, it was more often the norm to rock the car to start it, than not! Samantha and Brad would make any excuse not to be taken round to school in Mum's car! They'd rather walk. The last straw came when my car stalled about a kilometer from home and no amount of rocking would start it again. Eventually I walked home – it was a weekend – and got Keith and the pair of us pushed this car home! I had no idea there were so many undulations in the streets leading to our house. By the time we got home both of us had legs of jelly and were breathing so hard I wondered who would have the heart attack first!

Keith decided we would sell it, but being essentially a very honest man he would make it clear to a prospective buyer that the starter motor could be a problem. A man enquired about my beloved car on behalf of his daughter. We had at this time managed to start it again and when he tried it out, it burst into life without hesitating and he took it around the block and came back suitably impressed. We did tell him about the starter motor being a little uncertain but he said his son was a mechanic and would fix it cheaply. He gave us $400.00 – precisely what we had paid for it a year ago – and jumped in and drove it off – it never missed a beat and I sadly wished my car well on its way.

It was 1977 and Mum had been saying for a while that she felt she would like to retire – on what I have no idea because she had not saved any money all her life and had paid no superannuation or insurance. She was staying with us because she had set fire to her employer's house, by falling asleep whilst smoking in bed. The house was currently under repair thanks to my Mother and not surprisingly she had not been asked to return to her position so we helped her look for a flat. She wanted to live near the sea so we finally found her a nice flat at Scarborough, and hoped she would move in – soon! Things were pretty strained at home because Mum smoked the foulest smelling cigarettes called "Camel". Neither Keith nor I smoked and we did not like it around Samantha and Brad – Samantha was 6½ and Brad 4. We had moved Brad into Samantha's room and given Mum temporary use of Brad's bedroom. I had asked Mum time and time again not to smoke in bed, especially in view of the last debacle where she had nearly burned the place down.

I noticed that once again she was falling asleep very often and sometimes with a drink in her hand, watching television, she would go out like a light. Having experienced this in Moora we knew what was happening, so I asked Mum for her pills again but she vowed she was being careful with them and did not want to "have them doled out to me like a child"!! Things were pretty fraught.

One evening, late, before going to bed I checked on the children and then went to Mum's room to see if she wanted a cup of tea before I retired for the night. There she was sitting on the side of her bed, slumped forward – out cold – with a cigarette quietly burning a hole in her fingers and the carpet. I was absolutely beside myself with rage. Our children were in this area and the carpet could have gone up at any time! Mum was so drugged out she hardly knew what I was doing or saying as I none too gently pushed her into bed, removed all cigarettes, matches, pills everything from her room so she could not take anything and told her we would talk in the morning.

Next day, I was still very, very angry as I realized the extent of her drug problem. I told her we needed to get her to help. One word led to another and we had a dreadful row. At about lunch time I said I would have to leave her for a while before I said more that I would regret. After about 20 minutes I had calmed down a little and decided to go back and talk with her to see what we could do about her addiction. I walked into the bedroom and found her lying on the bed snoring very loudly with some pills which she must have had stashed around the place in a bottle in her hand. I shook her but she would not wake up – she had taken an overdose of her sleeping pills! For a split second, I have to admit to wondering whether I should let her die! But it was only for a split second as I rushed to phone Keith, who was at work, and told him what had happened. He asked if I had phoned for an ambulance and of course I had not. So he said he would call from work and then would come straight home.

Somewhere in the recesses of my mind I seemed to remember that you had to try and keep overdose victims awake if possible, so they would not slip into a coma. I rang my friend, Carmel, who lived down the street and asked her to come up and take Brad, who was at home at the time, back to her house to play with her daughter Naïve. She brought her older boy with her and he took Brad back to their house whilst Carmel and I tried to "walk" Mum to keep her awake. It was too late at this stage though because she was totally unconscious and unresponsive. The ambulance seemed to take forever, in fact they arrived at the same time as Keith did from work. They put Mum in the "recovery position" and took her off to Royal Perth Hospital. Keith gave me a stiff whiskey; because of course I was very upset by now. We followed the ambulance, but it stopped to resuscitate Mum not far from home. I was sure I would be told when we got to Royal Perth Hospital that she had passed away. It was therefore, with a great deal of surprise that I received the news that although they had had to work on her in emergency for 20 minutes, she was stable and in intensive care.

As soon as they told me she had required extensive resuscitation, my first thought was to wonder about brain damage. I asked about this and they, predictably, said we would have to wait and find out. After three days in intensive care, the doctor took me to one side and said that he was afraid there was brain damage because Mum was still unresponsive to stimulation. She was moved out of intensive care after a week and put into a Psychiatric Ward in a private room because she was hooked up to tubes everywhere to feed and irrigate her. She was breathing independently but was still in a coma. She remained that way for three months.

I was in a dreadful state, in one way wanting her to wake up and in another afraid to face her when she did wake up, because I felt so guilty about our row – it must have pushed her over the edge. Mum's friend, Ron, had said when he heard the news that he had been meaning to talk to me about Mum, because he had felt she had been on the verge of a nervous breakdown, so this did not come to him as a big surprise. When she had been staying at his house, in the enclosed garage (it had been made into a sort of granny flat) she had been convinced someone had been prowling around outside – which was the main reason she asked to come and stay with us. He had investigated on several occasions, but had found no sign of anyone around the place. She had also exhibited illusions of grandeur, feeling everyone was looking at her because she was so great! Something had not felt quite right about her. I wish he had spoken to us about it; we might have been able to get some help before this tragedy occurred.

When Mum did eventually regain consciousness, she spoke with a broad Scots accent! The damage to her brain was the immediate memory and she now believed she was a young woman living back in Glasgow, Scotland, where she was born. Everything was confused in her mind. Nothing worked properly. We had a real problem on our hands. Her speech was difficult to understand and she had to have speech therapy but she was not co-operative. She would look at me and get totally confused as to who I was. Her hand eye co-ordination needed therapy and she would give off these awful animalistic howls periodically, which were blood curdling. What had we saved!

Mum was in RPH for approximately 8 months then was sent to a Rehabilitation Centre. She nearly starved to death there because they were so busy, no one really noticed that Mum was not eating much and whatever she ate went straight through her. She became skeletal. Through all this Ron was still visiting her but Mum would ask who "that bloke" was who kept coming to see her? She didn't like him! Eventually, the time came when Mum was to be sent home – to where?

The Welfare Section of the hospital gave us a couple of places to try. They recommended a nursing home in South Perth initially. However, we found Mum's condition deteriorated after about a month at the home because they kept her sedated during the day and she was dribbling, and crying and unable to feed herself. So we took her away from there and referred back to the Welfare people. They gave us a short list of places to try. One of which was in an accommodation house in Bassendean. The lady in charge and my mother, took an instant dislike to each other so that was out.

We then found her hostel accommodation. However, after visiting her a couple of times it soon became obvious Mum was not capable of even hostel accommodation, as she never washed herself or changed her clothes.

We tried her at home for a while. It was not good. On several occasions Keith and I would be awakened at 2 and 3 in the morning by Mum putting on our bedroom light standing fully dressed ready to go to "work". I would steer her back to bed and tell her to go to sleep. On a few occasions I found her bed made and Mum nowhere in sight. She had got up early and walked up the road to catch the bus into "work". We would then receive a phone call from the police in Perth saying they had someone in the station who they had matched up to our "missing person" report. They would put her into a police car and bring her home. A police car on our driveway soon became a familiar sight!

I also became very friendly with the local newsagent, as Mum would frequently go "shopping", but unfortunately did not see the need to pay for anything. After the first time I found heaps of items in her bag – obviously from the news agency. I called and explained about Mum and took the stuff back. Thereafter, they would call and let me know Mum had "escaped" and was "shopping", so I would go and get her and bring her home. Sometimes Mum would protest at the confiscation of her items and would show the pieces of paper she had used to "pay" for the goods. One had to laugh, or would never stop the tears when thinking about her mental state.

Once, in a desperate bid to have some sort of normality, we left Mum at home watching television whilst we briefly visited some friends in the afternoon. When we got back we walked through the door to be met by a dreadful smell. We walked into the kitchen and found a melted aluminium pot on the stove containing something, which to this day we could not identify. Another pot – fortunately on a low heat, contained half a dozen chips floating around in a combination of sherry and cooking oil. Mum had decided to cook herself "some tea". We realized at this point, we had to make alternative arrangements for Mum somehow, our family life was disintegrating.

The children were afraid to be anywhere Nanna. Mum would often mistake Brad for the young version of my brother and would hit him for perceived wrong-doings! I was continually having to keep him away from her.

I rang a social worker at RPH and she came out to the house to see us. I told her that in all honesty I felt I was going to hurt Mum out of sheer frustration if we did not get any help somewhere. She was very good and we visited Graylands, and two or three "C Class" hospitals, as they were then called. Graylands was definitely "out": there was no way I could put Mum in there. Two out of the three hospitals stank of urine and exuded an air of hopelessness so they weren't options either. Then we found a hospital in Como. I liked the feel of the place straight away. It felt like a big hotel, rather than a hospital. The staff were very friendly and caring and most important of all, Mum seemed to accept it also. So we made arrangements and went home to pack her things. Although I still had to endure visits, this was to be the best outcome for us all and she lived there quite happily until the day she died – 12 years later.

It's funny isn't it how you get used to someone being around, even though that person's presence may cause incredible irritation. After returning home from installing Mum in her new home, the house felt really empty and I did not know quite what to do with myself. I had no one I had to dress, feed and tell what to do but I have to admit though, I soon settled happily into my own family group once more without the stress!

Even though we made the best of the situation, the experience with Mum had frayed our nerves somewhat and we felt unsettled in our house, so when, after five years there, Keith suggested maybe we could sell the house and start afresh, I was very pleased to agree.

In 1980 we put the house on the market and decided that we would return to the UK for a holiday. We had not seen the family for 12 years and felt it was time Samantha and Brad met their relatives!

Keith was due for some long service leave so in May we booked our flights for October that year, feeling sure our house would sell in the ensuing five months or so. It did sell but settlement was not due to take place until sometime during our vacation, so we borrowed some money to cover our fares and spending money and continued with our plans. We arranged for our furniture and belongings to go into storage and decided that when we returned we would book into the local motel, and look around for a rental for a while. Our friends, Fran and Robert took us to the airport and we were off!

I had never flown before so I was both apprehensive and excited at the same time. It was to be a long flight and the children were very excited. Take off was a rather painful experience for me as I did not know to swallow during the process so my ears were rather painful and in my ignorance I thought this was normal and wondering "why do people fly if it hurts so much?"

The flight was to have one stop over in some poor city with shanties lined up all along the runway and half naked, dirty children running all over the place. Unfortunately, we were not allowed off the plane due to some industrial dispute so sat in the plane on the tarmac for two hours. The trip was long enough without this extra delay, however, the children were very good under the circumstances.

We touched down at Heathrow some 30 hours later, exhausted and just longing to be horizontal and get a good sleep. What we had not remembered was the fact that Yorkshire, where we were headed, was another four hours away by car! Keith's brother, Sean, met us and duly piled us and our luggage into his car and thus began the endless journey up to Yorkshire. I think I dozed, as did the children, but we were awoken to have drinks and a 'pit stop' along the motorway. I can't remember what time it was, but it was late and very cold, I can remember shivering so uncontrollably that I couldn't hold my cup of coffee without spilling it!!

After what seemed like a lifetime we eventually arrived at Martha's tiny little stone cottage in Sutton-in-Craven. She only had the two bedrooms, so had arranged for Keith and I to go and sleep across the way at her neighbour's home, while Samantha and Brad shared the spare bedroom in Martha's cottage. Her neighbours, Ann and Kim, were delighted to have us and it worked very well.

After a suitable time of rest and recuperation it was time to catch up with the family. Martha really hadn't changed that much – just a little whiter in the hair – and Sean and Jennifer looked much the same too. The children were of course the interesting factor. We hadn't seen Mark and Sarah and they in turn did not know their cousins, Samantha and Brad. They all got on well, however, being much the same age – Samantha was the oldest of the four and it was great to see them interacting, playing games and chatting away in a very short time.

The thing that did strike us about England was how "grey and beige" everything seemed. Granted it was October, going into their Autumn, but by the time we had been in Yorkshire for about three weeks I was feeling very homesick for Perth. This truly brought home to me that I regarded Perth as my home now, not the UK.

We divided our five-week stay between Martha, Sean and Barbara, Keith's older brother Martin and his family and towards the end of our stay we travelled down to London and stayed with my brother for the last week or so. We also stayed with Ilene and Robert and their family, who had been neighbours of ours in Thornlie. They had returned to York in the UK about 18 months before our visit. Upon arriving in the UK, however, they realised they had made a mistake and were in the throes of re-applying to return to Perth. They had asked us to sponsor them, which we had agreed to do, so it was good to catch up with them. We hired a car and on the way south popped in on Jane and Malcolm (my dearest and oldest friends from my work days, pre Australia) and their two little girls. We finally found my brother's home – an old farmhouse in the middle of nowhere!

My brother at that time had a partner called Celia and she had a son called Russell (about Samantha's age). They leased this old farmhouse and adjoining land and ran horses. Samantha and Brad had never met their uncle before and they were somewhat alarmed on occasion when, as a joke, he would half lower one of his eyes and poke out his false tooth, thus showing an alarming face only probably seen in their worst dreams! Brad recoiled in horror! Celia was big into dressage and horse shows. There seemed to be a veritable zoo of animals, including 'Gloria' the swan, there was a ferret (or two), two Irish Wolf Hounds, and two lesser mongrels, about four or five horses and a few sheep. I am still not sure where their income came from. They certainly did not live high on the hog. When we were there my brother was endeavouring to get into breeding and selling dogs. He had a lovely little pup – Irish Wolf Hound pup – all ready to go to its new home when it became very ill and died. This was my introduction to "Parvovirus". A very bad virus that almost always killed young dogs and pups if they caught it. The UK was currently experiencing an epidemic of the virus amongst its dog population. In the years to come I would also experience the disease with one of our pets.

The children did not like Russell very much. Brad told me later that Russell used to thump him for no reason other than Brad was there to thump! However, they did enjoy the experience of living on the farm for a while.

The time soon came to say goodbye to all the family. It wasn't so bad saying goodbye to Martha this time as she had told us she was thinking of taking the trip over to Australia in the near future, so we knew we would catch up with her quite soon. Keith's brothers, however, were a different kettle of fish, being very set in their ways and not much for travelling. Indeed, I don't think Keith, himself, would have left the UK if it had not been for me making all the enquiries in the first place.

The flight back was not too bad this time. I learned about swallowing!! But it was still long!

When we got back to Perth, we were told by Robert and Fran that they had cancelled our booking at the local motel and were going to put us up at their place! As they lived in a two-bedroomed duplex I was unsure where exactly they were going to put us! However, they showed us the portable room they had at the bottom of their garden and how they had made up beds for us all in there. We would rather have stayed in the motel, but there was no denying it would save us a lot of money and they seemed very keen to have us, so we accepted their kind offer.

It was not a very nice feeling coming back to Perth with no home to actually go to. I would not recommend it to anyone else and I certainly would never do it again. Our stay with Robert and Fran became a little fraught after about a week. Fran really did not cope too well with people around all the time and I think they realised they had made a mistake with their misguided generosity! At any rate, fortunately, it was not long before we managed to find ourselves a rental property – through another couple of friends, Les and Linda.

Les and Linda lived in a house in Crestwood – a futuristic estate with all the backs of the houses opening up on to communal open space and parklands. It was lovely. Their next door neighbours wished to sell their house but it was currently empty. Les and Linda persuaded them to let us lease it from them. They had leased it before but had had bad experiences so were about to throw in the towel with leasing. However, Les and Linda persuaded them and we duly moved in. It was a lovely location. Tucked into the end of a cul de sac, opposite the High School and literally just down the road from the Primary School where Brad and Samantha attended. It was a three bedroom house, with a kitchen/dining area which opened out on to a small raised patio then out to the open space parklands at the back, an L-shaped lounge/dining and the bedrooms. It had wooden floors in all but the lounge area and we felt very at home there. We moved in at the beginning of November of 1980, pleasantly in time for Christmas.

Les and Linda had bought a small store in the hills and operated it seven days a week – how, I'll never know because they had four girls ranging from 7 to 15.

Because they had an endless supply of food (from their shop) they invited us to spend Christmas with them and have Christmas dinner. To my dying day I shall never forget the sight of their Christmas table, literally groaning with the weight of all the food placed on it. Rather than the table being set for ten of us, we could have fed a legion!

One of the good things about Crestwood was that it had a communal swimming pool and all residents had a key to the pool, so it was always available for swimming. The Crestwood gardener kept an eye on its maintenance so it was like having a pool without the bother of having to care for it – the only hitch being you could sometimes be sharing it with several other people. On Christmas Day after partaking obscenely of the food provided by Les and Linda, I decided to go for a swim to clear my fuggy head and took Samantha and Brad and Les and Linda's youngest with me. It was such a relief to jump into that cool water (it was as usual very hot) and this was reinforced in my mind when we all returned to Les and Linda's house to find the remaining occupants all sound asleep in their food-soaked stupor and who subsequently woke up feeling much the worse for their over indulgence.

We enjoyed our stay in the Crestwood house. The children loved it. The first negative experience we had there was to lose our Siamese cat, Cassandra. We had three cats, Cassandra, Big Puss and Gingerbread. We noticed after a while that we had not seen Cassie (as we called her) and immediately started hearing alarm bells. We searched high and low for her but we did not find her for a week. The Crestwood house was, as I have said, at the end of a cul de sac. The only road going past us at the end of the cul de sac was only busy at school drop off and pick up times. About a week after we had missed Cassie, Brad and his friend came running in to tell us that they had spotted a "dog" lying by the side of the road. As I knew the heartbreak we were feeling about the loss of our cat and not knowing what had become of her, I told the boys we should check for a collar and contact number, so we could notify the dog's owners, and they took me to where they had seen the 'dog'. As soon as I got within a couple of feet of the animal I knew it wasn't a dog, but was our beloved Cassie. She was partially obscured, which is why the boys had mistaken her for a dog, and all I could see was her one white 'toe' on one of her back legs! Our Cassie must have been hit by a car and because the area on which she was lying was slightly below the level of the road, we had missed seeing her when we had been out searching for her earlier in the week. I immediately burst into tears, which of course upset the children and so we were all bawling as I gently lifted her up and carried her home to be buried.

We buried Cassie with much sadness and ceremony in the garden area just outside of our back door and for a week shed many tears for our lost cat.

About this time I began thinking about returning to the workforce on a part time basis. We had bought another car for me and I needed a job to make the car payments each month. The children were getting older and if I could get myself a part time position within the school hours I would. I answered a few ads. and was asked along for an interview to a steel company in Welshpool, a convenient drive away from home. The position was as a part time administration/book keeper and the hours were just perfect. I duly started in the position and really enjoyed it.

During this time, Ilene and Robert, had returned from the UK. They arrived back in the June/July of 1981 and came to stay with us in our rental house. As they were the visitors, they got the main bedroom and Keith and I dossed down in the lounge. It was during this time that I began to suspect I was pregnant! I had only been in my new job for about three or four months and neither Keith nor I were exactly thrilled by the prospect of another baby, especially as Samantha was 10 and Brad was 8! I could not be sure though because I was 'spotting'!

On the afternoon of Wednesday, 29th July (the day Lady Diana Spencer and Prince Charles got married) I was working at my desk when I felt sharp pains in my abdomen, mainly on the right side. I tried to ignore them but they were very sharp. I felt I needed to get this checked out so immediately arranged a doctor's appointment as soon as possible that afternoon, then told my boss I was feeling unwell and needed to leave early, which he agreed to.

The drive to the doctor's office was not too good, but I managed and duly arrived, only to find my usual doctor was on leave that day and a locum was sitting in his place. The doctor was a female and she asked me about my symptoms. By this stage the pain was really unpleasant, to the point that I was physically sick at the surgery and they called Keith to come and pick me up as I was now unable to drive. She did not examine me and just told me to go home and take some Disprin!

That evening the royal wedding was being televised and as we did not have a TV Les and Linda invited us to their place to watch it. The pain continued and when it came time to go home, Keith had to help me walk, as I felt really quite lightheaded.

There was a lot of gurgling going on in my abdomen and I was convinced the pain was caused by colic – I suffered with the condition from time to time and knew it was very painful, although I had to admit I had not experienced anything quite like this before. I stayed in bed the next day and felt a little better resting. My doctor had in the meantime returned and was reading the locum's case notes from the previous day and had noticed mine. He telephoned Keith to see how I was and I by this time was feeling very silly thinking it was wind, told him I did not need for him to visit me at home. He must have guessed there was more to it, however, and asked me to come down to surgery later that day if I felt well enough.

By 5.00 pm I was not feeling the best so Keith took me to the surgery. When I got there I could barely walk into the doctor's surgery. He gave me an internal examination, which was dreadful, and duly rang a surgeon colleague of his, telling him he had a suspected ectopic pregnancy or ovarian cyst and wanted me operated on that night! He arranged for me to be admitted to a Victoria Park Hospital, so Keith drove me home to get some night things and to ask Les and Linda if they would look after Brad for us. Samantha wanted to come with us. This arranged I was ensconced in the back seat – unable by this stage to sit up – and we drove (what seemed at the time) the endless trip to the hospital.

They were waiting for us with a wheelchair for me and I was bundled into said vehicle and taken to a ward, where I promptly slid out of the thing in a dead faint (for the first time in my life)! When I came to, I was on a bed and my poor little Samantha was white-faced beside me asking if I was going to die! Vivid memories came back to me of when my mother was having one of her bad headaches, just after my father died and she was very depressed, and she told me "I think I'll be joining George soon." Such a thoughtless thing to say to a small child, and which instilled sheer terror in my young heart. So my one thought at that time was to reassure Samantha I was not going to die (even if at the time I felt like it!)

The surgeon duly arrived and did a cursory examination of my abdomen and immediately scheduled me for surgery that night as the "gurgling" I had experienced earlier on had actually been bleeding into my abdominal cavity! It was indeed an ectopic pregnancy and the fallopian tube had burst on the Wednesday afternoon at work.

When I awoke from surgery I was promptly sick and had tubes everywhere! They'd sent Keith and Samantha home with assurances that I was fine and in recovery. Poor Keith, I now know it is always worse for the person who accompanies the person with the emergency medical problem than for the actual patient. All the onlooker can do is anxiously await treatment for their loved one and watch the drama unfold!

Later that next day, I felt decidedly uncomfortable in my nether regions. I had had a catheter inserted into my bladder, but I felt the discomfort of a very full bladder. When I spoke to a nurse about this, she dismissed my statement saying, "No, you won't have a full bladder, you have a catheter inserted to drain your urine away." Nevertheless, ten minutes later I persisted with my complaint that I felt my bladder was full and I was uncomfortable. It was only then the nurse decided to check my catheter and found that the tube leading away from my body was twisted and no urine was draining away at all! With a quick adjustment the relief was immediate.

I was in hospital for ten days. I had my right ovary and fallopian tube removed, however, it was the left side which caused a problem as I developed an infection in the wound, which took weeks to clear up. I lost 5 kilos in weight and when I got home from the hospital I was 49 kilos and looked like a cadaver! My hip bones were sticking out like a skeleton and my trousers would not stay up! Fortunately, I put on about 3 kilos after about a week, so became a little more healthy looking but was still rather thin.

Prior to my having my ectopic pregnancy, Michael had called to say their little dog, Penny, was expecting puppies and as we did not have a dog, and her babies were sure to be little ones, did we want one. After deliberation, we decided Brad was old enough to have a dog so we said yes. During my stay in hospital, the puppies came of age and it was time to bring ours home. Brad had chosen a female and for some reason named her "Chubbs". When I arrived back from hospital I was joyfully greeted by this little round, brown ball of yipping pup! She was gorgeous, and although I had never been much of a dog lover, Chubbs and I made friends instantly. She was a hit with the childrens' friends too, as she was so small she would ride around in Samantha's bicycle basket and generally had a ball playing in the back park with all the children.

BUNBURY

*I*t was around the time I was recovering from surgery and later that year that we were informed that Keith had received a promotion and we were moving down to Bunbury! We were really thrilled with the move and Keith's progress through the bank. It also solved our immediate question of what to do about buying another house – we did not need to for a while after all! Also during this time we had acquired a spitfire Siamese kitten, who we named Pippa Ling and who delighted in waiting under seats until unsuspecting visitors sat down – like Ilene, who was not particularly fond of cats – and would then attack their feet. We had many a laugh at our friends' expense because of Pippa Ling until they became wary and would check under the seats before sitting down in our house. So now our animal family numbered 4, three cats – Big Puss, Gingerbread, Pippa Ling and Chubbs the dog.

Keith had acquired a VW beetle (a bronze one) from somewhere and had decided that as I was temporarily out of work, (my boss had apologetically called me after I was away sick following my ectopic pregnancy, to tell me they could not keep my job open for me), and as this was paying for my car, we would have to sell my Subaru (which I really liked) and I would use the VW beetle around Bunbury. I wasn't too happy about this, but I could not really argue as I had no job. However, this meant we had three cars! So a week before we were due to move down to Bunbury we drove the Subaru down to the house there then I returned with Keith in our camper van to Perth. The following week, when we were actually moving I drove the beetle down. It was kind of nice driving a VW again. They are unique. The driver and car feel like one unit. This car needed a bit of work, however, which we would have to get attended to in Bunbury.

Our house in Bunbury was a nice one. It was on Ocean Beach Road. This road followed the line of the beach but our house was situated driving away from the coast. It was on a really quiet road and faced open bush in front of a sand dune which led directly to the beach. The children subsequently found out that the beach in front of us and beyond the sand dune was designated for nude bathing!

The house had three bedrooms (all a fairly good size), a large lounge and family room, with a roomy kitchen/dining area looking out on to the back garden. It was in the Withers area of Bunbury and Samantha and Brad would attend the local Primary School.

They settled in really well at Withers. Samantha in particular, seemed to be ahead of her counterparts at the school, indicating what I had always suspected that her earlier Primary School was quite a superior educational school. Samantha was so much more advanced than her schoolmates that we were asked if she could take an exam for "gifted children" – much to her horror! Samantha never liked attracting the limelight and to this day, I believe she flunked the test so she would not appear to be "different"!

I joined the P and C and built up a brilliant rapport with the Principal at the school. The P and C was really quite an active body at the school and I enjoyed the activity. I needed to find a job, however, and let it be known around the place that I was interested in part time work. As luck would have it, a previous bank employee, Kevin, and his brother were partners in an hotel called the "Parade Hotel" and they were looking for a part time administration/book keeper – just up my street. Kevin had known Keith previously at the bank and they met up again, fortuitously, and he told Keith about the job and I went for an interview, which was successful, and I started at the Parade Hotel a few months after we arrived.

To this day, I can honestly say my job at the Parade was one of the best I had and would ever have. The hours were a dream – I could see the children off to school then go to the hotel and when my work was finished after lunch, I would go home again. So I was there to see them to school and there for them coming home, wonderful! By this time we had sold my Suburu to one of Keith's work colleagues and my bronze beetle was my sole mode of transport. The engine was running well, in spite of its advancing age. I loved driving it and the children absorbed my love for Bertie, as we called him.

I loved the work at the hotel. Each morning I would check the tills to see the float was right and would then tally up the previous night's takings, dividing them into their various categories in the huge, green cashbook. Hitherto, I had always thought I was useless at figures, having had a less than positive maths teacher at school, but to my joy I found that I was really quite good and accurate when dealing with the figures at the Parade Hotel and mostly managed to balance the books, to the cent. On some days the takings would be a couple of thousand dollars, but on Mondays, when I tallied up the weekends' takings there was between \$15,000 and \$18,000 most Mondays, which I would balance to the books and take to the bank.

I was also responsible for paying the staff, which as most of the staff there were casual or part time, and weekend workers, could be tricky, making sure their hours were at the right rate, etc. I loved it. Sometimes they were short in the bar and I would go and serve our customers. My pulling of beer used to be the subject of great hilarity amongst the regulars, with glasses of beer froth and very little beer to be seen. However, I eventually could pull a good beer and loved interacting with the clients. Some of them had been going to the Parade for decades and one particular fellow, was given his own set of six beer glasses with his name engraved on them for his 80th birthday.

Pippa Ling duly came into season. A Siamese cat in season is no fun and determination is its middle name. Pippa Ling miaowed herself hoarse! Yes, she actually lost her voice. We tried to keep her indoors, but eventually in desperation we let her out with the words "Go then, you tart, go find yourself a male and shut up!" In time, of course she was pregnant and ultimately gave birth to six kittens. All different combinations of brown white and black. All with the shape and ears of a Siamese cat. They were indeed beautiful kittens. We had no trouble finding homes for them and as usual, we *had* to keep one. Our longstanding Puss – Big Puss had recently died of advancing years so we could, at a pinch have yet another cat. After all, we were used to three cats and now, a dog. We decided to keep Pepe. She was a beautiful, black version of Pippa Ling – Pippa was a Torte Point Siamese. However, Pepe had more black than Pippa.

Pepe was not a warm cat! She reminded me of a beautiful woman but incredibly unfeeling. When you picked her up to cuddle her she would endure it without a struggle but you could tell she did not want to be there. This was really odd as the kittens had been handled since young and given all the love imaginable, but Pepe was cold.

One day when Brad and I were out in the back garden, Samantha and her friend Melissa came screaming home crying and saying Pepe had been knocked down by a car. Now our house was on a slip road and the road which adjoined it would have had, say, five cars a day along it. Would you believe that Pepe had chosen one of those five instances to run across the road and be skittled! Another cat knocked down – two inside 12 months!.

Samantha decided that she would like to try keeping mice. Fortunately, I don't mind mice – it is cockroaches and spiders that give me the creeps. So, we bought three mice and tried to keep them from becoming our cats' meal each day! I walked into the games room one day, where we kept the mice, and noticed one was missing! How it had got out I have no idea as the top was in place and there were no holes in the cage? Then I noticed Gingerbread sitting in the middle of the room staring at our vacuum cleaner! Suspicion crossed my mind – cats are very good at hooking things with their paws, was he the culprit? I picked him up and with difficulty put him outside of the room. I say with difficulty because he was so determined to get back in again, he would slip between my legs, like greased lightning, back into the room to sit and stare at the vacuum cleaner. Eventually I did manage to get him out and carefully lifted the cleaner and there, crouched in terror, was the missing mouse. I picked it up and put it back into its cage, but I think the fright must have been too much for him and he died, probably of shock, a couple of days later. The two remaining mice one after the other developed horrible tumours, so after a year of mouse keeping, we called it quits.

On occasion we would go up to Perth for the day or a couple of days, and most of the time we would take Samantha and Brad with us. There was one time when Keith and I had to go to Perth and we left Brad and Samantha with their friends' families. When we came back Brad was very upset and said that Gingerbread had been mauled by a large dog. He was indeed in a bad way, and we took him to the vet who told us he had not suffered any broken bones, but he was badly bruised. He ultimately recovered from this trauma, only a few weeks later to finish up being skittled by yet another car, outside our house. Having to put Gingerbread down was heartbreaking to me as he was a favourite of mine. When he was a kitten back in Thornlie, he was the noisiest of the lot and I would pick him up, put him in my apron pocket and walk around with him there for hours. He was mine, one of Cassie's babies and now he was gone too.

Before we left Perth, I had become a "born again" Christian and had wanted very much to continue my spiritual journey, but since arriving in Bunbury I had been unable to settle down to going to church. We had been in Bunbury about six months when a flyer was put in our letterbox inviting us to the Baptist church for Easter service. Each year I had dragged my family to church for Christmas and Easter and this year was to be no exception, so took myself to church on Good Friday with my protesting family in tow.

The Pastor of the Baptist church was a young, family man and I found his sermons both interesting and useful in everyday life and soon began to go regularly to the church. I was very interested in singing and the choir at the church was still a fledgling group, so I joined that group and we gradually emerged as "the choir" during the services. My family wasn't interested in attending church, so this was my 'project' so to speak. There was at this church another lady in similar circumstances to me, wanting to grow spiritually, family not interested in attending church, etc and the pastor could see we could be company for each other so he quite skillfully engineered our meeting and subsequently being "thrown together" on projects. Liz and I eventually became firm friends, but only after we both "held off" because I was a transient to the town and she did not want to get to know me too well in case we got on and then would miss me when we left! But, we both decided this was silly and began a warm and enjoyable friendship. I eventually was baptised into the Baptist church and became very involved in the church happenings.

It was about this time that I felt a little lost in my relationship with Keith. I am not sure what was wrong. I felt we were drifting in separate directions and something was happening in me. I was questioning "my meaning" in life – all very deep! I tried to speak to Keith about my feelings, but nothing seemed to make sense. I wonder now if deep down I had not mourned the baby I lost in the ectopic pregnancy, whether I smothered my wish to have another baby because Keith had expressed his lack of interest in having another child. He was happy with our Samantha and Brad and indeed, went as far as having a vasectomy just after we arrived in Bunbury. I feel the whole experience with me in hospital and being so ill, frightened him more than he ever expressed and he decided there and then that it would not happen again. I wonder whether, if we had talked more about the experience, we may have changed the future in some way?

Samantha had done particularly well at school. It was her last year at primary school and she finished Dux of her school. What a wonderful surprise that was! We went to the school's prize giving night. Samantha had not said anything to us – probably because she did not believe she was in the running. They had asked her class, as a whole, what they would like if they won the Dux of the school award, a calculator, a book or something else and she said they asked each child individually, so there was no clue as to who had won the award. There was another girl in her class, apparently, who they felt was in the running. But, on the night we sat there in stunned joy when they announced that Samantha Renton was Dux of the school for 1982. We were so proud of her!

Samantha went on to almost complete a year at Newton Moore High School in Bunbury before the call to move again came from the bank. Keith had been promoted to Manager at the Wagin branch of the bank. So sadly I resigned from my position at the Parade Hotel. They gave me a great farewell party and presented me with two pieces of Limoge china. I had not wanted to move the children around like this, it was too reminiscent of my own high school years, but there was nothing to be done, so we made our farewells.

WAGIN

*W*e arrived in Wagin in mid December 1983. The children were apprehensive at having to start another new school and particularly, Samantha, who was to start at High School level. She had enjoyed her stint at Newton Moore High School in Bunbury and was going through dreadful acne, brought on by her puberty blues. In short she was painfully shy and uncomfortable in new company.

Our house was on what was loosely called "Knob Hill" but was not particularly overwhelming in luxury. It was, however, on a large block and we were just down the road from a family the boys from which were to become Brad's best friends. It was also air conditioned which made life so much more pleasant to bear, particularly in the Wheat belt area of Wagin. In actual fact it was smaller than our house in Bunbury, as it did not have a games room.

To our delight we discovered that the tennis club was a thriving concern and despite the heat of Summer spent many an enjoyable hour playing tennis. I was no better at tennis than I had been in Moora, however Keith played pennant tennis. On some occasions it was too hot for me to play anyway. The good part about it was that Samantha and Brad were encouraged to play with the juniors, so it meant the whole family played together.

When Winter arrived practically all the tennis players would become golf players. I gamely tried to learn the stately sport of golf, even trying Monday afternoon lessons. Try as I may, however, I could never develop a liking for the game and indeed took so many swings per round by the time I got home I was fit for nothing, let alone cooking dinner for the family. Suffice it to say, when the Monday dawned wet and windy I was more than pleased to excuse myself from my golf lessons. Consequently, Keith and I saw very little of each other really – only evenings and maybe a part of Sunday. If it wasn't tennis it was golf. The bank was also making huge demands on its staff, particularly its Manager so we began to drift in different directions, I with the children to their various sports activities and Keith to his golf and bank commitments. It was around this time that Samantha had her first fall caused by a loose cruciate ligament in her knee. I normally went with her to netball but this particular day she had been taken by someone else. She was late getting home from the match and when she eventually arrived the poor girl was in agony because of her knee injury and also she had "chipped" her elbow bone. Unfortunately, that first incident led to several more in later life and only an operation at some stage would fix it.

As always I was interested in working and due to Keith's Lions Club connections learned of a part time position in town one or two days per week, acting as Office Assistant to the visiting Perth Lawyer, Peter and Ian the visiting accountant. The local Agricultural Advisor, also rented the rooms from time to time and I did typing work for him also. So, once again I was working part time and whizzing around the town in my re-sprayed, yellow VW beetle.

The shopping in town was a little bit wanting so sometimes I would pile the children into the car and we would drive to Katanning or Narrogin, both of which were approximately 45 kilometres from Wagin. On one particularly stinking hot day I was on my way back from Katanning and about 20 kilometers outside of Wagin the engine began emitting a knocking sound which really did not sound healthy. I stopped the car immediately and we jumped out! It was so hot and there was not a bit of shade anywhere. I had Samantha, Brad and a friend of theirs with me plus a boot full of shopping (including ice cream). I stopped a passing car and asked the driver to take a message into town, to Keith, for me. There were no mobile phones in those days. In about 20 minutes Keith arrived in the local breakdown truck to survey the damage. Upon investigation it was discovered that during the engine re-fit we had had done, a minute bit of metal had lodged somewhere in the engine and it had completely seized! The work was still under warranty so it would have to be towed to Bunbury for them to put the problem right, as it would have to be stripped right down. Keith went back into town to get his car and returned to pick up some very soggy people and bags of shopping. I was without my vehicle for three months, and began cycling everywhere – I think I would have been at my fittest around that time!

In Bunbury, after the sad demise of Gingerbread, Melissa's, (one of Samantha's friends) cat produced a brood of kittens. We were presented with a fluffy white kitten, which unfortunately was terrorized by Pippa Ling, to the point of emotional damage! We think Pippa thought it was a white mouse! It hid itself under Samantha's bookcase for the first three days, refusing to come out for fear of Pippa Ling, who sat in waiting for it. We had to shove food and drink under the bookcase to keep the poor thing alive! It never really was right after that.

We called this cat Snowball. In retrospect "Screwball" would have been a better name for her!

In the drive to find something to keep my brain from frying in the depths of the Australian bush, I enrolled in Long Distance Education Classes. I took up English Lit and Human Biology. I really enjoyed my English and did very well at it, but my Human Biol. was not too good. I could not make head nor tail of the slides I was sent to teach myself, so let that one go. I took myself all the way to almost sitting my exams in English Lit., however, half way through that year I also re-discovered my singing. One of the ladies at the tennis club was into singing and had heard about a local Choir which was being formed by a Community Arts Co-ordinator, in Narrogin. So, we arranged to present ourselves at the next choir rehearsal and ask to join. We were accepted and a small band of us would meet once a week in Narrogin to rehearse some pieces with an idea of putting on a small concert later in the year.

The amount of talent hidden in the country towns is quite astounding and we discovered some very good singers in our midst. Another lady from Wagin who also felt as if she was in a cultural desert, Maureen, also joined us so the three of us would commute each week come rain or shine. Maureen had a lovely voice and just wanted to use it. From these small beginnings the co-ordinator, Conrad, got the idea of putting on a Gilbert and Sullivan Opera – *The Sorcerer*. He had discovered another talented duo, Helen and Lee, from Williams. Helen was an experienced dancer/producer and Lee a natural acting personality. Between the three of them they planned *The Sorcerer* and the auditions for parts began.

Only those who have participated in putting on a play or a musical production will appreciate the comradeship that builds between cast members over the weeks of rehearsal. It was such fun and an outlet for people's pent up artistic interests. It also builds deep friendships but can sometimes distance people from their non-participating partners. Keith and I continued to pull in different directions at this time, which was (in retrospect) a recipe for disaster. I asked him on a few occasions to come with me to rehearsal, to see what we were doing, but he was not interested and cited having to be with the children as a reason to stay home.

Finally, the rehearsals were finished and it was the real thing! We played to packed houses in Narrogin and surrounding towns, for five performances. The standard of both the chorus and the Principals was pleasingly high and we were justifiably pleased with ourselves.

With the move to Wagin I tried to transfer my religious activities to the Baptist church there. It was difficult to settle in, however, after leaving such an active, forward thinking church as was the Baptist church in Bunbury. Unfortunately the

Wagin Baptist had been without a regular pastor for a long time, consequently the services were overseen by lay preachers, which were in most cases, farmers. Now I have nothing against farmers, as the saying goes, they are the salt of the earth but to a townie, they are incredibly difficult to talk to if you are not an authority on crops, animals or the weather. Their resultant sermons were taken completely from the bible with copious readings from said book. I have trouble now and had even more then, "getting into" the meanings in the bible. I have tried many times since then to settle into a reading pattern which would take me through the bible and gain meaning from it, but I can't. The main problem being that I read in bed at night, as it is the only time I find peace enough to do so, but unfortunately it is also a trigger for me to go to sleep. Now, add to this that I am not really finding what I am reading riveting, and you have me cross eyed and nodding off very quickly. So the sermons on Sunday were less than informative to me, and my religious activities with that church died a natural death.

What now! Well, I was christened an Anglican so I decided to go back to my roots, so to speak. I attended the Anglican church one Sunday and to my horror realized I was by far the youngest attendant there – by at least thirty five years. It seemed to be made up of widows and single ladies, as far as I could see as the only male within a mile was the minister, who did not look as if he would last too long either. Oh dear, this wasn't going to work.

There was only the Uniting Church left and the Catholic Church. There was no way I would go to the Catholic Church, which only left the Uniting Church. I felt I could not go there, however, as with Wagin being such a small town I felt sure everyone there would recognize me as the Bank Manager's wife and that I had been to two other churches prior to this. No, it was all too hard, so my religious activities ground to a halt. I was in just the state Satan wanted me in – real bait – with no support network in place.

We had brought Snowball and Pippa Ling to Wagin with us. Snowball was definitely neurotic but beautiful so we put up with her weird ways. She still hid under bookcases and treated everyone and everything with suspicion, but at least Pippa had stopped bullying her. Once again, however, we became aware that one of our cats was missing! Pippa Ling had been gone for a couple of days and we had no idea where she could be. We put out a call on the local radio station and advertised in the local paper to no avail. On one occasion a couple of months later, however, I was having a conversation with our hairdresser and the subject of cats came up. She said she had heard an interesting story from one of her clients, in that two boys had been riding their motorbikes in a paddock not far from where we lived and had accidentally run over a cat sleeping there. They said they had not seen her because she was just the same colour as the dead grass and bits around her – just the colouring of Pippa Ling. Now we knew what had happened to our beloved Pippa – exit cat number 5!

Snowball went on to have four kittens – all motley colours, but of course they were beautiful. One day Keith and I had come home from work to have lunch and on checking the kittens found that they had gone. She had moved them somewhere! But where? They were only two weeks old and naturally we were very concerned about their safe keeping and their neurotic mother.

We made a big song and dance about leaving to return to work, so the cat would hear us – she was sitting innocently in the laundry waiting for us to leave I believe. We then stole back on foot and watched what she did. Sure enough, after making sure we had left she ran out into the back garden and disappeared under the tiles into the roof cavity. She had them stashed up there.

That evening Brad was hoisted into the ceiling area to pass down the kittens to us. It was not a pleasant experience for him, as there was fiberglass insulation up there and he emerged red and itchy from his travaille. There was a problem though. One of the kittens was missing. We went outside to look for him (it was a male) and I could hear miaowing half way up the wall. I was horrified to realize that the poor thing was trapped in the brick wall cavity – it must have fallen down there. Brad bravely went up to look and said he could see the kitten perched on a piece of jutting brick. One move in any direction and he would fall even further and out of our reach, to die an awful prolonged death.

We were all very distressed and eventually Keith decided he would have to drill out a couple of bricks to try and get at the kitten. This he did, but it was higher up the wall and once again, Brad was the only one of us small enough to get his arm down into the space. It was awful for him because he said he could feel the kitten but could not get a grip on it. Eventually he did, however, and slowly and nerve-wrackingly he managed to lift the kitten out of the aperture! Our men were heroes. The kitten was none the worse for wear and settled in for a feed with Mum as if nothing had happened. He was of course the kitten we chose to keep and called him Ordie – short for Ordeal!!

Keith and I had been married 18 years at this stage. During that time I had been content with my life partner, but had recently been questioning the way it was going. I suppose women think about their relationships more than men and I was no exception. I started to question how we could improve on "just companionship". I wondered whether I was just undersexed or something. Not for me the licentious anticipation of a "dirty weekend" away with my husband – even in the early days of our marriage, I remember Keith not being particularly happy with our sex life. I always had to "work at" feeling sexy. This cast no aspersion on Keith, however, he was a caring and thoughtful lover, but somehow I always had to work on myself to want to "get involved". Consequently, I thought there must have been something lacking in me. During our time together, however, I never contemplated being with anyone else. Keith was always enough for me. Imagine then my utter shock and dismay to discover one day that I had sexual feelings for another man! Me, the respectable (although sometimes outrageous) bank manager's wife, found another man looming in her life.

For the whole time we had been rehearsing our opera and choir pieces, we had developed a humourous rapport with Conrad. The rehearsals were fun and he always seemed in good spirits. I seemed to amuse him with my antics but one particular night he seemed really out of sorts. Maureen and her husband Stan, had got to know Conrad quite well socially and later that evening she told me that the reason he was "out of sorts" was because he and his wife, Leanne, had just split up. I was so dismayed for him, all I wanted to do that evening was to make him laugh as I had been able to do in the past.

From time to time I would go over to Narrogin to shop, and I happened to mention to Conrad that when I was next in town we should go and have a coffee if he was free. He agreed and we left it at that. Nothing else happened for a few weeks then one day I did bump into him and he asked if I was free for lunch, I was as it happened so we went to lunch. He was still extremely down and is my want I got him to talk about things, and he told me he was in love with someone else, and that was what had finalized the split with himself and his wife. However, this other lover was unattainable so he was no better off. What happened I have no idea, but at that moment my feelings for him went from light friendship to something deeper, even though I knew he loved someone else, all I wanted to do was comfort him. I could not believe what was happening.

I hoped this momentary madness would pass and tried a few more times to get Keith interested in doing things within my interest, but he was always tired and out of sorts from pressures being put on him by the bank and he would not take seriously my talking about "our relationship" needing help.

Unfortunately, the intensity of my feelings grew for Conrad, the only light at the end of the tunnel being that his contract with Narrogin Council was due to end and he was trying for a position elsewhere in the country. At least this way he would be gone (although the prospect devastated me) and I would try to put my life together again. I continued to be his confidante, all the time wishing madly that it was me he was in love with, despite all the attendant difficulties that would have brought – but I was just a dear friend to him. He would kiss me and my insides would drop to my feet, but I was a married woman and it wasn't me he wanted anyway!

I might have managed to get over Conrad and gain some semblance of normality, if we had been left in Wagin for a while; I had my job and interests. Now I knew, however, why I did not have much of a sexual drive with Keith, the chemistry was just not there,. I had experienced the difference now. Not that I had acted upon it, but I certainly wanted to. The crunch came when we were notified that Keith had received yet another promotion and was to be the Manager at Manjimup branch. Good for him and in one way I thought it would be a new start for us, (and away from temptation for me). In another I was sad, as I enjoyed my work in Wagin and had made some good friends, who I would be sorry to leave. I was also concerned about the children being moved yet again. Samantha was going into Year 10 and Brad was just starting high school. Samantha was just beginning to forget about her acne and "be herself" with her friends in Wagin and we all enjoyed the tennis club. But, that is bank life for you and nothing – short of leaving the bank – could be done.

The choir was still performing here and there and we were due to move to Manjimup about the same time as we had a performance, so Keith and the children went in his car and with the furniture and I stayed over and drove down the next day in my yellow beetle. I had one more evening I could spend with Conrad before we would be parted for an indefinite period. We spent the evening together and I savoured every moment, even though I felt terribly guilty at feeling like this about another man! Nevertheless, I found that with someone with whom I was truly in love I could understand the longing to be with that person and no one else. But he could never be mine. I was married and he was still in love with someone else. How foolish can one be to get so caught up like that. We parted the next day and I think I cried all the way to Manjimup.

MANJIMUP

I still do not know how I got to Manjimup. I arrived in a pretty torn up state and if Keith wondered at my being so upset at leaving Wagin, he never asked and I never talked about it. Inside however, I had a physical pain in my chest from the sheer misery of having to say to goodbye to Conrad, I was desperately in love with this man and I had to pretend to be what I would never be again, the contented wife of the Bank's town manager.

Manjimup is located in a beautiful but very damp part of WA. When we told people in Wagin that we were going there they all laughed and said "Manjimup! It rains 9 months of the year and drips off the trees for the remaining 3". We laughed with them, but we found out they were not joking! It was so grey and damp! The children and I took an instant dislike to the place. We had left the dry heat of Wagin, where the tennis season was just getting going, to come to this place, which did not even have an operating tennis club and it was bigger than Wagin. I felt such an air of "hopelessness" about the town. No one was doing anything to give any kind of vibrancy to the place. The sole, main industry in the town was the fruit cannery and this had been ailing for some time.

Keith immediately slipped into his role and took up the inevitable golf at the weekends. The children and I would look at each other and wonder what we were going to do on those interminable weekends. We cruised around the area searching for a tennis club. We found several dilapidated courts on which we had a hit —after removing the broken branches and bits off the court first. Add to this, despite it being November/December it was cold and damp! You can wake up in the morning to bright sunshine in Manjimup but by mid-morning there is a grey, haze of rain falling. We kept the log fire going the whole time.

So, I had to throw myself into finding a job. Before leaving Wagin I had sent off several letters to businesses in the town letting them know we were coming and saying that I would be in contact to ascertain whether or not they had any positions they felt I might be able to fill. The idea was that I would contact them as a follow up. I did this with very limited success, however, one of the hotels was interested in my starting with them sometime – but they could not give me a date.

Probably because I was so unhappy personally, I was feeling extremely unsettled and indeed was losing weight at quite an alarming rate. I no longer wanted to be shifted from pillar to post and I wanted a life of my own, instead of feeling like an appendage or camp follower. I used to look with longing at the list of talks, conferences, seminars going on in Perth where the general public could go along to exercise their intellect and interests. In rural WA these just did not happen. I had tried several short courses through the years, but there was never anywhere to go with newly attained knowledge so it would soon be forgotten. I started to look in the "Situations Vacant" column in the paper and could not believe the salary that someone with my experience could earn in the big city. Slowly, but surely my discontent was building and I wanted to go to Perth and live another life; one that I had been denied living in the country regions. I had never been one to join craft groups, although I gamely tried to get younger women interested in the CWA in Wagin. My efforts were beginning to show results, with the younger women coming into the town, but when we were transferred all my enthusiasm for the project to be up and running went with me.

One day in late November I decided I wanted a break and told Keith I was going up to Perth for a couple of days. I would stay with Michael and his family, catch up with some friends then come back, hopefully feeling a little more positive. Eager to try anything to cheer me up, Keith was okay with this and I took our Ford Telstar car, which was better on the long hauls – and Manjimup was a long haul – at least 3 hours from Perth.

I arrived back in Perth where I had arranged to stay with Michael and his girls, and immediately organized to go to some agencies and have my capabilities tested and valued. I was pleasantly surprised by my typing speeds and comprehension and once again as a test case, I accepted the opportunity to go for an interview for a job – just to see how I would go.

I sat in the reception of the accountancy firm I had been sent to. I was offered a cup of coffee by the receptionist, which I gratefully accepted and waited, wondering what on earth I was doing there! Deep in thought, I heard my name called and immediately jumped, tipping over the coffee on to my dress. My potential boss was most concerned and ushered me into a ladies to clean up! Good start.

Five minutes later, having settled into a chair in his office, soggy but none the worse for wear – he apologized profusely for making me jump whereupon I of course told him it wasn't his fault but mine. The ice was broken quite well by the mishap really. We talked for a while, even got round to discussing starting dates, etc. and at the end of the interview we shook hands and I took my leave. I felt I had done okay, but then what I had done just hit me and I was very unsure what I wanted the outcome to be.

I went back to Michael's house somewhat bemused by the turn of events. I told myself that this was the turning point for my life. I would go back to Manjimup, wait for the job to come up at the hotel and get on with my life. Conrad was somewhere else and in any case was not interested in me. My life was with my family back in Manjimup.

Later that afternoon the agency called to say that the accountancy firm was very interested in me and the boss was calling them back early next morning with his decision. I felt as if I was being carried off on a tide with no recourse to shore! What would I do if I was offered this job?

The next morning I was getting ready to return to Manjimup when Michael's phone rang. My heart sank, I knew it was my decision time, I just knew. They wanted me for the position and wanted to know when I would start! I heard myself saying that as this was a Wednesday, I would need a week or so to get myself somewhere to live and sort things out in Manjimup. So a start date was agreed, a salary was agreed and I now had to go back and announce to my husband that I was leaving to take up a position in Perth. I think I was a little insane at the time, carried on an uncontrollable wave of destiny, taking me far from my comfort zone.

It is almost as if everything was meant to be. Under normal circumstances I could not have left the children and Keith for 5 out of 7 days per week. There would be no one to look after them, but Martha, Keith's mother was over staying with us for a few weeks, so the impossible started to look feasible. When I spoke to Keith about what I had done and more to the point, how much I had been offered in salary, although he was not happy about the situation he could see how ill and unhappy I had been looking lately and immediately said that no job was worth losing his family for and he would ask Head Office to re transfer him back to Perth. He had only been in Manjimup at this stage two months – understandably the bank was less than impressed and would not commit to when they would find him a spot in Perth or where. But at least they would look. In the meantime I would drive up to Perth on Sunday afternoon and then back down on Friday evening.

All of us came up to Perth the following week – Keith had some leave and it was getting close to Christmas and whilst I started my job we all camped in a unit in West Perth for a few days. During that time Keith looked around for a newer car for me to drive as the beetle could not be relied upon to travel back and forth on such a frequent basis.

I wanted something blue and a hatchback – I got a beige corolla sedan! But it was all mine and it was practically new so after the initial disappointment at the car being so obviously not what I had asked for, I was happily driving my new car along Riverside Drive, switching things on and off and giggling like an excited child (much to the amusement of Samantha and Brad, who were also in the car).

Samantha and Brad were not sorry to leave Manjimup. They too had hated the place and also the school that they went to there. They were, however, both adamant that they did not want to live back in Thornlie and indeed, neither did we. But where to go?

We had always lived "south of the river" whilst we lived in Perth so automatically started thinking about suburbs on that side. We had not been impressed by suburbs further North by the sea and all the inner suburbs were too expensive for us. My boss asked me one day why we were planning to live south of the river when I was working north of the river and would have to drive to work via the infamous Freeway every day! We suddenly thought "Why ARE we only thinking south? Force of habit?" So Keith and Martha began looking at townhouses (I like upstairs/downstairs houses) and eventually found an acceptable one in Floreat Park and we duly completed the paperwork and I was moved in. I loved it! Although initially I missed the children SO badly it was still nice to please myself when and what I ate and what I would do each evening, which on most occasions was nothing much. I was living on my own for the first time in my life and I really liked it.

I needed to go back to Manjimup each Friday night though and that was a journey I grew to dread – especially the last 45 minutes. I would stop in Bunbury for something to eat and then start the last haul home. How I did not run off the road during those trips I will never know as it was incredibly hard to keep my eyes open. I did this trip every week for approximately one and a half months, until it was time to bring the children up to Perth for the start of the school year in February.

I continued to miss Conrad terribly. I had seen him a few times when he had come down to Perth on business or to visit his parents but this love remained only mine as he was still hoping his "true love" would join him. In the end however, she returned to the UK with her husband and Conrad had to face the fact that it was not going to happen. However, being Conrad it was not long before he found someone else to help him cope with his love life going awry. Meanwhile I tried to pick up the pieces of my life but would never be the same again.

PERTH – A NEW LIFE?

*I*n the move to Manjimup we lost yet another cat – Snowball. She went out one day and did not come back – demise of cat number 6. We now had Chubbs the dog and Ordie, Because of the purchase of my Corolla, we had a surplus of one car – my beetle. So it was decided that we would sell it. The advertisement duly appeared and I had several enquiries, one of which was from a young lady who loved beetles. My beetle was an attractive vehicle and she came round to see it and pretty well decided on the spot to have it – despite the fact that when we tried to adjust the driver's seat it would not move – it had hitherto not been a problem. This did not deter her and she arranged for her father to come the next day and pay cash for the vehicle.

During my lunch hour, I drove back to the unit to meet my car's purchaser. It was almost as if "Bertie" had decided he did not want to go and was doing everything in his power to muck up this sale. When we walked out to the car it would not start! Overnight the battery had died. I was so embarrassed – there was nothing for it but to go to the nearest battery dealership and buy a new one. So we both jumped into my Corolla and went to pick up a battery. The new "owner" of Bertie put the new battery in and I of course did not charge him for it – how could I? Once again the driver's seat refused to be adjusted and I was feeling so frustrated at this turn of events. Add to this that the accelerator pedal had begun sticking, so there was a mad flapping going on to kill the revving that was taking place. At any moment I expected the man to turn around and tell me the deal was off. However, he didn't and I eventually closed the deal, gave him a receipt and waved him out the door with mixed feelings of relief and sadness.

After the initial settling in period into my townhouse on my own – I missed the children terribly and it was always hard to leave them on the Sunday evening – I began to enjoy my "single" existence. I saw a little of Michael, who having divorced his first wife, was now seeing a new lady and would come to sound me out on what I thought about this and that. It was mostly nice, though, just to relax after a day at work and take my time about deciding on what to cook for my meal. However, this was only temporary, as Samantha and Brad were coming up to join me at the beginning of the school year so I had to get a move on finding larger accommodation.

Just around the corner from my town house in Floreat, a new unit complex had been built comprising two and three bedroomed units, complete with a communal swimming pool. I had a look around them and as we wanted the children to go to Churchlands Senior High School, which was in the area, it was an ideal compromise until we found a house to buy when Keith was transferred up to Perth.

It was a difficult time. I was not happy, not having really got over my feelings for Conrad as yet. The children were unsettled and at a difficult stage in their lives and Keith was, of course, worried about when we could all be together again as a family. I managed to catch up with Conrad a couple of times during this time, as he was waiting to hear about the job he was after and was staying with his parents. However, in retrospect this was not wise as it just further unsettled me – he was still pining after his lost love, who had gone off to travel – with her husband – and had returned pregnant with their first child. When I look back at this time I can still feel my devastation at having to maintain a calm face in the midst of my churning emotions.

I was also finding it difficult to settle into my new position, as technology had far out run my experiences in the country and I was having to get used to memory typewriters. For the first six weeks at my new job I did not know what would happen first, my termination or resignation. It was also around this time that word processors came into the commercial world and I had to get used to using one of these things as well as everything else! The powers that be did not feel it was necessary to give the staff any training on these items of equipment and we were left alone to bumble along as best we could!

In April of that year (1986) the bank offered Keith a position in Perth Head Office, as manager of one of their CBD area accounts, and he duly arrived up in Perth. The children and I had, by this time moved into the bigger unit and we were trying to pick up where we left off.

It is hard for me to write about this time, as we were all very out of sync added to which our cat, Ordie, had disappeared. Once again, our unit was a block away from a busy road (this was always something we considered when choosing where to live, because of our cats!) Nevertheless, it did not save Ordie. Keith and I went out looking for him, and my heart fell to my boots as from a distance we saw "something" lying at the side of the road. We both knew it was Ordie and once again, we had to break the news to the children. Now we were left with Chubbs. We had lost 7 cats (and a kitten) in 5 years. (The kitten we lost was one of Pippa's, in Bunbury – Chubbs had jumped on the bed and accidentally landed on it!) I am sure there is a Renton Cat Club in Heaven, where they all meet to compare notes.

The search for a house, not too far away from Churchlands SHS and within our price bracket, began. We looked at countless houses in and around the Floreat/ Wembley area but nothing struck us as "the one". The children were beginning to think we would never find a house of our own. One day we saw an ad. for a rear townhouse on a duplex block. It was in Wembley Downs and not far from a house we were going to look at that evening – after work. We viewed the first house, which was quite roomy and had a spacious back garden, but it was on a busy road and despite the fact that the house was well set back from the road; it was something we were concerned about, given our immediate past history of demised cats! By the time we had finished at this house it was getting dark and it had begun raining. We debated whether in fact we would go and view the second place, but in the end decided it would be unfair on the salesperson we had arranged to meet there, so we went.

The unit was at the rear of what was once a large block. The front house was the original house and the owner had had the second unit built behind. The salesman was waiting for us at the end of the drive and we followed him down the drive (which seemed to go on forever!) The front door opened from the double carport adjoining the front unit and was singularly unspectacular. When we stepped inside, however, I knew this was it!!

The windows of the lounge/dining looked out on to the dense foliage of the back garden. There was an outside light which gave an inviting view of the trees and plants which grew in abundance out there. The interior walls were rough rendered and the roomy kitchen had an enormous number of cupboards. As we went through the house, everything about it told us it was to be "our house". The children were ecstatic as they excitedly ran up the stairs to explore the upper floor. The main bedroom was very roomy with one entire wall made up of storage cupboards and it was air-conditioned! We asked the price the owner would take, which was a bit more than we had budgeted for, however we put in our offer and waited with bated breath for an answer. This was, of course, "yes". We had found our new home.

At the same time as we were moving into our new house, I was also spearheading our firm's move to new offices. We were amalgamating with a larger accountancy firm and were all moving to West Perth. So I would leave packed boxes and chaos at home, to go into the office and find more packed boxes and chaos at work. The staff were essentially, quite young and looked to me for their support during this difficult time. Add to all this, the children were settling into school and a new house, and it was truly a tumultuous time in my life.

My firm duly moved into our new premises, which had been completely re-fitted to house us, and of course nothing worked. The switchboard had been incorrectly connected so was temporarily useless, necessitating the receptionist to accumulate a number of calls then go over the road to a public phone to make the calls! No one could contact us, which caused the partners of the firm no end of heartburn thinking of lost revenue and the rest of us tried to organize our desk areas as best we could. Several of the girls broke down in tears after a couple of days of this. However, by the end of the first week there was some semblance of order overall.

At this time we were all trying to overcome the "them and us" syndrome which always happens with an amalgamation of companies. There was the added difficulty that the firm we had amalgamated with was much bigger than ours and they still had an office in the city, so those staff members that were sent to join our firm ("them") were a little resentful and a trifle intolerant of the settling in chaos which ensued. This was not a happy time! There were several social "get togethers" organized in an attempt to bridge the gap, which were less than successful, with everyone seeming to huddle in their groups to discuss and survey "them". It was also becoming apparent that we had two captains to this ship, neither of which was inclined to defer to the other.

At home, amidst the chaos of boxes as yet still unpacked, there was a peace and tranquility prevailing. Our enclosed back area was such a joy to look at and experience. Apart from the fact that Brad's room was only marginally bigger than a walk in robe – the unit was very comfortable and even in the hottest weather we experienced a sea breeze. The upstairs window looked out over the tree tops and I spent many an hour just sitting up there watching the trees waving in the breeze. I needed this time to myself as I was still unhappy and lonely. Nothing seemed to fill the void that existed in my heart. On several occasions it all became too much for me and in order to avoid upsetting Samantha by letting her see me cry I would just take off in my car and find a solitary area somewhere and just let out all my pain and loneliness. I had to keep up a façade of cheerfulness and this was hard. Samantha was going through a bad time too, as the Nursing Course she had begun was the first training course run as a tertiary subject. To date the nursing training had been done on the job in hospitals, but in order to give nursing a more professional image, would-be nurses now went to college. However, they had not arranged the courses terribly well and the initial two years were almost exclusively made up with theory. There was no interspersed practical training during this time, consequently a lot of potentially wonderful nurses, both male and female, were lost in a sea of disillusionment and theory. It was Samantha's sheer determination that kept her going during these difficult years.

Brad was at that age, 14, when only a mother (or father) can really love him! I will say, however, that neither of my beloved children ever gave us a moment's concern about drugs or drinking. Any arguments we had were usually about their lack of enthusiasm to wash and put away dishes or their need to be somewhere and back at a certain time.

Keith and I were endeavouring to pick up the pieces of our relationship. I had almost left whilst we were in our unit in Floreat, feeling that I could no longer go on leading a "normal" life whilst feeling dead inside, I had told him I would be leaving. However we discussed things and decided to keep on trying to save our marriage, for everyone's sake. It was a hard time for Keith, seeing his family dreams fall apart, added to which he did not like his position at the bank head office, or the way that banking was going in its competitiveness.

I desperately needed to find something to fill my hours out of work. I heard about a choir called the Perth Oratorio Choir (POC), which met once a week and performed classical oratorios. I duly fronted up to a rehearsal for the POC, gave a very basic audition and was accepted into the choir. It was some 120 souls strong, but with a not too steadfast tenor section. At the time I joined the conductor was Peter Benton, but in due course he moved over east to further his career and we had a succession of choirmasters in the ensuing two or three years. I really enjoyed the rehearsals and performances, which were mainly held in Winthrop Hall at the University of Western Australia (UWA). It was an outlet for my need to sing and also filled a small void in my life.

At the same time I decided to take up guitar lessons, using the three-quarter sized guitar we had picked up during our sojourn in Moora, all those years ago. Conrad, who still continued to telephone me from time to time, put me in touch with a colleague of his called Stefan, and I attended classes with him for a while. Unfortunately, however, it became obvious that I needed to purchase a full sized guitar and as money was, as always, still a little tight with us, I gave up my lessons.

What next, well I could try going back to study – that would fill some hours. So I enrolled in a course at University which would ultimately give me a diploma in Social Services. The first two units were Social Studies and Theory of Multiculturalism! My lectures were at 5.30 on two evenings per week and I truly battled to keep my eyes open during this time! I had never studied at tertiary level before and the libraries and knowledge required to find books I needed, were a total mystery to me! I gamely kept going for approximately six weeks, but it was the time when students were being charged the Administration fee – which was approximately $280.00. Once again, money – or the lack of it – caused a problem as we were in the middle of negotiating settlement on our house in Wembley Downs – no money to spare. So with mixed feelings, I pulled out of the course after approximately two months.

WORK IN THE BIG CITY 1986 - 1989

*T*he amalgamation of our two firms laboured on for approximately two years, but having two equally stubborn "captains" for the one ship was disastrous. So, in 1988, two years after the initial merge, my boss and another of the partners pulled out and once again we were moving back to West Perth.

As before I was put in charge of the moving and fitting out of the new premises, including the décor for the boardroom and throughout the office. We were a small concern again and this suited me. I could do the work without having to think too much, as there was an unhappy void inside me which nothing seemed to fill. I had to recruit junior office staff, stepping carefully through the minefield of new legislation such as discrimination and equal rights. Finding just the right office junior proved to be the most demanding, as most of the youngsters coming for interview were fresh from secretarial agencies, where they had had their egos boosted and their expectations lifted. Consequently, gone were the days when a "junior" was content to do the *junior* work. This generation wanted to step into secretarial roles straight away. Eventually, however, our crew was complete and we were up and running.

Before our move I had experienced the *Big 40* birthday. I had loved turning 30. Some of the most interesting women (and men) I had met whilst in my 20s, were 30 and over, so the age held no fear for me. They had grown out of what I now term the "20s self-absorption" years and were outgoing and curious about things and people other than themselves. I was thus not really worried about turning 40 in the earlier years. Things had taken such a wild turn for me during my late 30s, however, that when my 40th birthday loomed I was in the biggest time void of my life. I felt, being 40, there were no further employment hopes for me – this was it! Being 40 I could only see my appearance and life careering downhill from there. In retrospect I realize that I was experiencing a depression. I was at work for my birthday. Several of my workmates had insisted that we go out for lunch to celebrate, although I really did not feel like it. However, one by one each of them was called away to do "urgent" jobs and suddenly I was alone and I spent my 40th birthday lunch hour, sitting in a café eating a curried egg sandwich.

Conrad called me to with me happy birthday and was surprised to hear me sounding so down. Little did he know that he could not "win" that day. His call upset me, and if he had not called I would have been upset because he had not made the effort! Dead if you do and dead if you don't!

I had told Keith I really did not want a party and he had respected my wishes, however, when I got home he had some champagne on ice and organized a lovely dinner – with just him and the children. I had a choir rehearsal that night and by the time we had eaten and I had quaffed a glass or two of champagne – and opened my lovely presents from them all – I was feeling much better and glad the whole rotten birthday was over.

The Perth Oratorio Choir (POC) was going through some changes. Peter had been the choirmaster for several years but was leaving to take up a post in Melbourne. We had several "try –outs" for choirmaster. One in particular did not last more than the first week, as everyone complained that he spoke so fast we could not understand a word he said, and when we did not adhere to his instructions he would have a tantrum!

We did utilize one gentleman for a while, however, during one of our performances I watched in disbelief as I realized he had forgotten to "bring in" the Sopranos at one particular point in the piece we were performing at Winthrop Hall. After this the whole choir lost confidence in him and he was past history.

Keith would dutifully attend the performances as a show of support for my singing. Samantha and Brad would be dragged along. I remember one particular performance – again at Winthrop Hall – where during the first half I could see my family trying very hard to look as though they were enjoying the music. For the second half, however, there was no sign of Brad. I asked afterwards what had happened to Brad and Keith, rather shamefaced said Brad had begged him to be allowed to stay in the car (and listen to the radio) rather than sit through the second half of the performance and as Brad was such a fidget when bored, Keith had decided it better to allow this than experience Brad's constant movement during the singing. I realized then how hard they were all trying to support me. However, I never again pushed them into attending any performances of my choir – it was just not their scene.

During this time and upon our return to Perth, we had not reinstated friendships with people we had known prior to going country. Whether it was pressure from the bank, or because our relationship was in such a state of turmoil,

I don't know, but Keith did not want to go anywhere at the end of the day, and I began to feel stifled. My mother had made me the focal point of her life and I had found this overbearing and now Keith was doing the same thing. I searched for things to fill my life – singing, study, learning the guitar, anything that would dull the ache I felt missing Conrad so much.

I had not been able to completely break contact with Conrad, because every few weeks or so he would call to say hallo. He was thoroughly enjoying his life in the fast lane in. He was the regular man about town with his little red MG car and single status. He had carved a niche with the "cultural bodies" of the town and had transferred his devotions to another love. A couple of times he had been in Perth for conferences or meetings and he had called to see if I was free for lunch. We would go and talk about things like old friends, but it would have been better for me if I had not seen him at all. I did eventually learn to live with the loneliness, but the discontent and emptiness got worse.

One day at work I was called by an old work colleague and asked if I would be interested in joining him in a new personnel agency venture he was taking on. I had not really thought about leaving my boss of the last three years so this was a bolt out of the blue! It would initially be less money but I would ultimately be trained as a personnel consultant – a new career! I thought about it for a while and then decided maybe the change would be just what I was looking for. So I told my boss I was leaving and he gave me a week or so to re-consider but I kept to my decision and I found myself in a new position.

The firm I joined was based in the eastern states and our offices were in Adelaide Terrace. Our company name was very similar to a government office based in the same building, so consequently as I was the receptionist I was forever re-directing people elsewhere. The owners of the building would not allow signage to alleviate this irritation. My work was repetitive and the months came and went with no indication that my administrative duties were to fall to someone else and my training as a personnel consultant would begin. As the head office was in the Eastern States the person who had recruited me in the first instance soon discovered just how little autonomy he had to run the business and hence forward my career, so unfortunately things did not develop as I wished.

Not long after I had joined this firm, my mother, (who in the February of 1988 was diagnosed with lung cancer) got worse. She had been in a nursing home for the past 12 years (I had to make the decision about her having or not having chemotherapy). Such was the brain damage my mother had incurred that she really did not understand on a logical plane, things that were happening to her, that I felt that chemotherapy would be cruel on her, as she would not be able to understand what was happening to her or why she would be feeling so ill. I opted not to have her condition treated and let the disease run its course.

Initially, the doctors kept her recurring lung infections in control with antibiotics. There was really no great deterioration in her condition for the first four or five months. Her energy levels went down a little and instead of scurrying from room to room on errands, which in her mind were most important, she tended to sleep a little more than in the past.

My visits to my mother had been very traumatic for me. Probably a deep seated guilt still remained that I felt responsible for her being in this situation because of our argument all those years ago. When we did visit her and she was asleep I felt ashamed at the relief that all I would have to do is sit quietly by her bed in case she woke up – so at least she would know we were there.

Keith came with me most of the time and if she was feeling up to it we would take a picnic somewhere so she could have her much cherished "cup of tea". Over the years she had become increasingly less enthusiastic about going into public and having "afternoon tea" at a restaurant – all of which suited me anyway.

By the September of that year Mum was having difficulty fighting off lung infections and the periods when she would have to take antibiotics grew longer. Her ability to walk any distance gradually waned also, and by the end of October we knew she was getting near the end.

In early November I was at work when they rang from the nursing home and told me that Mum was very low and I should come over. I left immediately and sat by her bed that afternoon on Friday the 4th November. At 10.30 I went home and returned the next day at about 3.00pm. She was on morphine now and I was dreading how the end would come. When she went, however, it was extremely peaceful. Both Keith and I were there when she took a shuddering breath and I sent him for the nursing sister, however, that was her last breath and she quietly faded away. I held her hand and cried but inside there was a gladness that at last Mum was with her George, my father, for whom she had never really stopped grieving, so there was a relief too.

Just how isolated Mum had grown became apparent at the funeral. My new boss and his wife came, for which I shall always be grateful – it was very thoughtful of them. However, apart from the all-caring Ron, who I had contacted when I knew Mum was really bad – there was only Keith and the children and myself to mourn her passing. From those first tears, when she initially died, I have never shed any further tears for my mother. For me, she died 12 years prior to her physical death – she was not my mother from that fateful day in 1977 – she was just someone with brain damage for whom we had the responsibility. I sometimes wonder at my reaction…

My disenchantment grew with the personnel consultancy as they had not fulfilled their initial plan for me; to train me as a personnel consultant, so after about nine months I looked for and found a new job as an administrative assistant/secretary – once again with a company whose head office was based in the eastern states.

For the first few months I really enjoyed my position with this new firm, until the head office started tightening the purse strings to the point where I was unable to pay any creditors and as this formed a major part of my duties, I was left twiddling my thumbs for much of the time. During my employment with this company I was yet again the main organizer for moving the office to a new location. In the past few years I had moved offices four times and house three times!

At about this time I received a call from Conrad to say that he had returned to Perth. I had very mixed feelings about this as I thought I had got over him and had picked up the pieces of my life. He and his wife, had got back together again, however, so I felt fairly safe. I would just avoid seeing him. Music threw us together again though. As he was working with the Music Department of his establishment and the POC was working on a project with them and suddenly I was seeing him at rehearsals. I still felt "cured" however so when he asked if we could have lunch I said okay.

I soon found out things were not going well with him and his wife and once again I became "the confidante". He kissed me and I realized I was not immune – I was right back where I started nearly five years ago. What a mess!

BOOK TWO

1990 – I GO IT ALONE!

*I*n January of 1990 I finally left home and started in a new position all in the same week.

The strain of living a lie to my feelings had become too much and I decided I needed time and space "to feel and express what I was going through". Only those that have taken the painful decision to walk out on a long-standing marriage and family can understand the devastation we all felt when I finally announced I was moving out – by myself – to try and sort things out. Even writing about it now, all these years later, has not dulled the pain I felt and was felt by all the members of my close knit family. I did not want to leave Samantha and Brad but I could not afford to rent a place big enough for us three and I felt I could not ask Keith to leave so I would have to go by myself.

Brad had graduated from High School (in year 12) and was unsure what he wanted to do and Samantha was in the "home stretch" of her bid to become a nurse, so I felt I could leave without causing their studies to suffer, although of course there is never the "right time" for a mother to walk out. Apart from the sadness I felt about what I was doing I had to cope with the guilt of knowing that I was breaking up my family unit, but I had to get away; to be free to have my crying fits when they came, free to just think about what I wanted without worrying about what everyone else wanted.

At the end of 1989 I had applied for and obtained a position as Administrative Secretary at the Geology Department at the University of WA. Part of the contract with the Geology Department was the necessity to undertake a medical examination. I duly presented myself to the appointed doctor and everything was fine, until we got to my blood pressure reading, it was so high he took it twice with a short time lapse in between to ensure the equipment was not faulty. He asked me if I knew of any reason why my blood pressure should be so high. When I explained that I had just split up from my husband of over 20 years, moved out of home, leaving my two children with their father and started a new job over the past week and a half, he nodded and asked me if I had had any counseling to cope with all of this!

Up until this point counseling was not something I had known or thought about. Money was very tight as Keith needed my salary to keep our house going and support the children, neither of whom were yet working full time. So paying out vast quantities of money to a psychologist was not something I could realistically contemplate. The Doctor, however, had recently undergone a marriage break up himself and had found a young lady who he had been visiting for counseling. The problem was she was not registered for any medical rebates, but by the same token she did not charge as much as the recognized counselors did either, so I duly took her name and said I would ring to make an appointment, just initially to talk things through.

The previous occupant of my position had been with the Department 30 years and had retired the previous November, consequently there was no "hand over" or induction into the position. Add to this that the Head of Department was new to both the position and the State and you have a case of "the blind leading the blind"!

Just what the new Head of Department (HOD) wanted of me was a little confusing. On the one hand he wanted to know everything that was happening and see all the mail that came into the Department. On the other hand he needed to get on with his own interests and studies. With no one with whom to really check out what had previously been the regime I bumbled along as best I could, letting him see all of the mail (circulars and all) even though I could have handled it (but thought he wanted to know about it.) I also found out that there were a few people around who were not particularly happy with the HOD's appointment so was also aware of friction within the Department. Add to all this my newness to the tertiary institution and its way of doing things, and it will be realized the first few months at the University were far from easy.

In my search to find somewhere to live which I could afford and was also acceptable and close to work, I had discovered a small bed sitter built on to a house in Nedlands. It was very convenient to work and within my price range. It was also roomy and had its own bathroom and little kitchen. The negative was that the bed sit was connected to the main house by just a door and it was one which I could not lock from my side. I have to say now, there was never any problem with the owners coming through unannounced whilst I was there, but I am sure they checked out my bed sit when I was away! I did not particularly like the husband of the couple who owned the house, so not having a lock on the door was rather a disadvantage. However, the accommodation and its own little verandah overlooking the garden, and a well-placed chair under the door handle of the connecting door, made up for this and I settled into my new life.

Up till this point in my life I had never had a problem sleeping so it was a shock to me when I found it very difficult to fall asleep – sometimes still lying awake at 3.00am in the morning! I experienced true sadness for myself, Keith and the children. It was just such a dreadful feeling knowing I had inflicted this circumstance on everyone. In those early days, in the wee small hours I could have easily just packed up everything and gone home where I belonged. However, having caused such heartbreak to Keith there was no way I was going to return before I was totally sure it was what I wanted to do. I just had to get through this patch.

I did begin to see Conrad, but the way was far from smooth. He was still with his wife so I am ashamed to say I became "the other woman". My conscience troubled me but my love for him overcame any virtue of conscience I had.

My blood pressure continued to stay high, not surprisingly, so I was a frequent patient at my doctor's surgery. On one occasion I mentioned that I had been feeling unwell with no particular symptoms, just out of sorts. He stated that as a precaution with his patients of child bearing age he gave them a pregnancy test, just to eliminate this as being a cause for feeling "unwell". I laughingly agreed and he duly took my blood.

A couple of days later, whilst in my office, I received a call from the doctor congratulating me on being pregnant! To say I was speechless with shock is putting it mildly. I was aware of the doctor on the other end of the line talking to me but I didn't hear anything he said after being told I was pregnant! I managed eventually, to acknowledge what he was saying and in a daze replaced the receiver. Pregnant… age 41, recently separated from my husband and embarking on a life supporting myself, in a new position….Pregnant? What was I going to do? It was impossible! I only had one fallopian tube – badly damaged from the Dalkon Shield and the father – and I knew it must be Conrad's – had hitherto been unable to father any children and indeed, had come to terms with never being a father! He was also married to his lawful wife! I needed time to digest this latest turn of events.

The following day, after an extremely restless night, I contacted Conrad and told him the news. Predictably, his response was "but that's impossible!" He probably had a moment of wondering whether or not it was his – although he never confessed to thinking this I'm sure it crossed his mind. He was adamant the pregnancy could not go ahead and as can be imagined things were pretty fraught between us. I needed time to think about things and I did not need Conrad panicking around me so we agreed to stay away from each other for a few days! As it happened I lost the baby a couple of weeks later. One weekend I took myself to King Edward Memorial Hospital for a checkup because I had begun spotting and in 24 hours I had lost the baby. As can be imagined there was a mixture of feelings of loss and relief, although the hurt I had felt because of Conrad's (understandable) reaction lasted for a while.

Around this time I contacted the counselor recommended to me by the doctor and made an appointment to see her. Kelly was a young lass and one of her best assets, was of course, her ability to listen. I told her about my confusion as to how I could "fall out of love" with Keith after all these years, to the point where I could want someone else. She explained that from what I had told her, I had never really voiced my opposition to any decision Keith had made in our marriage. I had accepted everything whether or not I wanted it. Sometimes I would have felt resentment at a subconscious level, which would have stayed with me even though I would have thought I was going along with plans quite happily. After many years of "little resentments" building up, it begins to take the place of love – rather like a milk jug that starts filling with water, gradually, and eventually there is no room for milk. I could identify with this idea. Kelly said I needed time to do things for me, to gradually empty out the water from "the milk jug" and make room for some new "milk".

From the day my father had died – when I was 10 – I had taken on the responsibility of trying to ensure those around me, who I loved, were happy. Initially, it was my Mother who I was always concerned about. I could only go out and leave her if I was sure she was either watching a television programme she wanted to see, or was with someone else. If neither was the case I was unable to really enjoy myself whilst away. As I grew up I transferred these feelings to Keith, then to Samantha or Brad and ultimately to Conrad. I have never really been able to shake off this sense of responsibility. Maybe if I had been more like my mother and less like my father I would have been able to stand up for myself and say what I wanted to say to people, even if it was not what they wanted to hear. I also believe that I married when too young.

My conscience was badly troubling me because I had walked out on my children, particularly, so most weekends for the first couple of months, I would go over to the Wembley house and helped clean up the place, change sheets, do some washing, etc. They were difficult times and I was very unhappy but unable to do anything about the situation.

When I had been in the Department approximately five months, the previous occupant of my position came in to see her colleagues and mentioned that she was looking for someone to house sit her home while she went on a world trip for a few months. After making some further enquiries I decided this could be just what I was looking for to enable me to get out of the bed sit so I offered to look after the place for her. It was fully furnished of course. It only had one bedroom but there was a closed off area in the lounge which could be used as a sleep over bedroom for Samantha. She had built the unit at the back of her original house just a stone's throw from the University so it couldn't have been more convenient. The front house was let to a single mother and her daughter and in due course I moved in to my comfortable new abode.

I continued to see Conrad some evenings, after work. I was still his other woman and this did not sit well with me. As far as friends were concerned I was in a no man's land as all of my friends were married or in pairs, and although my life was a little solitary at least I could be myself, and there was actually no one around with whom I wanted to spend time.

Keith was having a bad time at the bank. He had been unhappy there for a long time and of course our situation was not making it any easier. One day he contacted me and told me he had been offered retrenchment – at 48 – he was being put out "on the scrap heap" as he put it, which was another blow to his self-esteem. He could refuse it of course, but he would then be given all the "scrap" jobs no one else wanted, so in reality he did not have a choice. He decided to "take the money and run". It was a really hard time for him as he still badly needed security and even that was being taken out from under him. After looking around for a while he bought a small business, which was a supply and collection of garden bags to householders. It suited where he was at the time and he built it up over the next two years.

I had been on my own for approximately six months and decided a weekend away at a "Retreat" was the answer. The Extension Service at the University was running a weekend retreat in the June and I decided to go. The retreat was somewhere in the hills and it was supposed to be tailored to enable the participants to relax, meditate and put themselves together again, like the proverbial Humpty Dumpty. The food was vegetarian and we had workshops and chat groups, etc. I found out several of the participants were suffering from Schizophrenia. Talking to a couple of the ladies suffering this condition was a real eye-opener. To most of us, if someone has Schizophrenia they are perceived as "dangerous" doubtless due to our ignorance of the condition. In actual fact, I learned that weekend that the people that suffer the most are those with the condition, as they get no rest from these insistent and persistent voices telling them very negative and self-destructive things. Mental illness is so badly misunderstood and supported, for the sufferers and those that love them.

One of the activities we had on the Saturday morning was a session of lively aerobics, into which I threw myself with gay abandon, with no thought for the painful aftermath as my muscles recovered! The following morning I was awakened by excruciating pain low down on my left side. This was muscle spasm gone berserk! I had to ease myself into chairs and lift myself up very slowly to avoid pain shooting all through my abdomen. This lasted for most of the day, so the last day of my "meditative relaxation" was anything but! I did, however, go home a little freer in the mind, armed with some "tools" which I could use when things got too hard to cope with.

Earlier in the year – about March – my son, Brad had decided to try his hand at being a Jackeroo. He won a contract to go – with the Department of Training – up to a homestead in the middle of nowhere, somewhere in the north of Western Australia. The first of my pigeons was leaving the nest and saying goodbye to him was one of the hardest and heartbreaking moments of my life. Keith and I cried together for hours afterwards.

Samantha was also going through some crisis in her young love life and was on the verge of marrying someone to enable him to stay in Australia as her husband. She was sure she loved the man, but fortunately he had the moral fortitude to admit he did not love her and would not let her sacrifice herself for him – although Samantha did not see it that way. This also hit me very hard and once again I spent the better part of a day crying my eyes out, although if someone was to ask me why, I would not be able to put my reasons into words.

Around the middle of July I once again felt "unwell" and as before I unbelievingly underwent a pregnancy test! I was relieved to see it was negative and waited another week or so for nature to take its course – it didn't! The impossible had happened again, I was pregnant.

This time, I was sure I could not go through with it and when the doctor sent me off to see the Gynecological specialist to arrange for a termination, due to high blood pressure, this was the plan. To this day I can only say that this baby was meant to be. By the time I got to the specialist (two hours later the same day) my blood pressure was absolutely normal! After my previous experience of miscarrying I fully expected to do the same, however, the specialist – Louise – decided to give me an ultrasound anyway, and there was the heart of my baby beating bright and strong, just where it should have been. Somehow this new life had pushed itself along my one remaining, damaged, fallopian tube and into my uterus and was hanging in there for dear life! When I thought back to my weekend retreat I realize the pain I had experienced was my very determined baby pushing its way along my one remaining fallopian tube! Nonetheless, I made an appointment to go to a termination clinic and duly turned up for my pre-termination counseling. The woman I spoke to there told me she felt I was not totally sure it was what I wanted to do, and if this was the case, the termination would be mentally traumatic for me so I was told to go away and think some more about it!

At this stage, I was beginning to make tentative plans as to how I could manage to keep this baby and bring it up on my own, as I was in no way relying on Conrad to be there. This had to be something I could do on my own if I needed to. I decided to have the amniocentesis test to see if there were any genetic problems. This in itself can sometimes cause a spontaneous abortion, but, if I lost it, so be it. I was sure this baby was a boy. Conrad was overseas when the results of the test came through. I was informed that the baby was perfectly healthy and as a matter of course I enquired as to its sex and was told I was having a perfectly healthy baby girl. That was it then. There was no way I was going to terminate a perfectly healthy baby. It is funny how circumstances make you realize what you have believed all along but were not aware of. I could not terminate this life – I was going to be a mother again and amid all the uncertainty I was thrilled. My health continued to be wonderful whilst I was carrying my baby, who we decided to call Alexandra. I did not suffer any discomfort, apart from occasional heartburn, and no nausea at all.

Our relationship, however, fluctuated madly as Conrad came to terms with the fact that I was going to go through with the pregnancy. I told him I would manage on my own if I had to but was determined to have my baby.

When he returned from overseas – I had rung him and told him the baby was a girl and was healthy – he had decided to end his marriage. As is his way he wasted no time in doing this, arriving back in the country on a Thursday and moving out of home on the Sunday! I had made arrangements for him to stay with Michael and Helen, his new partner, when he moved out as I felt it was not the best idea to move in with me straight away. I firmly believe people need time and space to adjust to being "single" again. However, he spent more and more time with me until eventually in the December he just never left!

Our relationship was still a little fraught, I was very unsure of his true feelings for me and would have panic attacks every so often when I thought about what I was intending to do. I was also feeling rather self-conscious about being pregnant "at my age". Here I have to say my daughter, Samantha, was a great support to me and for this I shall always be grateful. Samantha was really looking forward to the baby and would urge me to go shopping for clothes and when I shied away from this, would point out I did not look my age and didn't even look very pregnant. Indeed right up until seven months, there were people in the Department at the University who were totally unaware I was even pregnant!

We were unsure how Conrad's parents and family would take the news of the baby. They had long since grown used to the disappointment that they would never see a child of his, so this would be quite a shock to them. Being staunch Salvation Army people, when Conrad did tell them, they were concerned about the moral situation with Conrad and I still being legally married to other people, however, after the initial shock they became truly supportive and looked forward to this unexpected gift from God.

Having lived with Keith for so many years I was under the impression that he was typical of most males. I was soon to realize he was rather the exception when it came to his thoughtfulness and regard for me. Conrad was opposite in every way to Keith. He had his good points too, but it seemed that every time I needed some emotional support, he was having his own little crisis and was nowhere to be seen! We continued to have counseling to sort ourselves out but we had a long way to go.

We had some happy times too. These were mainly spent with Michael and Helen who, during this time, were unfailingly "there" for me. Once, when I was approximately eight months pregnant we had a great weekend at "The Vines" in the Swan Valley. I had left work on maternity leave and was happily anticipating the birth of our baby, but amidst all of that there were times of uncertainty about my future but never uncertainty about the rightness of having my baby.

After Conrad moved in with me in December 1990 we settled into a semblance of a relationship but at all times I needed to know that I could fend for myself in the event that he would not stay around. Life with him was so different to what I had experienced with Keith.. We had some laughs and a few arguments but I loved him so much and was looking forward to our baby, so none of our problems seemed important and I knew there was no one else I would rather be with.

ALEXANDRA MARIE

*A*lexandra entered the world at 12 minutes to 3 on Friday afternoon, the 8th February 1991 at a respectable 8lb. 2ozs (the same birth weight as her brother).

We were hoping she would arrive on both our birthdays, the 9th, and left to her own devices I think maybe she might have done. However, after a wonderful and trouble free pregnancy, my blood pressure started creeping up on the 7th February and even though I had felt nothing my labour had actually started when I went for my weekly checkup that afternoon. With my previous two children my waters had broken and was the first indicator that they were about to arrive. With Alex, I had no indication, physically, that anything had started.

My checkup that day was in the middle of the afternoon and my specialist, Louise, told me to go home and wait for developments. So I did, but nothing happened. We were at Michael and Helen's house all evening but by 11.00pm I still was not in labour, so we contacted the hospital, who in turn contacted Louise and she instructed them to admit me because my blood pressure was up. She had talked about giving me an epidural, which I did not want and unfortunately this played on my mind to such an extent that I think I drove up my BP by worrying about it!

Samantha wanted to be with me for the birth so she sat and waited and waited and waited. By 3'oclock that morning, however, I told the poor girl to go home because nothing was going to happen before dawn and she had to go to work that day! She was now a nurse at Sir Charles Gairdner Hospital.

I concentrated on trying to keep down my BP but by lunch time on the 8th it was high so Louise induced me by breaking my waters. This was at 1 o'clock. By 1.30 I had started labour but nothing particularly painful at this stage. Conrad returned to the University thinking it would be a while until Alex would be born. At around 2.15 a specialist came in to tell me that he was preparing to give me an epidural but as my labour had progressed quite spectacularly in the last 40 minutes, I told him (none too politely) that I did not want his epidural, it would be a waste of time and he should go away, at which point he flounced out of the delivery room announcing that there were plenty of other patients who needed his services! By 2.30 I told the nurses to contact Conrad and tell him to come back if he wanted to witness the birth of his daughter. They did not believe me, but when they checked on my progress decided I might be right after all!

The rest, as they say, is history. She arrived quietly, hardly making a noise – much to Conrad's concern "shouldn't she be crying or something?" he said. However, with a whimper from Alex she was taken to be assessed and pronounced healthy and not traumatized because of the ease of her birth! I don't remember getting much of a hold at that stage as they took her away to clean her up while they cleaned me up. I was then wheeled back into my room to rest and have a well-earned cup of tea. A dream pregnancy and a dream birth.

When Samantha and Brad were born "rooming-in" was not practised. Mother was in her room and baby was in the nursery, so having Alex with me night and day was a lovely experience. The feel of that soft downy head against my cheek and the knowledge that she was "all mine" are two feelings I think I shall remember for the rest of my days. It was love at first sight for me. We had a brief scare with her on day 1 when she began to cough and splutter a bit and I rang for the sister in panic, who duly took Alex away to the nursery to "suck her out". Some mucous had managed to find its way into her throat, but she was fairly quickly returned to me safe and sound.

The parade of the relatives and friends began. Samantha was the first to hold Alex after Conrad. I thoroughly enjoyed my days in the hospital and quite honestly was not fussed at getting home too quickly, however, after five days Conrad began agitating for me to come home with Alex so I decided I would go. What a home going that was!

Conrad was late picking me up and my post maternal blues had kicked in quite solidly, so by the time he picked me up I was upset to start with. There was obviously something upsetting him too, as he hardly said a word to me on the way home.

Even when you have had children previously it is always daunting arriving home with a new baby, and I was 20 years out of practice. Firstly you are physically still tired and recovering from the birth and secondly, there is the moment of panic when you realize you are in charge of this little bundle and your support system has disappeared, and you have to think of something to cook for your meals! When I got home all these feelings were churning around inside me and when Conrad took one look at Alex and burst into tears, I did not know what to do, except ask what was wrong? He told me that his wife, had called on him at his work that morning and they had a blazing row. What exactly had upset him, I do not know but he was upset anyway. He eventually calmed down and left to return to his office, leaving me desperately needing a reassuring hug but feeling totally alone!

I cried and cried – it is a wonder I had any milk to give my beloved child. When I eventually stopped, to my horror someone called to see me. It was Tom. Tom worked with Conrad and we had spent some enjoyable evenings in his company. He too, had eagerly awaited the birth of our baby. He arrived armed with a huge bunch of flowers, however, I was so upset I did not want him to see me this way and so I did not open the door and eventually he left the flowers and went away. In retrospect, I probably should have opened the door, as I know I would have got a hug from Tom!

Alex slept in with us for the first six weeks. She was a good baby right from the start and only woke to feed every four hours, for the first three weeks or so. I thought back to the babyhood of my first two children and am amazed that I even dared to put them into a separate room straight away, it just seemed so natural to have Alex in with us.

At about two months Alex developed the dreaded colic and Conrad and I would take it in turns to eat, while the other paced the lounge moving her around on our arm to ease the pain. I am sure, to this day, that Conrad thought she was just being naughty when she cried. It was the first real argument we had when he would yell at her to be quiet!

Prior to Alex being born, the occupant of my home returned from overseas. As it happened the tenant in the front unit had moved out, so I moved in there. When Alex was about two months old the woman from whom we had been renting our house came down to tell me that as Conrad appeared to have moved in and she had previously told me she would not tolerate de facto relationships, we would have to move. I wasn't sorry as she was one of the few people I can honestly say I grew to hate. I always felt, with her living behind us since her return from overseas, that she was spying on who was coming and going to our home. So the search for a new house began!!

It was hard getting out to view places to rent, which were close to the University. As I would be returning there at the end of my year home with Alex and Conrad was still at the Music Department. After about two weeks of soul destroying searching I found a town house, in a group of three, literally in the same street as the University. I walked inside and that wonderful old feeling of "this is it" came over me. With mounting excitement I ran up the stairs and stepped into a truly great main bedroom with built in robes all down one wall, with plenty of room for our furniture and a dear little balcony which looked out over the beautiful garden next door. The second bedroom was ideal as a nursery and again, had a built in robe. It was lovely and just what we were looking for. I put in for it on the spot. So on Anzac Day 1991 we moved into our townhouse.

Where we lived was within walking distance of a small shopping center, the grounds of the university and the Health Care Centre which I took Alex to for her monthly checkups. Michael had found a neat pram and Alex and I would go for a walk every afternoon, sometimes through the University grounds or round to the shopping center for a couple of items of groceries. The local shopkeepers grew accustomed to seeing Alex and I out for our walk and as she grew and became more aware, noticed her little face peering out of the back of the pram watching to see what was happening.

The year of maternity leave I had with Alex was just tremendous. I was a little lonely as my friends were, of course, not bringing up babies anymore and worked, but I really enjoyed her and she was a fun baby. I was supporting myself through a single parent pension but had to be very careful as there appears to be always someone out there ready to stir up trouble and because Conrad was spending most of his time with me (he still had a room at Michael and Helen's) he was seen as supporting me. One day I received a letter from Welfare informing me that there had been a complaint made against me, that I was receiving my pension under false pretences. An inspector duly came out to see me and informed me that they only investigate a person if they have received two independent reports about someone. I could only assume that my previous landlady, maybe, had reported me for some reason and maybe Conrad's estranged wife – who was very bitter about their break up. Fortunately, the investigator believed me and the complaint was not acted upon. Just as well as I would have had no means of support without the pension. What it did do, however, was harden my resolve to become independent as soon as possible.

My independence was eventually achieved when Keith gave me the proceeds from the sale of our house in Wembley Downs. It was with the greatest relief I informed the Department I no longer wanted their money and repaid Michael the loan he had given me and cleared my debts.

I was breast feeding but, like Brad, Alex was an impatient baby and sometimes my milk would not "come down" fast enough for her and she would get very frustrated. The end came when she was about four months old when during one feed she glanced up at me with this cheeky look and then proceeded to bite me! Ouch…that was the end she went on to the bottle.

Conrad was getting very restless in his position and was agitating to leave. This worried me immensely as he did not appear to worry about finding another job first. Fortunately a friend of his, Jim, talked him into being a little more responsible with regard to Alex and I and he stayed on, but his habit of acting first then thinking later worried me.

Conrad was very busy with the work and his musical involvement in the choir and in July of 1991 they went away on a tour of Asia and were away for three or four weeks. I missed him terribly and it was during one of those weeks I had my first migraine for a long time and it was as bad as any I had had before. Fortunately, I had Conrad's parents to help me and they came and looked after and put Alex to bed for me while I painfully experienced and finally got through my migraine. But it is at times like that you realise that you are "alone", suddenly you can feel very insecure in the realisation that you are responsible for a helpless child all by yourself.

In September of 1991 I realised I had to do something about birth control. Much as I would have loved to have another baby as company for Alex, financially this was out of the question. I was unable to take "the pill" because of its adverse side effects. Conrad did not appear to want to have a vasectomy, so the only thing I could think of was to have my tubes tied. I have to admit to not wanting to have this done and was very apprehensive about this leading up to the operation. I have always had a morbid fear that during an operation I will wake up and be aware of everything that is happening. It has never happened of course but even now I still fear the same.

I duly went into hospital and had the operation about midday. I must absorb a lot of anaesthetic because I was still out to it at 8.00 that night and have only a vague recollection of Conrad coming in to see me with Alex, and I was sent home the next day, feeling very sore and sorry. It took a while to recover from the operation, feeling very sore and bloated for at least two weeks afterwards. I remember feeling very depressed as well, probably postoperative depression, but it wasn't a very pleasant sensation. Conrad did not know quite what to do with me, but then, he always seemed to be having his own crises whenever I needed him, so once again I had to draw on my own emotional resources to get through.

Michael and Helen got married in 1991. They utilised our townhouse as their headquarters because their house was full of people preparing food, etc. for the ceremony. They had the reception at their house, in the garden. For weeks prior to the wedding we were putting together table decorations and a garland for their archway, under which the ceremony was carried out. Conrad sang and Helen's cousin Leanne and I were the accompaniment. It was a lovely day, although Michael's two daughters had very mixed feelings about the whole affair. I have to admit to wishing Conrad wanted to marry me, but he never did ask. I realise now why, but at the time, I thought we were happy and it was a logical conclusion to me.

Alex was always very advanced for her age. The infant health nurse was amazed at her muscle tone, even as a little baby. Inevitably she was pulling herself up on the furniture and "walking" around at eight months, crawling (briefly) at nine months and was walking by the end of her tenth month, just about Christmas time. We put up a Christmas tree in our little lounge, which we eventually had to barricade because Alex would not leave it alone and I had visions of her pulling it over on top of herself. She also liked crawling into baskets and many a time I would look for her, eventually peering into a laundry basket lying on its side and their grinning out at me would be Alex. A marvellous game!

We had stairs in our townhouse so pretty smartly I put up a gate to stop her getting up the stair but I still remember a few times when upon checking to see what she was doing she had spotted the fact that the gate was not up and was halfway up the stairs.

As my year got closer to its end I became more and more depressed. I really wanted to only go back to work on a part time basis and spend most of my time with Alex, but I could not do this. My job was a fulltime position and part time work then was really difficult to find and in any case I had to have a full time wage coming in to live!

Nevertheless, the first year of Alex's life is one I shall always remember with joy – it just did not last long enough and the day was looming closer when I would have to return to work and put her into child care. I was due to go back to work at the beginning of February 1992 but on Australia Day Alex came down with a dreadful tummy bug, which lasted for the ensuing week prior to my going back to work! She had only just got over it in time to go to the day care but I felt very, very bad taking her there on my first day back at work.

1992

*A*lex's cries as I left the child care center tore me apart and I was in tears by the time I got to work. It was so hard to concentrate on work. I would find myself staring out of the window wondering how she was and if she was okay. I rang a couple of times and they told me she had stopped crying soon after I left, which I am sure is true but nevertheless, the day dragged intolerably until I could go and get her again.

Only a working mother of a small child can understand the sheer hard work and emotional stress caused by such a circumstance. By the time you have finished work and picked up the baby, she is tired and you have no idea what has gone on during the day, so when baby is cantankerous you do not know why! You are tired so less able to cope with things and the hours between 5.30 and 7.30pm can become a whirlpool of stress. Of course, they are also open to new health bugs and viruses so the inevitable times off work because the baby is ill add to the whole miserable experience of being a working mother. We staggered through the first two months of my return to work and got into some semblance of routine.

In early April of that year, just prior to Easter, Conrad felt unwell. We thought it must be a stomach virus and waited for it to pass but one Saturday evening as he was getting ready to oversee a concert at Winthrop Hall he experienced violent pain in his chest and we all wondered if perhaps he was experiencing a heart attack! Fortunately, as luck would have it, Samantha and Conrad's parents, Alan and Joan, were over visiting us. So Samantha took Conrad to Sir Charles Gairdner Hospital to be checked out, whilst I went to Winthrop Hall to let them know they had to oversee themselves, while Alex was cared for by Alan and Joan. I then went on to the hospital to see what was happening.

Conrad was still in the emergency area. They were checking for enzymes from a heart attack but this did not appear to have happened. He was still in a lot of pain, however, so eventually they found a bed for him and he was admitted. Over the next couple of days they tested him for a stomach ulcer, then the pain moved to his abdomen and from there on it seemed to hit all his major organs in turn. They could not find anything as a cause and just kept him on pethidine. One day I went in to see him and Conrad told me they were going to discharge him. I was frantic, who was going to look after him while I was at work? – He was still unwell and we were no further forward into finding the reason for his pain. He did return home and went straight to bed, however, he was far from well and by now had developed a dreadful headache.

On Good Friday I went upstairs to check and see how Conrad was and became extremely anxious about his condition. His headache was awful, he could not bear to look at the light and his neck was unbearably painful. That was enough for me and I rang for an ambulance immediately and then rang the doctor who had been treating him in hospital and told him I was returning Conrad to Sir Charles Gairdner as his condition had deteriorated drastically. I organized care for Alex and followed to the hospital as quickly as I could.

Once again he was still in emergency and they were carrying out more tests. Eventually they did a spinal tap and confirmed that Conrad had viral meningitis. The very name "meningitis" instilled fear into me and I asked what was to happen now. I was told that there were in actual fact two forms of meningitis, viral and bacterial. The bacterial version is truly bad news and is the one that can kill. The viral meningitis makes you very ill and causes a great deal of pain but eventually goes. However it takes a long, long time to recover from it as we were to find out.

Prior to Conrad becoming ill, we had embarked on trying to get some sort of marriage settlement for him to enable final closure on his marriage. His wife was obviously still very bitter about everything and was fighting tooth and nail against him having any kind of share in their mutual property. There were two conferences scheduled for the time when Conrad was in hospital, one he managed to attend but nothing was settled. The ensuing hearing was due but he was too ill to attend. The upshot of it all was that he was threatened with having to pay a backlog of maintenance to his wife a couple of years down the track – she had claimed mental depression and thus was a dependent of his – if he pursued his claim for anything. So two miserable months and thousands of dollars later we had to discontinue the claim. This did not help his recovery and I was considerably out of pocket for nothing.

Conrad was eventually allowed home but was still very weak and ill. The spinal tap had left him with violent headaches so every step he took was an endurance test. I was still trying to maintain my job, care for Alex and was worried sick about Conrad so it was not a good time.

About the middle of May I was at work when I received a call from Conrad telling me I had to come home because the house was flooded! I hurried back to the unit to find Conrad standing in the courtyard at the front in his dressing gown and pyjamas looking very pale! I asked him what had happened and he told me he had come downstairs to make a coffee and was struck by the dreadful smell coming up to him. It wasn't until he stepped down into the lounge that he realized the whole floor was covered in about four inches of dirty brown water! It had not been immediately obvious because our carpet was brown. At about the same time a couple of men from the Metropolitan Water Supply (MWS) knocked on the door to ask if we had any water inside. They got their answer when upon opening the door filthy water rushed out to meet them. Apparently a sewer pipe had clogged further down the street and the backwash of sewerage had come up through whatever opening it could find, *viz:* our toilet and overflow outlets in the floor! Our ground floor was covered in raw sewerage! What next!

The MWS booked us into an hotel while they pumped out the sewerage and dried the floor. The carpet had to be ripped up and the lino in the kitchen removed. It was an absolute nightmare. The smell was unbelievable and I was very worried about the germs we were in the midst of, as meningitis is caused by just this sort of dirt and here we were trying to get Conrad well. By this time he was near collapse, so I quickly sat him in the car and went upstairs to gather up some clothes for us all to take to the hotel overnight. We settled him into bed at the hotel and I then set about letting our insurance people know that a claim from us was imminent. They were very prompt and met me at the unit later that day – after the MWS had removed the floor covering and tried to sanitise the floors as best they could in the short term. All the bottoms of our furniture were water swollen and a couple of the pieces were badly water damaged, so we had to make estimates of replacement value, etc. By the end of the day I had nearly finalized the insurance papers and it was time to pick up Alex from child care.

Alex did not take kindly to the change in routine or bed. The hotel walls seemed to be paper thin and every noise we heard and probably we made, seemed to be amplified tenfold. Conrad's headache was very bad because of the activity and Alex cried a lot of the night, consequently I was not feeling the best the next day, but did realize we would be better sleeping in our own beds and camping upstairs if need be. I could still use the kitchen to cook, etc. We went back to the unit and I settled Conrad back into bed and barricaded Alex upstairs with him whilst I went downstairs to sort out what was to be done. I was worried about having time off from work, but really there was nothing I could do about that. I realized that babies still need clean clothes, etc. and checked the washing machine to ensure it was okay. There was a slant to the bathroom floor and fortunately water had not risen high enough into the machine to cause electrical damage. I moved the machine to get at something and pieces of raw faeces rolled out at my feet. Up to this point in the proceedings, I had managed to cope with the emergency, but this was just the last straw I just stood there and cried. I had never felt so alone in my entire life!

When I had recovered from my episode of self-pity, I rang the MWS and asked them to return and do a more stringent cleanup, which they duly did. The smell was nearly gone by later that day and with the damaged furniture out in the back courtyard the carpet layers were agitating to get into the unit and replace the floor coverings. Our little family "camped" upstairs for a total of about four days before we could eventually come downstairs again. A nice light brown carpet was laid in the lounge but somehow the unit never felt the same again, and as soon as Conrad was up to it we would be moving.

A few months after the sewerage overflow my daughter Samantha expressed a desire to move in with us. She and Brad (who had returned from his period as a Jackeroo) had been living with their father in a rented house in Wembley since Keith had sold the house, but now he had bought a two bedroomed duplex half in Karrinyup and there wasn't enough room for them all. This was okay, I loved having Samantha around me and she and Conrad got on pretty well. As luck would have it friends of the family, Brian and Vi, owned a house in Nedlands which they rented out and this was becoming vacant very soon. I had been looking around for somewhere with three bedrooms in it so when they suggested we might like to go and look at it we happily agreed. It was roomy and had air conditioning in the lounge and main bedroom. The second bedroom was just big enough to hold Samantha's stuff and the third bedroom was an ideal size for Alex. It was close to the University and Sir Charles Gairdner Hospital, where Samantha worked, so all in all we were happy to rent it.

Things were ticking along quite nicely. Conrad was able to return to work initially very part time and gradually increased his hours back to full time – his meningitis had taken its toll on him and he never really regained his total vitality after the illness. Towards the end of the year he was agitating once again to leave the university. He now wanted to go into a small business. I still had some money so I said we could use some of that to pay for a business. I was very apprehensive about the move but could not dissuade him from resigning from his job.

He looked around for something he would like to get into and eventually discovered a desktop publishing company, which was affordable and specialized in wedding stationery, business cards and stationery, etc. Still very apprehensive about going into small business I went along with the plan and in November of 1992 we were a small business owner and considerably poorer!

1993

*A*lex was a true example of "the terrible twos". Maybe it was the frustration of being in child care or my not handling her as well as I would otherwise have done had I been home, but she had truly awesome trantrums!

I had experienced Brad's tantrums but I knew at the time that his were "normal" – loud but short. Samantha had been a comparatively quiet child, although she too had had her moments at the same age. Alex, however, was something else! When I heard about a lecture to be held at the University on the condition ADD, to which the public was invited, I decided I would go along and see if maybe Alex was suffering with this condition. Whilst at the lecture, however, listening to the various case studies and symptoms of a child suffering with ADD, I realized that whilst Alex was extremely strong willed and stubborn, she did not have ADD. That was a relief, however, I was still left with the question of how best to deal with her temper tantrums.

So many times I could feel my own rage well up as Alex continued to scream and scream. I knew this was a dangerous situation so would propel her down the passage to her bedroom and shut the door on her until I had regained my control, for I knew if I smacked her I would not stop. The problem was that her bedroom door was a sliding door and hence I could not lock her in and go away, I had to hold the door closed. There was one time I remember when I held that door closed for 45 minutes and Alex did not stop screaming the whole time. In the end you just had to admire her stamina! Samantha still says that Alex was the best birth control she and her friends could have had – if this was what it was like to have a toddler they were all staying childless!

I did not see a great deal of Brad at this time. He was going out with a lovely girl, Carolyn (Caz), and working at the Wembley Hotel as a barman. After his sojourn up north on the cattle property he had returned home unsure of what he wanted to do. At one stage he had suggested going into the Army. I was quietly horrified but I have made it a practice never to interfere with the childrens' decisions about what they want to do with their life, however, I did not want him to go into the Army. It was with immense relief, therefore, that when he decided against it and he mentioned he would like to train in bar work, we were glad to pay for him to take a course.

He informed me one day that he and Caz were getting married. Again, I was not happy about this as he was only 21 and Caz 20 – so young to commit for life. About eight months before the wedding, however, Brad realised he could not go through with it and he and Caz broke up. I had to admire him for being so honest about his feelings but I sadly comforted Caz on a few occasions as she cried and asked me if I knew "what had gone wrong". I told her nothing had gone wrong, Brad had just realised he was not ready for such a big commitment in his life. It was a sad time for both of them, as I know from my own experience that not only the person being left is hurt, the person doing the leaving also suffers as well. Brad did not see anyone for quite a while, then gradually he started seeing Jo, who was to be his partner for several years.

Conrad and I were also having our problems. The business had gone fairly well for the first eight months or so. He had maintained the existing contracts for stationery, etc., and the wedding stationery was being publicized by our stands at various Wedding Expos, etc. There were still some annual reports being ordered, which generated good fees – and Conrad was very good at the actual production of the documents. It was, however, a year when a lot of businesses began producing their own annual reports, in-house, and with this money drying up there was less to spare to be part of the wedding expos, hence we were losing publicity from this avenue. We were living mainly on what I earned but this was not enough to cover our expenses. By July 1993 we were really struggling and getting into financial difficulty. I still had some money in term deposit but I was desperately trying to keep that to put towards buying a home of our own, however, with dipping into it every so often to "catch up" this was dwindling away.

At this time I also felt very strongly that I wanted to go to the UK to visit my brother, who I had not seen for 12 years and who was now married with a family. It looked very much as if I would not be able to go, but at the last minute Conrad got a good tax rebate windfall and we were able to afford the fares for Alex and I. So hoping things would improve whilst I was away I booked to go to England in the October and hoped that being apart might repair some of the damage financial problems and a strong willed child was inflicting on our relationship.

The UK

My plan was to spend the first day or so in London, hire a car and drive up to visit my mother in law in Yorkshire, come down via Warwickshire and visit my friend Jane then on down to Cornwall and spend the bulk of our stay with my brother and his family.

The flight from Perth to Kuala Lumpur was good. I wasn't sure what sort of traveler Alex would prove to be but she was very well behaved. We arrived in KL at about 1.00am and took off again about 1.45am I hoped Alex would sleep for most of the long haul to Heathrow and things started off fairly promising. About an hour into the flight, however, Alex woke up crying and without warning, vomited. Call it bad planning or sheer optimism but I had not bargained on her being sick in flight so did not have a change of clothes for either of us! She continued to have problems for most of the flight, so much so towards the end the air hostess attending to us asked over the PA if there was a doctor on board the plane. We were worried about Alex being dehydrated. Unbelievably, there was a doctor on the plane from Great Ormond Street Childrens' Hospital of all places! He examined Alex and said she was not dehydrated yet, but I should keep a close eye on her for the next few hours and told me the symptoms to look out for.

To this day I do not know whether or not Alex was suffering travel sickness or had caught a 12 hour bug in KL but from the moment we touched down in Heathrow she stopped being sick.

We had a lot of stuff with us and I was not particularly flush with money so we had to get on a bus to get into London Central from Heathrow Airport. Fortunately, there were a few willing hands to help as they saw me struggling to hold Alex and load my copious items of luggage, pram, etc. on to the bus. When we got off the bus at Victoria bus station it was just too hard to carry and push Alex and all our belongings so I hailed a taxi to take us the short distance to the small hotel I had booked for us. When I look back on this trip I wonder how I managed!

It was 7.00am when we arrived at the hotel and I had been without sleep for over 24 hours – I was absolutely exhausted and although Alex was bouncing about wanting to do things, by this time I was beyond caring and told Alex I had to sleep and she could do want she wanted! Fortunately, she too realized she was tired and fell asleep beside me.

We both woke up at about 4.30 in the afternoon and I knew we had to find a Laundromat to wash our puked upon clothes. So loading Alex into her pusher and carrying a plastic bag full of disgusting items of clothing I set off in search of a Laundromat. We did not have far to go and after negotiating the complex payment machinery and delivery of w washing powder I put in the clothes and we went off to explore for a while.

Being October it was rather cold and we were rugged up against the cold outside, but of course all the shops are heated so every time we went into a shop we cooked in our coats, scarves, gloves, etc. Neither of us was particularly hungry but I tried to get us into a routine for the evening by getting us both something to eat and trying to get Alex tired enough to go back down to sleep in the evening. It is very stressful when everyone else in the hotel has gone to bed and you have a 2 year old bouncing around full of energy and wondering why there is no one around to play with. She eventually fell off to sleep at about 11.30 but was awake again by 4.30 – her body clock was going berserk!

At the time we were over in London Conrad's parents were also staying on the outskirts with Alan's brother and his wife and on our second day we met up with them and spent a most enjoyable day wandering around looking at the sights of London. Alex was of course an immediate hit with her relatives and had a wonderful time with Bamma and Bampa and Uncle Cyril.

I had organized a hire car for the following day and we duly packed up our goods and chattels and left the hotel. We took a taxi over to the hire car offices and loaded up. I had worked out a route to take, as we were going via Hertfordshire where my brother, Peter, and his family were visiting with friends for the day. It was only a flying visit as I was catching up with them later on anyway. All was going well until I took a left turn too early and found myself caught up in a traffic jam, due to road works, and on the wrong road. I noticed that the fuel gauge was getting lower quite rapidly and it wasn't until I had been driving the car for about two hours that I realized I had left the choke out! No wonder the fuel was practically dripping from the car! Apart from this hiccough, however, I enjoyed driving the car, a little Ford Festiva, and felt terribly adventurous!

To this day I do not know how I found my way to the address in Hertfordshire I was aiming at, as my sense of direction is notoriously bad and I took several wrong turns, which on the English motorways can prove most unforgiving, as you have to travel miles before you can get off the motorway and turn back. However, find it I did and we had a lovely half a day catch up with family and friends. I did not want to stay too long though because I had a fair way to go to get to Bingley in Yorkshire before it got dark.

The trip up to Bradford was fairly uneventful and we stopped a couple of times for a break and freshen up. Alex was a wonderful traveler, though rarely sleeping but somehow quite happy to sit and watch the miles go by.

We reached the outskirts of Bradford at dusk. I had hoped to arrive there earlier but I did take a couple of wrong turns and had to double back. The smell of the place is unmistakable even to a 2 year old, as Alex asked "What is that funny smell, Mummy". I explained that there were lots of Indian people in Bradford and they cooked lots of curries and that was the smell around the city. I followed the directions to Keighley and found myself in vaguely familiar territory but the last time I had been to Martha's was 12 years ago and Keith had been driving the car. I took a wrong turn and as it got darker, by the minute, I found myself motoring up on to the moors which definitely did not feel right. The time was only about 5.30 but it was dark and felt like about 10.00 at night! I realized I was going the wrong way and turned around, trying not to let my alarm convey itself to Alex. Upon returning to the village I had just passed through I saw the sign I was looking for – faded with age and halfway up the wall of a building – in the fading light no wonder I had missed it! At last I knew where I was and soon Martha's cottage and street came into view.

Martha

Despite the break up with Keith, Martha had maintained amicable contact with me and indeed she had been over in Perth when Alex was about five months old and I had visited her. She admitted she had begun to get worried about our whereabouts when it began to get dark.

Martha's cottage was a tiny building with a minute hallway (big enough for only one person at a time) leading into a small lounge/sitting room, with the kitchen running across the back. As with a lot of homes in England the kitchen usually contains the w Andrew ing machine so is a combined kitchen/laundry. Upstairs there were two small bedrooms and the bathroom. All very fine for one person but when this expands to two people plus a lively toddler things become a little crowded.

Whereas Alex was a wonderful traveler she had to let off steam at some time and when we were in situ this is when it happened. She was still having problems sleeping through the night, which was hardly surprising as we had only been in the country three days and her body clock was still adjusting. The stairs were a magnet to her so consequently I had to watch her like a hawk! It was really hard to keep her quiet at 4.30 / 5.00am. I had to stay awake as long as she was awake in case she took it into her head to go to the stairs! Most mornings we were reading books in hushed tones or drawing pictures, as quietly as possible, until it became a respectable hour to move about. I must admit to finding this all a little stressing. Martha was very good about it but I was always aware of the fact that she was not completely well and used to living peacefully on her own. Alex wasn't even a blood grandchild, which would normally be reason to make allowances for behaviour.

One day we went into Keighley. We had been at Martha's a couple of days and Alex had had a couple of tantrums, so Martha was bravely trying to cope with these experiences as well. For some reason Alex was particularly cantankerous on this day and in the middle of the shopping mall she gave her all to a tantrum truly awesome in decibel level and energy! Martha really could not cope with this and stated she thought she might go home a little sooner than planned! I realized she needed "space" and stayed in town with Alex the whole day, returning only at 5.00 that evening, so Martha had time to recuperate from her ordeal! I was also hoping to wear out my daughter so she would go to bed at a reasonable hour and give Martha and I some time to talk.

All in all the visit passed quite well but I was keen to set off down South to visit Jane and then ultimately, my brother. So we left Martha's after about four days, leaving her I am sure with mixed feelings of relief and sadness, as we were close and neither of us realized it would be the last time we would see each other.

Jane and Malcolm

Jane is my oldest friend. We worked together when we were 16 years old and her husband, Malcolm, was supposed to be my date all those years ago but I chose to go out with Keith instead and Jane met her life mate!

They lived in a lovely detached house in Warwick, which reflected how well Malcolm had achieved in his chosen field of car design. Jane and I had not seen each other for 12 years but in that time neither she nor Malcomn appeared to have changed in any way. Jane fell in love with Alex from the start and admitted later into our visit that she was feeling quite clucky because of her! It was fortunate she got on so well with Alex because the day after our arrival I awoke in the morning with a dreadful sick headache.

We had only had a couple of glasses of champagne to celebrate our reunion the night before so I felt extremely hard done by to think I was experiencing such an excruciating hangover! It was Jane who suggested that maybe I was having a migraine! I realized straight away that was what it was, but as I had woken with it I had not experienced the vision disorder, which is my normal warning sign that a migraine is imminent. I further realized that this was a classic happening as since arriving in the UK I had been rather stressed out and had also forgotten to take my Inderal (my blood pressure medication), the side effect of which was to lessen the severity of a migraine when and if they came. Being with Jane and Malcolm I had totally relaxed and this is, of course, when a migraine will hit! So I took to my bed for the rest of the day and Malcolm took over the role of Mother to Alex. They had a wonderful time apparently, drawing, reading, going to the park, etc., I was not missed neither did I miss the activities as I slept away my headache and my day. All too soon, however, we had to take our leave of Jane and Malcolm. I was in two minds about leaving as I loved being with them but I also wanted to get down to Cornwall to my brother and his family.

Alex was becoming a seasoned traveler by now and as soon as I made one of my wrong turns and made an exclamation of dismay because of this, her little voice would reach me from the back of the car asking "Are we lost again, Mummy?" Fortunately, she did not have to ask this too many times on the trip down to Cornwall although it seemed an awful long way. We were traveling all day and hit the damp environs of Cornwall once again, just as dusk was falling! I managed to find my way to my brother's home and as soon as the car pulled up, out tumbled a noisy welcoming committee of children, dogs and people!

CORNWALL

*J*en, my brother's wife, and I hit it off straight away. She was and is a lovely person, an earth mother! She had three children from her first marriage, Carol, Ashley and Matthew and Peter and she had Dennis who was about 12 months younger than Alex.

Throughout his life Peter has had varying fortunes. Following his accident at 17; when he had fallen from the third floor of a block of flats, whilst cleaning windows, the doctors doubted whether they could repair his broken bones well enough for him to walk again. He proved them wrong, but has suffered painfully all his life since that time. As he grew older, of course, the joints and bones deteriorated and the pain grew worse and more incapacitating. He and Jen met when they both lived in Hertfordshire and were both working and comparatively comfortable financially. After they were married they decided to move to Cornwall and go into business, however, this was not successful and now they virtually lived on Peter's disability pension and what money Jen could make from car boot sales.

Peter could be difficult at the best of times – I remember this well from my childhood – but constant pain had made him sometimes rather moody. All in all, however, they appeared to be happy and our time with them was fun. Alex enjoyed the interaction with the older children but was a little put out by suddenly not being "the baby" in a group, so took a little while to settle down.

We drove around the area quite a bit and took the dogs and children for frequent, and very pretty walks. I had not been to Cornwall before but remember well that it was a very damp county, particularly in the Winter. We mainly traveled around in a big old Bedford van, that housed all of us, though not particularly safely as there were only seat belts in the front and the rest of us rolled around and hung on for dear life as best we could in the back! I sadly relinquished my little car back to the hire people in Bodmin so was reliant on Peter and Jen for transport. I had arranged for another hire car to drive us back up to London at the end of my trip.

Alex on the whole was fairly good but she had her moments of tantrum, sometimes I coped with them okay and at other times I could quite happily have left her somewhere and never gone back! It was great to spend time with my brother but I was getting tired and towards the end of my trip was missing Conrad and ready to return home, but we had two last stops, and they were to visit Madam Tussaud's and Harrods in London. I had promised Alex she would visit the Queen!

The day finally came when we had to leave for London. It was a sad day as Alex had definitely won a place in her aunt and uncle's affections and I did not know when I would see them again. We went to the car hire firm to pick up our transport for the last leg home. It was a brand new, white Ford car (I can't recall the model) and, illogically, I hated it on sight!

Alex and I were due to fly out of Heathrow on the Saturday and I had allowed two nights and a day in London to visit Madame Tussaud's and Harrods. Even though I had lived in London until I was 12 years old I never visited the famous old prestigious store, Harrods. I had been taken to Madame Tussaud's but was so young at the time could not remember it really and I had to take Alex to see the Queen and Princess Diana!

We set off from Bodmin, tearfully, hoping we had allowed enough time to get up to London – once again – before dark. I was still uncomfortable in the car, although I could not say why! We had only been driving for approximately 20 minutes when I scuffed a sharp piece of kerbing and blew a tyre! Panic! I did not want to drive up the motorway with no spare tyre and I looked around for help to change the tyre. Now if something dire like this was going to happen it could not have happened in a better place, as my puncture had occurred right in front of a home-based garage! Taking Alex out of the car I walked across the road to the workshop and told them what had happened. The fellow in there could not have been more helpful and did not charge for changing the tyre. I enquired where I could get another tyre as a spare, thinking that this expense would be reimbursed by the car hire firm, and he said the nearest big town to get this new kind of tyre was about 30 minutes away. I was concerned about this because it meant at least an hour's delay getting underway to London. Nonetheless I had to get a tyre so off I went.

I eventually got to the town he had mentioned and was looking for the street where the tyre suppliers were located but I was finding that this was not a tourist/stranger friendly town! I drove round in circles hitting dead end after dead end, getting more and more stressed by the minute! After an hour of circling the town

I eventually found the tyre supplier and bought the new tyre which, being for a new model, was very expensive! Another half an hour and I eventually flicked off the mud of that town and was at last on my way back to London. The car had not endeared itself to me at all.

We had to stop a couple of times for food and nappy changes but it was not a good journey, I was terribly uptight and by this time getting awfully tired. I had rung the landlady of the B&B where I had booked us in to let her know we were running late, as she was expecting us about 5.00 and there was no way I was going to get there before 7.00 that evening, which meant we would be trying to find our way around a strange suburb of London in the dark!

We had been traveling for what seemed like hours and once again I missed a turn off the motorway and was trying to make my way back on to it again when Alex became extremely upset because she was thirsty – hardly surprising, the poor mite had been in the car most of the day. So we pulled into the parking area of a pub/service station and I took Alex inside to get a drink. After a break of about ten minutes, for us both to stretch our legs I returned to the car but where were the car keys? I remembered going to the ladies, had I left them in there? We looked but they were nowhere to be seen. I retraced our steps but there were no keys to be found. I was now really panicking. Where had I put them, had Alex picked them up? She said she hadn't seen my keys. I hadn't locked the car so sat on the driver's seat and cried. All the frustration and worry of the day suddenly too much! After about 30 seconds, something told me to pull myself together, I was in charge of a small child here, if I fell apart what would happen to her. I re-traced my movements, in my mind, and remembered I had opened the boot to get a map from my bag, perhaps I had left the keys in the boot lock? It was with immense relief I found them sitting in the lock, where I had left them! I gave Alex a reassuring hug and once again set off towards London. I had somehow gained additional stamina from the whole trauma, probably the adrenalin rush of fear!

After a few wrong turns I managed to find my way to our B & B and knocked on the door – no reply – now what? I went next door to ask if they might know where their neighbours were and found a note addressed to me telling me to knock on the door! Weird! Anyway we found our landlady and she showed us into a big, double room with the most inviting double bed I had ever seen, made doubly wonderful because of our sheer fatigue and relief at finally getting to lie down. We had arrived!

After a good night's sleep and a nourishing breakfast of cereal, fruit, toast and tea we prepared for our day as tourists! I had to return the car first and I had ascertained that the nearest and most convenient depot for its return was about ten minutes away near the London Underground. I really was not sorry to see the back of the car, it had truly been a part of the worst experiences of the trip so far. I went inside and presented my paperwork, plus the receipt for the new tyre, telling them what had happened. It was then they informed me that replacement of the tyre was not covered in the contract and they were not going to refund my money! The tyre cost approximately $150, which I had paid for out of my own pocket. I argued quite aggressively with them for half an hour but to no avail and with the knowledge that this was completely wasting my valuable time. I swung out of their offices in high dudgeon vowing to get my money replaced one way or the other – but later – in my time!

The quickest way for us to get up to London was via the famous underground service. I did not, however, anticipate the feelings of claustrophobia or anxiety which I experienced as soon as we had boarded the train and the doors had closed. Not having traveled on a train for a very long time, let alone the underground, it felt very un-nerving being jammed up against so many people in such a confined space. Memories of recent news stories about IRA bomb explosions in the underground in London came flooding back to me and try as I might I could not settle down and just enjoy the experience with Alex! By the time we reached our destination I could not get off the train quickly enough!

We were deposited within walking distance of Madame Tussaud's so made our way there. You cannot just walk in at any time there, they have regular "tours" starting at different times, and as we had some time to spare before the next "tour", I decided to find somewhere to get a drink and snack. Food is very expensive in London and everywhere seems full of people! I could not live there again – long term – it is too crowded for me!

During our time in London we had taken a few bus tours around and I was awestruck, when seeing some of the old buildings, at the sheer age and history of it all. I must admit there were times when I thought how pleasant it would have been to go to one of the old, quaint pubs with Conrad and sit and drink and savour the atmosphere. The buildings there have been standing for hundreds and hundreds of years. Living in Australia we don't realize how "young" everything is here, until you go to somewhere like London which is steeped in history.

We queued up with everyone else to wander through Madame Tussaud's. Once again, it was very crowded so I had to keep a close hold on Alex, who was dying to get away and explore at leisure, but if she did I would never find her again! She was definitely a little confused at all these people in funny clothes, just staring ahead when she spoke to them and at one point she came up to me and said "Mummy, these people don't say much do they?"

Eventually, we came to the Chamber of the Kings and Queens of History and I led her over to the "Royal Family". There I pointed out the various members of the Royal Family to Alex and she stared, awestruck, at each one in turn. Predictably, she liked "Princess Diana" the best! King Charles II, with his chiseled, hard features and black flowing hair intimidated her a bit, but not for long.

Time was passing and we had only the afternoon to finish our trip to Harrods. I had "history overload" anyway so I decided to leave Madame Tussaud's. I could not face the underground so decided we would find out which bus would take us there.

Making one's way around London on public transport is a time consuming and confusing experience, however, one's sense of adventure is heightened because you never know where you are going to end up. You know where you wanted to go, but that is not necessarily where you arrive! After asking several people which bus I should take to get to Harrods, and after walking around in circles a couple of times I did what I should have done in the first place, and waited at a bus stop and when it stopped, asked the conductor which bus to take! This I eventually did and at last found ourselves on a bus heading around Hyde Park corner en route to Harrods' famous store.

It doesn't seem to matter what time of day you walk around London it always seems to be teeming with people. Back in Perth you can tell what time it is almost by whether or not you can get on a Red, Blue or Black cat bus without standing nose to nose with your fellow passengers. In London people seem to be moving about all the time. Add to this the seemingly endless road works being carried out and you will understand why the majority of London commuters choose to travel by underground, in spite of the IRA threats. It took us about an hour to negotiate the London traffic and road works but eventually we arrived at the distinguished doors of Harrods. Backpacks are not allowed into the store so if you have one you have to hold it and pretend it is some sort of handbag. I do hope they have revised this rule as it is ludicrous, you can stash ill-gotten goods into a bag whether a backpack or hand held equally as well, so what's the point?

When you walk into Harrods it reeks of opulence and money. Items are vastly overpriced but we pay them anyway. It was dicey taking Alex into a store like this without tying her hands behind her back, so it was a constant watch to make sure she didn't pick up a colourful cup and saucer, for instance, as I would be out of pocket for my airfare to pay for any damage! We did buy a couple of things; a tee-shirt for Alex (which adorns one of her teddy bears to this day) and a Harrods (plastic) bag which I could flash around when I got back. There wasn't much else I could afford, so I just enjoyed being in the midst of such opulence for an hour or so.

Outside the store there is a beautifully emblazoned horse and cart which can be hired by the tourist for the purposes of having one's photo taken in it. Once again, finances would not allow this for us but I watched as several people availed themselves of this attraction. Once or twice Rolls Royces pulled up at the door and the grandly dressed doorman would rush to open the doors for the occupants. I did not recognize any of them, but I am sure they were worthy of such attention, their cars certainly were anyway.

Soon, however, it was getting dusk and we had to find our way back to our digs for the last night of our sojourn in London. I had ascertained the appropriate bus so knew where to go to catch this and by the time the skies had darkened for the evening we were arriving at our bus stop. Alex was, unbelievably, still wide awake and I had great hopes that she would collapse in a tired heap for the evening, as we had an early start to get to Heathrow to catch our plane and I had some packing to get through that night.

We Go Home

We woke bright and early and rang for a cab to pick us up. We paid our bill and thanked our hostess for her hospitality and headed for the airport. I still feel confused when it comes to tipping, not being used to it here in Australia, but I felt I tipped fairly generously as the airport – using the last of my English pounds.

We did not have too long to wait and it was with relief we sank into our seats on the plane. This time I had taken the precaution of giving Alex some travel medicine and mercifully she slept part of the way to Kuala Lumpur, which was our one and only stop.

We had a couple of hours to kill before boarding our flight for Perth and stayed in the KL airport sightseeing and generally letting Alex run off steam in preparation for another few hours seated on the plane.

Eventually, we arrived at Perth. We were home at last. I was looking forward to seeing Conrad and so was Alex. We had no problems getting through customs and suddenly there he was grinning from ear to ear and looking better and more relaxed than I had seen him for months! Being on his own really suited him.

1994 TO 1996

The next couple of years have got to be a low point in our relationship. The business continued to gradually die and Conrad made the decision to move it into the dining room of our house to save costs. So we moved out the dining table and chairs and moved in the desk, filing cabinet and paraphernalia attached to the business. Our main service by now was wedding stationery but it was a less than ideal arrangement because clients (such as there were) had to walk through the house in order to view wedding stationery, etc., and I always felt really uncomfortable when Conrad had people in for an hour at a time. It was okay during the day when I was at work but in the evenings, which is when a lot of young couples would come, I was trying to get meals cooked and out of the way before they arrived, and I was always aware of the smell of cooking when people came.

Our money was by this time gone as I had "consolidated" our debts on several occasions and this just ate into my house nest egg. We had our good times, when Conrad would get a few orders at once so there was a little extra to work with but somehow I was always sheering up our expenses out of credit cards, so I would clear them and then need to use them again to pay pressing bills or even just to eat. It was a vicious circle. We just did not have enough money to live on!

Samantha was staying with us and her board helped a little but there were times when I was at my wits' end wondering what to do next. I spent many a night crying in quiet desperation at our situation wishing Conrad and I could deal with the situation together, but instead of us being a unit, we drew apart.

Samantha

Samantha lived with us in Nedlands until she left in 1994 to go over to the USA to get married.

She had always been vehement that she did not want to move away from Perth, as we had always been a close family and she loved it here anyway. She liked her job at Sir Charles Gairdner Hospital and it was convenient for her, living so close to work. Because she did not want to leave Perth, whenever the US naval fleets were in town she would not go out because she did not want a long distance relationship with a US sailor! She had had a couple of relationships, which had not worked out very well and indeed, she had been quite hurt. Her main activities were going out with her girlfriends and netball.

One Friday evening in 1993 her friends called to say they were going to a particular night club a little out of town and did she want to go? As the US navy was in town she said "no" but they persuaded her that this place was not on the usual route the sailors followed, so she eventually agreed to go. Her friends were wrong, two lone US sailors were in that bar Dan and Jeff.

They managed to get themselves invited into Samantha's friends' group and a good evening was had by all. Dan asked her if she was free the following day but she said she was working all weekend (which she was). He was persistent, however, and found out she actually finished work at 3.00pm on Sunday and he told her he would call her at home at 3.30.

Samantha really did not want to see those guys again. Not because they weren't nice, they were, but because she really did not want to get involved with someone from overseas. When she got home from work on that Sunday she was really hoping he would not call and when, after she had been home a few minutes and it was past 3.30 and he did not call, she heaved a sigh of relief. Her relief was short-lived though as at 3.50 the phone went and she froze! It was Dan, full of apologies because he had not been able to get to the ship's phone, there was always a queue of sailors wanting to use the phone and he had had to wait his turn! He wanted to see her again. In fact both he and Jeff wanted to catch up with the whole group and spend time with them until they sailed on Tuesday.

Samantha and her friends spent some great times with the two guys over the next couple of days, mainly around Fremantle, and they all saw them off at the quay on the following Tuesday. Samantha was not particularly sad, as they had all just had great fun and now they were going…end of story.

A few days later Dan called from the eastern states and asked if she would write to him because he wanted to write to her. Once again, she could see no harm in this and began writing to him and he would ring her whenever he was in port somewhere. The rest, as they say, is history. It became obvious that Dan was interested in more than a pen pal relationship with Samantha and after a few months she began to wait impatiently for Dan to call!

She went on a trip overseas with a friend at the end of 1993 and on the way back she detoured to Japan where Dan was currently stationed with his ship, and spent a few days with him there. She knew he wanted to ask her to marry him but she kept steering him away from proposing as she was still unwilling to commit to anything further than a long distance relationship.

In April 1994 Dan took a couple of weeks leave and came over to Perth and formally proposed to Samantha and this time she accepted. The following few months were very, very hard on everyone. Samantha wanted to be with Dan but there were lots of formalities that had to be got through. She would have to be able to work when she went over to the USA as naval pay is not very good, so she applied for a fiancée's visa, which would give her permission to obtain a Green Card (to work). It meant, however, that she would have to marry Dan within 90 days of arriving in the country, or she would be summarily returned to Australia again. Over the ensuing months she sat for and passed the nursing exam to enable her to work as a nurse in the USA and madly tried to save money, although this was next to impossible because Samantha had always had a problem over spending and she had a massive credit debt which she was trying to clear. We were all very sad to think that Samantha would be marrying in a strange country with no one from her family or friends to see and be with her. The idea of our daughter marrying and neither her father, mother or brother being present was heart breaking but there was no way our family could afford to fly over to the USA, stay and then return. They did not want to wait so there was nothing for it but to grin and bear it but Christmas 1994 was a sad time for all of us.

The early months in the USA were very, very hard on Samantha. Dan was frequently away at sea for weeks at a time and she had to fend for herself in a strange country with no friends or relatives to fall back upon. She always took a while to get to know people as she had always been very self-conscious from a very early age, avoiding the limelight. Through all of this, however, she has proved to be incredibly resilient and I shall always admire her for that.

She and Dan settled in Seattle for a while and Samantha managed to get some work, but unfortunately it was not easy for her as the hospitals wanted people with USA experience, however, she did eventually get a job which helped with their finances. At one stage she returned home to Australia as Dan was going to be at sea for five months. This was a testing time for her but at least she had her friends and relatives around and could work on a casual basis back at Sir Charles Gairdner Hospital. As the time drew nearer for her to return and for Dan to return from his sea duty, she became more and more anxious. Samantha had always had a problem with deep, sad moods but this was different. She was "hearing" people at her window and was experiencing panic and anxiety attacks. I eventually convinced her that she should go to the doctor and he prescribed Prozac for her. The change in her demeanour was remarkable. We suddenly realized that our daughter had been battling Depression all her life but we just thought the personality we saw was "Samantha". The anti-depressants helped so much, she was a different girl.

While she was home we planned a re-avowal ceremony to replace the wedding we could not have. We chose and booked the reception venue – Samantha wanted this to be AQUA at Hillarys, the service would be conducted by a celebrant in King's Park and she picked out her dress. We could do this because Dan's ship was scheduled to call into Fremantle on R and R which is when we would have the ceremony. Alas, however, it was not meant to be as his ship was re-directed to the Taiwanese to ward off trouble brewing there. Once again she did not get her wedding.

Samantha returned to the US and she settled back with Dan. She still wasn't happy though and I suspect she took herself off the anti-depressants, which would not have helped. The changing point in Samantha's happiness came when they applied for and achieved a draft to Hawaii and they left the chill of Seattle for the never ending warmth of Hawaii. She liked it there and eventually found a terrific job in a lovely private hospital. The money woes, however, continued and began to take their toll on Samantha and Dan's relationship.

I had been back at the Geology Department for two years since my Maternity Leave. I was not particularly settled as things were not too good with the HOD and I had applied for a position in private industry in the November of 1994. I did not get it, but the agency that had sent me for the interview obviously remembered my application and one day in early January of 1995 I received a call from one of their consultants asking if I was still in the running for a position.

Since applying for the job back in November 1994, however, the HOD had been replaced by one of the other Lecturers and we were getting on very well. I had decided to stay put and get on with my job. Now this! I said no initially but the lady was very persistent and called again asking if I would just go and talk to this potential employer as she felt I was perfect for the position and what was more, it paid considerably better than I was currently being paid at the University.

Eventually, I capitulated and went for an interview. The position was with a cleaning company and I was to meet with the Chairman of the company. We hit it off straight away, but I was still staying put at the Department. Several phone calls later, with the agency emphasizing that I was the one he wanted for the position, I began to wonder if I was knocking back opportunity for the sake of security? I decided I was and with a heavy heart I went and informed the new HOD that

I was leaving. Everyone, including myself was upset and there were many times whilst serving out my notice, when I wondered if I was doing the right thing.

The Cleaning Company

I shall not name the company or the personnel for obvious reasons, however, working there was a real eye opener. The first thing that hit me between the eyes was the foul language used by both office staff around me and the Contract Managers and executives. I can honestly say I had never worked in such an environment before and really had to "close off" sometimes as the expletives came thick and fast. It appeared to be their normal mode of language!

It was very noticeable that there was a communication problem between the partners, The Chairman and Managing Director and the rest of the staff – a real "them" and "us" situation. It was also very apparent that the interaction amongst the office staff was at times, somewhat hostile! I had fallen into a really stress-filled situation, which I obviously did not need. Somehow, however, amongst the discontent and at times fraught situations that arose, we managed to form a bond amongst ourselves. The company was also in the midst of changing over the Payroll system to an electronic one and this was causing immense difficulty for our overworked Payroll Section. The only thing that kept that Section buoyant was the unfailing good humour of its (new) Payroll Manager, Tony.

The turnover of staff at the company was mind boggling. Tony and I kept a track of numbers and during my first year there were no less than 23 people left and were replaced, with the leave-taking, without exception, far from amicable. I always felt like the meat in the sandwich between the partners and "the rest". The Chairman was basically a very honest man who tried to keep the peace but throughout his life, and who knows maybe it is just the cleaning industry, he had been 'ripped off' to the point where he really trusted no one and was always very money conscious. The Managing Director appeared to care for no one and did not mind who he verbally tore to bits in order to get what he wanted, whether or not it was possible! I did not work for The Managing Director, he had his own secretary, Trudi, who by the time I joined the company had grown to hate the Chairman and indeed appeared to be bitter and twisted about the whole organization. I asked her on many occasions why she stayed and never really got a straight answer! I was seen as part of "The Chairman's camp" so wasn't really trusted by the Managing Director and Trudi Duo! In spite of this in the initial couple of years, Trudi and I managed to work together quite well and indeed, shared many a laugh.

Let's face it, if someone could do anything else to earn a living why would they turn to cleaning? The company was a very big organization – the biggest privately owned cleaning company in Australia. Our cleaning contracts varied from shopping centers, high rise buildings, to schools and banks. Our work force was enormous and each Contract Manager had their set number of contracts to take care of and as most of them had started their career as cleaners who showed a bit of leadership quality, they were expected to and did muck in whenever there was a shortage of manpower at any of their contracts. They worked tremendously long hours and they had to deal with an incredible scale of matters to do with the running of their contracts. They did, however, really back up each other when the need arose.

One such occasion came when we decided to enter the annual Corporate Dragon Boat Race to be held down in Bunbury. The whole thing started as the result of idle discussion about the merits of "doing something together – a team effort". From those musings came the commitment to field a team from the company. There were approximately 16 of us involved, the mover and motivator was the State Manager, Diane, and the first "practise" was at Trudi's unit where we all sat on the floor, one behind the other, and pretended we were in the Dragon Boat! Needless to say this "practise" disintegrated into a laughing, helpless disaster. Nothing was learned but we had a heap of fun pretending it was.

The weekend dawned and we all duly arrived in Bunbury in the early morning, in time for the sponsored, cooked breakfast. The actual event was very well organized and there were many teams. We could tell at a glance those teams that took this very seriously, as they would be decked out in colourful uniforms, complete with serious headbands. They would charge to their dragon boats with fire in the eye and determination in their well practised seating plan. We on the other hand wore our complimentary tee-shirts and whatever bottoms we could muster up and leapt to our feet, certainly not lacking in enthusiasm but certainly in organization, to jostle for positions in the boat. Coming close on several occasions to capsizing the thing even before we left the bank!

We watched the "well-oiled machines" fly down the estuary, thinking we could do that, however when we came to actually trying we would manage to co-ordinate our "oar movements" for approximately 10 seconds at a time, after which the people at the front of the boat would be moving in unison with the caller, but those at the back had a fractional second delay before they heard the count of "1, 2, 1, 2" so we would then get out of sync and oars would be splashing madly in the water in their own time. All of which would set us off into hopeless laughter fits, rendering us helpless as the rest of the field flew past.

During one race, we were actually leading for about a quarter of the way, however, as soon as one of the crew realized this and ecstatically told the rest we lost all rhythm and finished last. We finished 32nd out of 33 teams, but at least we did not capsize the boat once and a great day was had by all.

The cleaning business is very cut throat and when it came to quoting in order to obtain a job the partners would go in as cheaply as it was possible to run the job. Sometimes they quoted too cheaply and when awarded the contract it became apparent that it was not workable, given the number of hours quoted to do the work. This put incredible strain on the Contract Managers as they tried, valiantly, to keep their contracts on budget. The manpower in this industry was mainly made up from newly arrived immigrants, desperate to find work. The was understandable but it made life very hard for supervisors and contract managers when trying to give instruction. The majority of them had a very poor grasp of English so understanding it and speaking it was a matter of trial and error. In later years when Occupational Health and Safety conditions became more stringent, this was an ever increasing problem. The company would provide training, which the new people would attend but how little they actually understood became only too apparent when they were put into their various positions. The consequence of this, of course, was a skyrocketing Workers' Compensation bill every year. We got to know the nationalities not to trust. Some were really out to just milk the system for all they could get and this did not improve The Chairman's (or The Managing Director's for that matter) belief in the goodness and honesty of human nature.

My role at the company became one of mediator, and consoler of distressed staff members after emerging from "interviews" with the Managing Director! I had no influence with the Managing Director so if I needed to pass comment on something I had to go through the Chairman – who really did not like confrontation. Neither did I, but sometimes things seemed so badly unfair I could not contain my indignation on behalf of some member of staff, chewed up and spat out by the management! One such person was Diane. Many a time I found myself consoling her in the restrooms as she gave me a word by word account of the Managing Director's caustic comments! I took all this on board, but needless to say it took its toll on me.

In 1998/1999 my working relationship with Trudi completely broke down! Consequently, for four months, until she finally was forced to leave, we barely exchanged a civil word and the atmosphere around our area, extending into the partners' respective offices, was poisonous! In all my working career I have never had an on-going fight with a colleague, it is just not in my nature. Such was the undercurrent amongst the "The Chairman Camp" and the "The Managing Director Camp", however, that Trudi and I were inexorably sucked into the in-fighting. She should have left at least two years before she did. Trudi was not happy either at work or at home – her recent marriage had proved a disastrous affair not long after the actual ceremony took place! During the time we were on better terms, I wondered often why she married her husband in the first place, but never voiced my questions as I did not want to cause Trudi any further stress than she was already experiencing. I made allowances for her vindictive tongue and moods, but at the end even I could not excuse her manner or behaviour towards the other staff.

When I look back at my time at the company, I wonder that I stayed as long as I did – four years! There were several complete changes of staff during my sojourn there and a change of office venue. I had been in charge of several office moves, all of which went perfectly well, the last move, however, did not. The Chairman was, by this time (it was in 1999) feeling the strain of an ever disintegrating relationship with the Managing Director and would not make decisions on things quickly enough for me to convey them to the Consultant they had appointed to co-ordinate the move. Consequently, there was an on-going breakdown in communication and when we moved into our new offices, it was chaos. The Management ever ready to blame anyone but themselves, targeted me and the Consultant. By this stage though I was beginning "not to care".

I think maybe one of the contributing factors to my longevity at the company was the bond which had grown between several of us. After Trudi left, the Managing Director went through a few secretaries, all of which must have been brighter than I had been at the beginning, and realized that the company was not a company to stay with and left! Then came Hillary.

Hillary was over 6 feet tall, a practising Christian and was (and is) a lovely person. We hit it off straight away and together with a few other members of staff grew very close, in the midst of the on-going turmoil. The last Christmas we had together, Hillary and I performed a skit – singing a ridiculous song and looking even more ridiculously dressed as "sisters"! It was great fun and is one of the brighter moments of life at the company. A group of us from the company and a sister company Hospitality (*not its real name*) (who shared the offices) stayed in contact for some time after I left.

ELLENBROOK - 1996

$\mathcal{W}$e had been living in our rented home for over three years and comfortable as it was, it was not ours. I now wanted, somehow, to get a home of our own. Hitherto, I had always thought of an established home, which was now out of the question, as we did not have enough money for a deposit. To help finances a bit Conrad had begun working part time for the Company in the morning and evening five days per week and I had made my last bid to "consolidate" our debts. At the beginning of 1996, we had approximately $1200.00 in the bank and I had cleared all our debts.

Sue, one of the girls that worked at the company was seeing a representative from Homeswell Builders and she suggested I go and talk to him about building. You could borrow a far larger percentage on a newly built home and plus, the Government was giving a $3000 home grant to first home buyers. We, as a couple, would qualify as first home buyers, so would be able to apply for the grant to help with the building. So, I duly went to see her friend and he told me what land was available.

I was shown some blocks in Kenwick Heights, Beliar Heights and a place I had never heard of, Ellenbrook. I had lived in Thornlie and did not want to go back in that direction, so Kenwick was not a consideration. Beliar Heights was south of the river, which would mean a trip down the freeway twice a day so that was not a consideration either.

I had been taken out to Stratton, near Midland, to look at land, with another representative earlier in the year, but had hated the suburb on sight, so Ellenbrook, which was also in the Midland direction, did not hold any interest for me, however, we decided to take a ride out to Ellenbrook one Saturday afternoon. We seemed to travel for miles and hours. In actual fact it was only 40 minutes but it seemed to take forever to get there although the drive took us by Whiteman Park and was a very picturesque route.

The entrance to Ellenbrook is very impressive and as we wound our way along the main entry road to the suburb we were struck by the way the tree and plant landscaping had been carried out. A great deal of thought and planning had gone into this development and our interest was beginning to spark. We found our way to the Sales Office at the center of Ellenbrook and went inside to look at the future model they had made there. The idea was that over a ten year span Ellenbrook would consist of approximately ten separate "villages" with a couple of town centers, growing in capacity to a city and population about the size of Bunbury. The Gt Northern Highway was to pass by the development and the railway was to be extended up to and past the suburb.

The owners and developers had been of Japanese origin and coincidentally at that time I was interested in the belief of Feng Shui and harnessing the natural energies of the universe by the way of landscaping and design. The developers had definitely incorporated this belief into the design of Ellenbrook as was demonstrated by the undulating roads and hills and the introduction of manmade lakes and bridges. Kerbs were rounded and not squared off, another trait of Feng Shui. By the time we had spent a couple of hours in Ellenbrook we were very interested in knowing more, so upon returning home we contacted our friend and asked him to come around and see us about building. We had already spoken to the on-site representative and knew which block we would like to buy. From beginning the investigation into buying, building and moving in it was a total of six months. In August 1996 we moved into our first new home together.

We had met our neighbours, Will and Tasha, a few times as we had been out to the block to see progress on our house. They moved in about six weeks before we did and they seemed very pleasant. We had a bit of a scare early on in the building when we came out to the block and the bricks for our house had been delivered. They looked nothing like the colour I thought they would be and indeed we were singularly unimpressed with them as they sat in their packs. I immediately checked the name for our bricks against those delivered and they certainly were the same but we had chosen ours because we thought they were more of a grey colour and indeed, had chosen our roof tiles based on the colour we thought we had ordered for our bricks! These looked more beige than grey! An anxious week went by until we could go out to the house again and it was with baited breath we rounded the corner to our street, anticipating a first glimpse of the bricks we were going to be stuck with for our house! Fortunately, out of their packs and laid, they did not look too bad at all so we heaved a sigh of relief. They were, however, not grey but a mottling of beige, white and brown!!

We had made a few alterations to the house, for example, we wanted a double carport and a bay window in the main bedroom and had asked for a "step down" into the lounge and main bedroom. This ate into the money which the builders had allowed for floor coverings, so we had to sacrifice them. We had signed up for insulation before the house was built with a 12 month delay before actually having it installed. Money, of course was very tight and costs involved in moving into a new house are incredible. Our debt free status soon became a thing of the past and it seemed that every time we received mail it was a demand for more money! When we were in situ, however, we were very pleased that we had made the structural changes, as imagining the house without them it would not have been nearly as nice.

I got used to the drive to and from work and in some ways it was good as the 35 minutes or so it took me to get home, gave me time to unwind from the stresses of working at the company! They had managed to move Conrad's work place from somewhere near to Nedlands to a school closer to Ellenbrook and then, when the company gained the cleaning contract for Ellenbrook Management Offices, Conrad was the obvious choice to do the work, although this was a seven days a week contract, which ultimately put a lot of strain on Conrad and our relationship generally.

I had thought that when we moved into a place of our own that Conrad would take more of an interest in doing things around the house and garden, but I was wrong and beginning to realize that his weekends were for relaxing, rehearsing and lying in! I found this really irritating as the sand pile which resembled our back garden stayed the same week after week. In all fairness we did not have much money to spend on plants, etc., but there were things we could have done, if we had both pulled together. Part of the Ellenbrook deal was that the front of the house was landscaped – and indeed, having experienced living in a new house (back in Thornlie) and the hard work involved in putting in a front garden, this was one of the things that decided me on buying in Ellenbrook.

We were months in the house before we could afford to put up a fence along the back of the carport. Basic fencing had been included in the package but not the additional fencing. Gradually, Conrad put down 2 feet square concrete slabs along the side of the house in preparation for a patio and he did a wonderful job utilizing the last of our driveway bricks to make a pathway to our front door. Having the front step concreted was also one of the things we had to sacrifice in favour of the structural changes so we erected a slab of concrete on top of several bricks, and this stayed as our front door step for nearly five years.

The problem of Alex's care during the day loomed as she was as yet not at school. I made enquiries into childcare and there was a child care center starting up but Alex was too young to go there and in any case it was for before and after school care only. We found a home-based child care for her, very conveniently down the road from our house and for the latter half of 1996 I would drop off Alex in the morning and pick her up at night. It was not a registered child care center, however, so I could not get back any allowance for her care, so this was an added expense which we had to cope with. Fortunately, because Alex was to start school the following year, she was allowed to go to the school holiday care programme at the recognized center for the Christmas break, so with a sigh of relief I dropped her there during the month of December and she loved it so did not mind going.

There were only a few houses in our street and as the blocks were sand, causing a sand storm on windy days, we were understandably pleased to see houses, one by one, go up across the road. The Ellenbrook Management, however, were very good in that they stopped a lot of sand blowing into our houses by spraying the surface with a mixture of green debris, which hardened to form a crust on top of the sand. I longed for someone to move into our street with children! Alex was quite lonely, although she was used to making her own entertainment, living in Nedlands but it would have been nice if she could have had a friend close at hand.

Things did not get much better for Conrad and I. His working seven days a week left him physically exhausted and when he was performing with the Opera or with one of the choirs with which he sang, we would not see each other very much, and I found it a lonely time. An added irritation was the amount of time he was spending performing with yet another group – a quartet. This consisted of himself, Suzanne and another couple. Performances with this group were in the evenings and at weekends most of the time and when rehearsal time was added to this it became an all-consuming interest to him. I have to admit to becoming increasingly resentful of the time he spent with his group. It seemed to me that all the "good" and "enjoyable" times Conrad was experiencing were with anyone and everyone but me. I felt like the "spoilsport" in his life as I represented the reality of trying to make ends meet and pay bills.

It was after one of these performances that my world, as I thought it was, fell in pieces around my feet. Sometime in the middle of 1997 his group Suzanne arrived back at our house late in the evening after a "gig" at a local vineyard. It was late and I had gone to bed and was half asleep when the noise of their arrival woke me up. I heard the other couple leave and after a while I became aware of low, mumbled talking coming from the kitchen/family area. I got up out of bed and walked through to the kitchen only to be confronted by Conrad and Suzanne in a passionate clinch against the kitchen bench. Suzanne saw me first and of course was horrified at being discovered in such a compromising position. I was speechless and within seconds felt quite sick at what I had witnessed. I went back into the bedroom in a dazed and breathless state and sat heavily on the edge of the bed not quite wanting to believe what I had seen. There were scurried movements by Suzanne from the kitchen and Conrad asked me for my keys – he was going to lead Suzanne and her car out of Ellenbrook (it could be very confusing to find the exit) – I threw them at him and gave Suzanne the worst look of hatred I hoped she would ever experience.

When Conrad returned I was waiting for him and asked him how long "that" had been going on. He lied and just said it was a once off – a heat of the moment behaviour. I did not believe him, but at the same time I could not believe what I had discovered. I suspected he had been having an affair for heaven knows how long!

The hurt I felt was a physical pain in my chest, which lasted for days. I felt so many emotions, hurt, anger, disbelief all at the same time. I know that had it not been for the fact that Alex was in the house and I did not wish to disturb her, I would have left Conrad then and there – at least to go away and consider what I was going to do. I had plenty of friends to whom I could have gone but this would have meant taking Alex out of her environment as I most certainly would not have left her behind.

As can be imagined, things were very strained between us as I struggled to come to terms with what I now knew about Conrad's affair with Suzanne. My hatred for her knew no bounds and I did not know what I felt for Conrad. We carried on as well as we could – I frequently wished I could have been free to walk out on the whole situation but this was not possible, so I decided to try and understand how it could have happened and pick up the pieces. I was not to know the true extent of the affair for a few months to come.

In November of the same year I returned home from work one Friday night to find Conrad very upset and agitated. I wondered why he was still at home because he was due to go to a gig that night with his group. He told me that he and Suzanne had had a blazing row that afternoon caused by something someone had said about him to her. Had tried to call her because he had left his mobile phone at her house and a policeman had answered the phone, saying there had been an accident, but that was all he would say. Later Karen, a friend of Suzanne's called Conrad and told him that she had been found dead in her car in the carport. She had committed suicide! I wondered at the time how much Conrad had played in her finally going "over the edge". I could not feel grief. Shock, yes but not sorrow – I hated the woman. I was glad she was dead.

1999 – 2000

*A*t the end of 1998 I was informed that the stormy relationship between The Chairman and The Managing Director was finally coming to an end.

We knew there was "something in the wind" but as usual The Chairman and The Managing Director were tightlipped. When we saw the respective wives arrive at the office, however, we knew things were coming to a head.

The Chairman arranged to speak to myself and Dianne, one of the long-standing contract managers, prior to an announcement to staff later that day – on the 15th December 1998. He informed us that he had sold his interests in the company to a third party, who was to be a "caretaker" director for some, 12 months, until The Managing Director could afford to buy him out and thus be whole owner of the company. This, in essence, left Dianne and I out of a job because we knew we would not be working for The Managing Director in the new *regime*.

I was extremely hurt that The Chairman had not given me much more warning of his impending departure. He assured me, however, that he would be staying on at the company in an advisory capacity and would need my services and this was why he felt there was no urgency. I knew otherwise. Sure enough just before we broke up for the Christmas break The Managing Director called me into his office and most ungraciously told me that he would be sacking Hillary from her position as his secretary, and I could consider it if I wanted to. I knew, however, that he did not really want me to take the job; he was merely covering himself against having to pay me any redundancy payment. I went away ostensibly to think about it, but in reality there was no way I would stay and work as The Managing Director's secretary and I knew that he knew that too.

So I was given "as long as I needed" to find another position – 2 – 3 months however long it took. The new director asked me to re-consider taking the job with The Managing Director as he did not want me to leave, but by the end of January

The Managing Director was beginning to ask when I was leaving. He could not get rid of me quickly enough. I was a leftover of the "The Chairman" era and such was his hatred for The Chairman by this time, (and I must admit the feeling was mutual) that he wanted everyone associated with him out of "his" company.

In early February a friend called and told me to contact someone called Lauren at the ArtsWA agency of the Ministry for Culture and the Arts. I did and she informed me that I had come highly recommended and there was a position at the agency I could fill on a temporary basis and then apply for when it came up as a permanent position with the public service. So, with a few misgivings, as I was not sure I wanted the job at ArtsWA, I finished at the company on the 26th February 1999 and began at ArtsWA on the 3rd March. There was really no choice, I could not afford to be out of work.

The job wasn't bad but I did not really "fire on all cylinders" because I felt I could not instigate changes to systems until I was on permanent staff. Initially the plan to apply for the permanent position fell flat as a "re-deploy" employee of the Service wanted my position. By the time she could get an interview, however, she had obtained another position. So I was "on again".

Applying for a public service job entails supplying a mini-book answering a list of "essential" and "desirable" criteria, in addition to one's résumé. The interview process consists of every candidate being asked the same questions and doing a typing test. The suitability of a candidate does not seem to enter into the equation, in the effort to appear totally unbiased! I made the mistake of assuming they knew my capabilities and thus did not really "sell myself", consequently did not get the position. I did not gather enough "points" and I was looking for a job once again!

Things at home were somewhat fraught also. Conrad was very "down". The strain of working at his cleaning job 7 days a week relentlessly, was taking its toll and we were getting dreadfully short of money – again.

The bright spark at this time was that my eldest daughter, Samantha, was currently visiting from Hawaii and her company was invaluable. Alex loved having her "big sister" on tap and I loved going out with her, even though she was stressed over the downhill roll of her own marriage. It was very hard to say goodbye to her at the beginning of August, and I was still essentially, unemployed, just registering with several agencies for casual work whilst applying for permanent positions. I was losing my best "girlfriend". The thought of her returning to Hawaii on her own, knowing she had to find somewhere else to live, as she and Dan were separating, worried me immensely. She was very sad and not a little frightened by what was waiting for her back there.

Conrad's state of mind was gradually getting lower and lower. One Friday in August, after Samantha had left, I returned from my casual job at a solicitor's firm to find him once again, very upset and agitated. He mentioned having had an argument with the husband of a colleague in his choir. Alarm bells rang somewhere in the back of my mind, however, I was more concerned at his apparently very bad depression.

The whole of that weekend he was very low and mentioned a couple of times that he wished he was dead. He failed to return from a cleaning session on the Saturday and Alex and I drove around Ellenbrook until we found him, crying in his car. We brought him home and did what we could to settle him down.

On the Monday morning he was once again very low and I was very loathe to leave him to go into Perth to put in a timesheet for hours worked the preceding week. I had no alternative, no timesheet, no pay. He assured me he was okay and I left for Perth full of misgivings. By 10.30 that morning these feelings were so terribly strong I knew I had to return home. As soon as I opened our front door, I knew I had been correct in my fear. The smell of gas was overwhelming. My stomach was a knot as I ran inside and noted the gas taps on the hotplate were off, where was the gas coming from? Then I saw him, Conrad was stretched out on the lounge with a plastic bag over his head, which I removed straight away. I immediately flung open the doors and windows and shook him, I could not tell how long he had been like this. He was barely breathing. I ran to the phone and called an ambulance, then that done, I proceeded to shake, shout, and apply mouth to mouth resuscitation to Conrad – anything to keep him from slipping into a coma. He was deeply unconscious. After about 20 minutes the ambulance arrived and the ambulance men checked his vital signs. He was breathing very shallowly and I was so afraid he might have suffered oxygen starvation to the brain, as my mother did so many years ago. It was like a recurring nightmare.

At this point my wonderful neighbour, risking being told to "mind her own business" came over to see if I was alright. I tearfully told her Conrad had tried to commit suicide. Tasha was great and immediately told me to go with the ambulance men to the hospital, she would get her nephew to drive my car behind and she would follow to bring him back. She would also pick up Alex from school later that day and keep her there until I returned.

By this time the ambulance men had stabilized Conrad, although he was still unconscious, and we all left for Swan Districts Hospital. August the 15th, I shall never forget that date.

At the hospital I telephoned Erin, Conrad's younger brother, and told him what had happened. He left work immediately to join me at the hospital. We waited for about an hour during which time they tested Conrad for oxygen content in his blood. It appeared to be okay and by this time, he was conscious. When we went in to see him, he was very emotional, which was to be expected and we all cried together.

The doctor wanted to transfer Conrad to Royal Perth Hospital for psychiatric treatment and for ongoing checks on him physically. He left by ambulance and Erin and I went separately to the hospital to meet up later in casualty. We were waiting five hours in casualty before we could go through to see him in his ward. He was still very upset and obviously drained – as we all were.

He said he had had no conscious thought of what he was doing at the time. He heard a voice telling him that he could kill himself now and no one would find him until it was too late. "The voice" reckoned without my divine intuition. For I know it was God giving me the urgency to get home. If I had been 15 minutes later it would have been too late. Obviously, God was not finished with Conrad yet. In a way it answered a question I have often asked myself about people who commit suicide "How could they do it, knowing how much pain and heartache it will cause those left behind?" The answer, in my mind is that they get to such a level of despair and depression they are no longer capable of considering anyone or anything but the need to end it. In a way it is a comfort knowing that they are not conscious of hurting their loved ones by their action, although it doesn't make it any easier for those left behind to wonder "why?"

Conrad had been in hospital about a week, receiving psychiatric counselling when I received a phone call from the husband of this colleague I mentioned earlier. He rang to ask me if I was aware that Conrad and his wife, Greer, had been having an affair on and off since the trip to Asia in 1991! I was once again devastated that Conrad had been leading a double life and seeing another woman. Only a partner who has been told such news can understand the turmoil of emotions which one goes through: Heartbreak, a feeling of unreality and then – rage!!! It was really hard for me because I could not let Alex know what was going on. Fortunately, being the wonderful child she is, she took her father's illness in her stride and came with me to visit her Daddy in hospital.

On the following Monday, I called Conrad's psychologist at RPH and told her the only way Conrad was ever going to get over this episode would be if he was scrupulously honest with her. She said he had told her about the affair with Suzanne and I asked her whether he had owned up yet to the fact of being discovered with his current lover by her husband, and this had preceded the suicide attempt. At that point he would have known I would find out quite soon, and that was what had tipped him over the edge. She told me he had not. We discussed what would be the best way of tackling this and she suggested I should tell him I knew and that would open up the way for him to be totally honest in his counseling sessions. I did not want to see Conrad that Monday, but arranged to go and see him, without Alex, the following day. I told him I had been informed of his latest affair and that he had to be completely honest with the Psych. during their counseling sessions. He was, to put it mildly, somewhat taken aback by my knowledge of the affair and we mutually agreed not to see each other for a couple of days to let things "settle down" a bit.

A week or so later, he rang to say they were releasing him from hospital. We were both horrified at him being sent home so soon. He was not ready and I most certainly was not ready to deal with his depression and our situation on a daily basis. However, despite my phoning the hospital, he was sent home – they had been told to "empty beds of anyone not in physical need of one" which is ludicrous, as this was a Psych. Ward. In most cases the patients are physically ill because, they are desperately mentally ill.

Conrad's return to home was the beginning of a nightmare six months. He desperately wanted to be anywhere but with me – he was consumed with guilt and self-loathing. His medication just would not work properly and our time together was fraught with atmosphere. To add to our torment Greer's husband was ringing and generally making things worse. His hurt was taking the form of harassing me when he could not get to Conrad. I eventually had to have our telephone number changed to a silent one to stop the calls.

In the midst of this there would be times when Conrad would be in such a "black" mood of depression I would be apprehensive about leaving him alone in case he had thought of some other way of attempting suicide. My Pastor and his wife, Mark and Ann, were on occasion my only lifeline to him. He maintained he would not have tried again, but prior to his first attempt we had spoken about this and he had said then "suicide is just something I would not do" remembering the hurt Suzanne's suicide had caused her loved ones!!!

Every weekend was a torment of (my) contained frustrations and his inactivity around the place and his irritation that he could not be left alone to sit and smoke cigars in his chair on the patio, and do crosswords. Living with someone who is deeply depressed is just awful. A part of you understands that their lack of animation and energy is part of the illness but it does not help you live with it any better. Sometimes the inward rage has to bubble over. It did with me several times, but I knew I would pay for my "release" by enduring another period of the "blacks" as I grew to call his moods.

We staggered on in our relationship until the beginning of February 2000. Never had I spent so much time praying to God asking for patience and healing as I had over the past six months. He was my soul comfort. He gave me the strength to continue, but He finally recognized on the 5th February I was really at the end of my tether. I seemed to spend most of that day, off and on, in tears. I almost did not get to church on the Sunday (the 6th) because I was embarrassed about my appearance. I am not one of these lucky women who look "pretty" when they cry – I do not and my face seems to take forever to recover. However, Alex and I did go to church, kissing Conrad goodbye before we left.

The service passed. I was feeling very down. We eventually went home and noticed Conrad's car was not in the carport. This in itself was not unusual as he often took the car down to the lakes and sat in one of the little shelters there. I went into the small bedroom to get something and noticed a pile of baby rugs that were usually in the red suitcase on top of the wardrobe. This was missing and realisation began to dawn on me as I noticed things missing from the bedside table and of course, when I went into the bathroom none of his shaving items, etc., were on the shelf. He had left. I was numb. How was I going to break this to Alex?

I sat in the lounge for a while and presently Alex came through and said "Mummy, Daddy is taking a long time for his walk". I took a deep breath and talked to her about how he had been feeling, and that he needed to be by himself for a while. Then I told her that I thought perhaps he had found himself somewhere to get better, by himself, and he would not be back today. She thought for a while and then said "Oh well, as long as he has found somewhere to rest and is alright then I don't mind." Then she wandered back into the family room to resume her video watching! I looked after her in wonderment. This little girl had been through so much; seeing her beloved father change personality almost before her eyes, not knowing quite how he was going to react towards her and now he had just left! She had accepted it all, but I would have to watch her to ensure she was really alright.

He rang later that day and told me it had been the only thing he felt was right to do, for all our sakes. He did not want us to finish up hating each other, which would have been a strong probability if he had remained. Although painful, I felt it was truly a move of God as Conrad had managed to find a place to stay, which belonged to a friend and was presently unoccupied, and he had time to look for somewhere to live, which we could afford. It was God's way of organizing the separation, whilst holding us all in His hands to comfort. We all needed space but I was yet to learn that once you have saved someone from suicide, in essence, you are responsible for them for the rest of their life!

2000 – I AM ON MY OWN AGAIN.

*D*uring my period of working for a secretarial agency in the preceding year, they sent me on assignment to work at the WA Industrial Relations Commission for a three month period, replacing someone on long service leave.

After the turmoil of the previous year, this time at the Commission was a real break. I loved the people I was working with and what was more, felt I was really doing well there. During the beginning of my time at the Commission, however, I was approached by The Chairman, who by this time had washed his hands of the company and was Chairman of the company his son had begun – Hospitality (*not its real name*). He was looking for an administrative person for his company and knew I was doing temporary work. I thought about it and hoped this might be the last job for a while. I knew all the staff at Hospitality. I asked if I could be relieved of my assignment at the Commission, halfway through, with some regret as I was enjoying the job and they graciously did not cause any problem for me. They did express their disappointment that I was not staying – which was very good for my, by this time, badly battered ego, and left the door open for me to contact them if I was ever in the market for a position again. As the position with Hospitality was offered as a permanent one, however, I was hoping that the Commission's offer would be one I would not be taking up.

At the end of February I started with Hospitality as receptionist and administrative assistant. A new PA to the Managing Director, Stephen, started the same week. I enjoyed the work I did, the only problem was that the hours were 8.00am until 5.00pm and as it took me over 35 minutes to get to West Perth from Ellenbrook, and as I could not leave Alex before 7.30am in the morning, I had to make special arrangements to arrive a few minutes late every morning, but made up the lost time by shortening my lunch hour. This was agreed to by everyone, although I could tell that Stephen was not happy about my late start even if it was only about 10 minutes.

Working at Hospitality was almost like a continuation of the company! The same heavy handed management, with staff coming and going and not being replaced. The new PA was sacked after about four weeks, (there were *personality problems* between her and the MD – *viz*: her self-esteem was good, so would not take the sometimes rude attitude displayed towards her.) I took over some of her workload. As the MD was quite often overseeing his eastern states offices and was away, this was manageable. The company was expanding at a rapid rate so there was always a budget crisis – everyone was under pressure.

To add to my worries, Samantha had called to say she was pregnant! During her separation from Dan she had been in contact with Dan but they were seeing other people and she had fallen pregnant. So it was "me" all over again! Samantha was endeavouring to work out how she could become a single mother as well! The baby was due in December and I wanted to be there for her.

As time wore on I began to get really stressed because of the time factor in getting into work and Stephen began to get very cross when I was not there on time. He had no sympathy with the fact that I was on my own with Alex and that she was so young. I began to make enquiries back at the Commission to see if there were any positions going there, because I knew it was only a matter of time before Hospitality and I would part company. After negotiations regarding my starting salary, I was offered a 12 month contract. I also suggested to them that it would be a good idea to have "a floater" in the Commissioners' chambers; someone who could fill in when needed on a temporary basis and they seemed to think this was a good idea.

After about six months, following a particularly difficult week, with delays at home, making me really late getting into work – which caused Stephen to get really angry, I finally called it quits and resigned. I had negotiated a position back at the Commission. My contacts there had told me there was a position coming up as Chamber Liaison Officer (CLO) to one of the Commissioners, and was I interested? Was I ever! I applied and returned to the Commission in September 2000.

Conrad seemed to be much happier on his own. His health had noticeably improved since moving into a unit in Leederville. He was on medication which was causing him some irritation because of the side effects, but he was definitely better than the previous year!

It was a difficult year for Alex and me. In retrospect I realize, even though she was putting on a brave face about things at home, Alex was very "sad" and had quite a few health problems over the year. She struggled at school somewhat and could not seem to settle down into friendships or lessons. Her teacher, Donna

Simms, was a lifesaver to Alex – always ready to lend an ear and hand out some sympathy. I kept her informed of what was happening at home so she was aware of the problems and heartache my little girl was experiencing.

Towards the end of September, however, I started to relax a little as the atmosphere at the Commission was so different to what I had experienced for the past six years. I enjoyed the work and it was not by any means "taxing". My position with the Commissioner however, was changed to CLO to the Chief Commissioner as my position as "floater" started to fall into place. The Chief's permanent CLO was on extended maternity leave and I was filling in for her, whilst also helping out at a couple of other Commissioners' chambers when needed. For the first time, I felt no pressure at work and this aided greatly in my beginning to relax a little and, yes, maybe start to look forward to "life after Conrad".! Eventually. Financially, things were still a struggle, particularly so because Conrad and I had negotiated a new loan for the house, ostensibly to consolidate debt and help pay off the house quicker. This seemed to take forever as we started negotiations in July – when Conrad began full time work with the Cerebral Palsy Association (as a "Carer"). We mistakenly believed that his having a full time job was enough, but the lending authorities wanted the initial three months' employment to pass before they would consider his position permanent enough to give us the loan. So, three and a half long months passed as we waited for his probationary period to be up. The loan settled in November 2000 but in the meantime Samantha's baby's due date in December was drawing ever closer and she wanted me there. Where would I get the money to go?

Keith paid my airfare to Hawaii and after much soul searching I decided that Alex must come for part of the four weeks I was hoping to get there, so Brad and his then girlfriend, Jo, paid Alex's fare. My fare was booked for the 15th December. Baby was due on the 17th December.

I arrived home on Friday, 1 December 2000 to a phone message from my son in law, Dan, saying that Samantha was in substantial labour and the baby would be born within hours! I was thrown into a spin! I was due to help at our church's "Vineyard Café" that night so phoned back Dan to ask how Samantha was – by which time she was pretty well advanced – and to ask that he phone Samantha's Dad, Keith, as soon as the baby was born, who could then phone me at the Vineyard Café. I needed to be with my friends whilst I waited so excitedly went down to tell everyone my Grandmother status was imminent!

When Holly was born, everyone in that Café knew – I yelled at the top of my voice "I'm a Granny!!!" to all who would listen! It was a lovely evening, despite my not having been there after all.

When I got home that night I called Dan and Samantha to give them our love and congratulations and ask how mother and baby were going. Holly was very small but okay, Samantha, however, was still having problems with her blood pressure and was facing complete bed rest to avoid hemorrhaging. How I wished I could be there for her, but at least I would be in two weeks' time!

I spoke to Samantha on a daily basis the following week. She was obviously very tired and because of her blood pressure problem was taking a while to recover. She was also very apprehensive about going home with a brand new baby and me not being there. I spoke to the powers that be at work and they were very helpful in trying to find ways I could bring forward my departure date and still get paid leave. In the end, however, the airlines put an end to my plans by telling me that unless I could prove it was a medical emergency (which fortunately, it was not) I could only change my flight by paying them an additional $350.00 which was not possible. By the time Samantha had been home for half a day, however, she was sounding much more confident. Dan had managed to get a couple of days off when she came home and this helped – knowing someone else was going to be there. So my departure returned to status quo.

I still had the problem of what to do with Spot (the dog). Back in February, in an effort to cheer up Alex, who had had a bad year, I suggested we go and look for a puppy – a small one –for her. I made all the provisos – "only looking....", "may not get a puppy today......" etc., etc. The first place we went to was filled with adorable little puppies with very large price tags! I wouldn't even let Alex hold one of these pups, for I knew that would be cruel. So dragging a very tearful Alex from the shop we made for the pet shop in the Wanneroo markets. The only thing there resembling a puppy was a "dogfish". So once again a tearful Alex and I made our way back to the Malaga markets. By this stage of course I had realized my mistake but was fast drowning in the certain knowledge that we would have to return home with a puppy TODAY!

At the Malaga markets there were two puppies in a cage. One was completely black and the other was black with blue heeler, grey spotty markings on his chest and paws. He was gorgeous. We were told he was a Stafford Terrier/Blue Heeler cross. Mistake number two, assuming it wouldn't grow too big!!

Suffice to say that over $120 out of pocket later we carried home Spot the dog.

I have always believed that if you have a dog it becomes part of the family but that they sleep outside. However, Spot was only 7 weeks old so we made a bed for him in the laundry. I was determined not to let him out of the laundry no matter how much whimpering he did, so when Alex came in to me at 11.30 crying because she could not sleep as Spot was making so much noise, I told her to climb into bed with me. Fortunately, our neighbours slept on the other side of their house so at least we weren't causing them aggro because of our whimpering dog.

He cried for a few nights but ultimately realized he was dealing with "Mrs Tuffy" here and eventually settled down. The mess in the laundry each morning, however was something else. I had to get up at least 15 minutes earlier than usual in order to clean up torn paper, wee and poo. Fun!

We had had Spot a week and I knew I had made a dreadful mistake getting a dog. He was adorable and we loved him but being so young he was a lot of work and working full time is not conducive to having time for yet another chore! Plus he broke his heart when we left in the morning – it was an ordeal leaving him. Todd, the cat, did not know what had hit him. This black whirlwind suddenly appeared from nowhere and hurled himself (playfully) at Todd. Todd is not a particularly "social" cat anyway and this was the beginning of nine months of hell for him. Even at 7 weeks of age Spot was almost the same size as Todd already – ominous!

By 10 weeks the laundry could no longer contain Spot! My fluffy duster had been de-fluffed, the bottom of the blinds had to be lifted in order to save them from his merciless teeth and what he did to newspaper was nothing short of awesome, so we made a bed for him on the patio. He demolished three cardboard boxes over the next few weeks and set his sights on Conrad's pride and joy – his brown rocking chair. It wouldn't have been so bad if Spot had just adopted the chair as his bed, but he gradually tore it to bits, leaving himself with an ever decreasing area on which to lie and much to Conrad's dismay!

We could not take Spot out much at this stage because of the fear of Parvovirus. He had had two inoculations so we would take him out for a quick walk around the park to ease his boredom. However, one Sunday we visited friends who had a young dog and Spot and he played literally for hours without stopping. By the time Spot was bundled into the car to return home he was tired out.

The next morning instead of eagerly wolfing down his breakfast he just looked at it and I thought he must have really tired himself out! However, when that night and the next morning he did not eat I knew he was not well. We took him to the vet on the Tuesday and they kept him in overnight for tests. They all showed that somehow he had contracted the Parvovirus and was a very sick pup. Despite our desperate financial situation I knew, after taking one look at Alex's desperate face, that we had to see if we could save him. I think it was his sheer strength and stamina, also that even though he had not finished his inoculation course for the virus, he had had two inoculations, and this is what saved him. By Friday evening we were able to pick him up, almost his old self – also the bill which was horrendous, and took me three months to pay!

Spot was getting very strong. So in an effort to "train" him we went to puppy social classes at the local vets, followed by RSPCA "training". The social classes were just an excuse for bounding puppy bodies to have an incredible game of chasey around the vet waiting area! The problem being that as soon as we put Spot into the car he would bark continuously until we got to our destination. Even at his young age his bark was incredibly cruel on the ears especially in the closed confines of the car. The car trips were a real ordeal. By the time we got where we were going I was ready to throttle the rotten dog!

Poor Alex's dreams of owning a dog to take for walks and spend joyous play time together, became a nightmare as Spot was far too strong for her to take for walks, added to which, because he was shut up so much during the week he would pull unceasingly on the lead, making walks a most unpleasant experience for all concerned. I could only just hold him, so there was no way Alex could walk him. He was like a pesky younger brother when she played with her doll's house or had anything on the floor. Anything and everything was fair game to Spot and belonged in his mouth! Alex's anguished "Mum, take him away!!!" became common place.

Dog training was another experience not to be repeated. Again, because he did not see another dog for days on end, when he did get out he was uncontrollable! We tried gamely to keep going but near the end of the course, I was wearing some shoes which did not have much "grip" on them and Spot pulled me over and dragged me quite badly, and I could not go back again.

The main problem was he needed people and regular walks and he got neither because of my working full time. I found owning a dog incredibly binding too. If I or we wanted to go anywhere straight from work, for instance, I would find myself thinking "No, we have to go home and feed Spot – he has been on his own all day". Even taking him for a walk now was a problem because he was too strong to take on a lead, so the only alternative was walking in the nearby pine plantation, which was fine as long as no one else happened to be walking there as well. As soon as Spot saw "people" he was off – he loved people and was very friendly but to a stranger, who was not aware of the dog's temperament he looked a frightening sight bounding towards them, indifferent to my calls of "Spot! Here…." I had a couple of heated exchanges with people who were angry because my dog was frightening one or both of them to death! Also, Alex was still a little young to leave on her own for any length of time, and suffered quite badly with asthma that year, so I had to take her with me and this usually meant returning home with her experiencing a full blood asthma attack because of the pine trees.

The time was getting near to visit Samantha and my new granddaughter, and I had to make some provision for Spot's care.

I advertised him in the "Quokka" and received a few enquiries about him, some of which were quite promising. However, after nearly a fortnight we still were no further forward in finding a new (ideal) home for Spot. It was the Friday before I was due to fly out to Hawaii and I was just about to leave work for home. The problem of a new home for Spot was playing on my mind and as per my usual regime, when desperate - pray! So I did. Just as I was about to leave the office the phone rang and it was a young fellow enquiring about Spot! He lived fairly close to home and wanted to come and look at him. I told him when I would be home and a couple of his friends said they would come and look at Spot on his behalf as he had to go to work (he was a shift worker). I was concerned about Alex's reaction to Spot going, but when I picked her up from out of school care she asked if she could stay down and help set up the Vineyard Café, which was on that night – couldn't be better, she would not have to witness his leaving. I went home just as the young couple picking up Spot arrived. They took one look at Spot and new their friend would love him. I left strict instructions that if things were not right with dog and new owner they were to call me over the weekend. The funny part was, it was not a particularly sad parting for me either! The only explanation could have been that this was an answer to a prayer, as I telephoned over the weekend and new owner and dog were getting on famously! Alex? She did not even notice he was gone for two days – as it was the same night we heard that Samantha had had her baby and we were too excited about that.

2001

While I was in Hawaii, staying with Samantha, Dan and Holly, I have to admit that I did not really miss Conrad, or anyone else for that matter. He wasn't exactly a barrel of laughs – hadn't been for a while – and indeed, whenever I spoke to him on the phone he always seemed to be peeved at someone's perceived stupidity or act against him! I found out that he had stopped taking his medication since before Christmas and gradually the residual effect of the drugs was running out, thus making him the way he was. We had to go through another couple of "blacks" in order for him to accept that he had to change his medication but keep going as he was going nowhere fast without it. He had, however, made some effort to tidy up the back garden and keep the house in a reasonable condition and when I returned in January, I was pleasantly surprised at how acceptable the back garden looked, tidied up a bit!

It became obvious he was still endeavouring to sort out some kind of future with Greer and his depression lifted or dropped according to how his romance was going. He was still a worry to me as I was not at all sure he would not try suicide again in one of his black moods.

One particular time, Greer had once again come to stay then decided to leave and he was very low. I was somewhat alarmed at his tone of voice when I spoke to him on the phone and when, later that day I tried to contact him on his mobile and received no reply I once again went into panic mode.

By the time I went to see his doctor to get some advice or help, I was in a dreadful state of fear myself. I spoke to the doctor at length and confessed that I knew I would have to go round to his flat and see if he was okay, but was terrified at what I would find! Bless him, he even offered to go in my place but I refused of course. Once outside the surgery I tried once again to call him and to my immense relief he answered, but by this time I was a blubbering idiot, unable to string two words together! I went round to his flat, had a stiff drink and he told me that although he was very down, he knew the "danger signs" and would call for help – this was on the Wednesday night. As I left his flat that night I knew, this had to stop. I could not allow myself to get into such a panic each time I could not contact him and I vowed to pass on this responsibility to his family, particularly Erin and Nick, his brothers. I had to let go.

On the Friday of the same week, I received a call from Royal Perth Hospital telling me that they had my "partner" there in emergency. He had called the ambulance after unsuccessfully trying to cut his wrists! The doctor reassured me it could not have been a real attempt to kill himself but still, they wanted to know if they could release him into my care! I was beside myself with rage at Conrad. Two days earlier he had sat in a chair opposite me and told me he "knew the signs when he needed help" and now, this! It is fortunate that it takes 35 minutes to get into Perth from where I live because it took all of that for my rage to calm down a little. How could he do this to us again! If I could have got my hands on Greer at that time I would have helped her on to eternity for sure. She was the cause of this. My Christian forgiveness was in very short supply that night!

My saving grace during 2001 was that at least at work my stress levels had diminished. I was really enjoying working at the Industrial Relations Commission and loved the people with whom I worked. At home, however, it was a different story. Trying to keep up appearances of calm and normality for the sake of one's child is a terrific strain when things are anything but calm and normal. This year, Alex had really settled down after a difficult 2000 and was doing well at school so I did not want anything to do with her father to upset that equilibrium.

I was in regular contact with Keith, who was over in Hawaii with our daughter, Samantha, and her family. At least I did not have to worry about the quiet pressure he was applying for us to get back together again and would be away until the end of the year – or so I thought.

By June/July Keith was saying he wanted to return home, as he felt he had done as much as he could to help sort out Samantha and Dan's financial position. By August he had returned.

Brad was still in Keith's unit but was in the throes of applying for a position in the country with CALM, so Keith came and stayed with me for approximately four weeks. It was a funny time: Alex loved having someone there when she left for school and came home and he really was a terrific help to me. Particularly helpful in that I had once again decided to sell the house and I had a vast amount of stuff I had to move out of the place to make it look more saleable. However, my personal life was in turmoil still and the last thing I wanted was for Keith to want a decision from me about "us". As far as I was concerned there was no "us" but I hated hurting him. After about four weeks, though, he sensed that I needed to be left on my own and he moved back to his unit with Brad – where he and Brad had some sorting out to do, also. Brad was used to his own space and the unit really was not very big! Fortunately, Brad did get a position in the country, at Monkey Mia near Denham and he was ecstatic! He needed to get away from the metropolitan area. Things were still fraught between him and Joanne and he was hurting rather badly. Moving away was, although painful, the best thing he could do in the circumstances. In October we saw him off to his new position.

My life stumbled on from there with not very much happening. Conrad's romance continued to ebb and flow and I tried to keep myself as much apart from him and his love life as much as possible.

Not long after Keith got back from Hawaii, he won a competition for two people to go to Las Vegas for 5 days, with accommodation, air fares and some entertainment included. No money, unfortunately but the prize (the first either of us had ever won) was certainly worth considering. There was a time limit on it – which expired in March 2002 – so we had some hard thinking and planning to do. Samantha's second baby was due in February of next year so the timing to go and see her would be perfect!

In November/December of 2001 I was traveling on the train after work and (unwillingly) found myself the object of conversation with a stranger. He had mental problems and, as is normal with me, I was not really keen to strike up a conversation with him or anyone as I just enjoy reading or unwinding (on my own) on the train. However, he had other ideas. During the trip it transpired that he had at one time accumulated a fair amount of money, however, had become mentally ill and his affairs had been taken over by the Public Trustees. He had to go to them whenever he needed money for anything and was currently living in a hostel in Midland. He was very frustrated as he felt he could now take over his affairs but getting out of the clutches of the Public Trustees is not such an easy affair. I listened with interest as he told me of his efforts to reclaim his finances and indeed, his life. I am not sure what happened during that conversation but later that evening as I was talking to Keith somehow the conversation got around to "us" and I felt I was "ready" to try again. Keith obviously was very happy and I was optimistic that this was a new start for us.

We had arranged to go to the movies on the Saturday of that week, Alex, Keith and I and before the film Keith produced a ring! It was a beautiful gold, diamond and emerald band and I loved it but at the same time it scared me as I was not THAT "ready" – he was moving too fast for me. However, I hoped we had turned the corner and put on the ring. It transpired that I wasn't ready and transferred the ring from my left hand ring finger to my right – rather than not wear it at all! But the planned trip to Las Vegas took on a new dimension as we discussed the idea of having a re-avowal ceremony over there.

2002/2003 – THE US!!

I have grown to understand over my time with Conrad that "wanting" something to be so does not necessarily "make it" so! In a way, realising this was why I could understand Conrad's feelings for me and grew in the knowledge that without that extra something that comes with actually being in love with your partner, there is not the commitment to that relationship. As much as I wanted to re-form a relationship with Keith, when it comes to matters of the heart you cannot make it happen. I was still trying to get over my split with Conrad. I was very, very hurt and unhappy so sought some counselling to try and sort out my feelings. It was a mixed success as I am not good at totally opening up to counsellors; only telling them what I want them to know. However, from this counselling session came the direction that maybe it would be best to completely divorce both partners, as up till this time Keith and I had never actually divorced, and of course I had never actually been married to Conrad! It was suggested, however, that I draw up some "divorce" papers to serve on Conrad, as an act of finality to our relationship and actually divorce Keith properly, which I duly did.

In view of my divorce, therefore, it was a difficult decision to utilise the winning tickets to Los Angeles and at the same time incorporate a trip to see Samantha. I say "difficult" because I had just "finalised" everything with Keith and it also meant I had to leave Alex at home this time, as taking her was out of the question both from a monetary but mainly an accommodation point of view. Samantha and Dan were still in the little one bedroomed flat and there simply was no room for Alex. It broke her heart and mine to make this decision. I hated leaving her and she definitely hated being left! I organised for her to stay with Ann and Mark - our pastors. She got on well with them all and was indeed regarded as part of their family.

The trip to the airport was fraught with emotion! Both she and I were dreading the "goodbyes". I think even up till the day before we left we were both secretly hoping that by some miracle she could go, but it wasn't to be. By the time we were due to board the plane both Alex and I were in tears and it was the worst farewell imaginable – I vowed that I would never go over to visit Samantha again without taking Alex with me as long as she was in my care and it was with great reluctance I relinquished her into her father's care.

We arrived over in Hawaii to find an exhausted Samantha! She was so pleased to see us as Sandra's birth had left her very anaemic and tired. My little Holly had grown into a gorgeous toddler, although when we first arrived she was still refusing to walk. During our stay we bought her a little push along pram and with this she gradually started walking and by the time we left she was standing quite happily. She walked about a week after we left. I loved my time with Holly. Samantha said she was normally a reticent little girl when meeting someone for the first time, but within minutes of our meeting she was on my lap and happily letting me give her a cuddle. I think instinctively she knew I was an extension of her Mum!

The apartment Samantha, Dan and family was occupying was meant for one person! For one person it would have been very roomy but when you have four adults, two babies and all the paraphernalia that goes with babies and 3 cats, then the area shrinks to minute proportions! We soon, however, got into a kind of routine but trying to get out anywhere was really difficult as Holly would need naps at a different time to Sandra and it seemed as though we were continually getting up a baby, feeding and changing it, then doing the same to the other one. It was lucky we had been to Hawaii before as we did at least get to see some of the island then, because subsequent visits had been focused on looking after babies and being with Samantha and Dan.

I found myself feeling very edgy quite often so would take myself off for a walk around the area, just to get some space. I put my edginess down to the cramped conditions, missing Alex and the looming departure, when we would have to say goodbye to Samantha again, but in retrospect I realise I was not ready to spend a lot of time with Keith. My "healing" time was taking longer than I wanted it to.

We did share the same bed – had no alternative really – but as far as I was concerned "sex" was of no interest. We managed, however, and enjoyed the time we had with Samantha.

Las Vegas

We took our tearful leave of Dan, Samantha and our grandbabies and left for Las Vegas. How I hate those airport "goodbyes"! We were booked through Los Angeles but because of the time frame did not see much of that city en route to

Vegas. The security at the US airports, however, is very strict and we must have been earmarked from Hawaii because at each stop we were searched, including removal of shoes, before being allowed through to the departure lounges.

The flight from Los Angeles to Vegas is not very long and we watched the changing landscape below us, including the famous "HOLLYWOOD" built into the hills of LA. The whole experience of flying past that sign was unreal, only experienced by us before via the limited viewing of American television programmes and movies. There was a long vista of desert then after flying over some mountains we suddenly saw in the midst of desert and isolation a city, vast and sprawling and vibrant with colour!

We had to mentally pinch ourselves several times as we drove in our taxi towards our designated hotel the "MGM Grand" (otherwise known as "Emerald City" because of the fact that its three "legs" are built from luminous emerald coloured glass), not really believing we were in Las Vegas. We were very, very tired when we arrived – early in the morning – and unfortunately our room was not ready so we deposited our luggage at the hotel and went to look for a coffee and maybe some breakfast, although all we really wanted to do was shower and have a rest. We were told to return to the hotel at about 11.30, so unwillingly we took ourselves out the door and went to explore!

What a place Las Vegas is! We formed the view that everyone should visit Vegas at least once in their lives. It is truly a town of make believe. As we walked along the Boulevard we looked with awe at "New York, New York" a casino built incorporating the famous New York skyline with the Statue of Liberty and "the Manhattan Express"; a roller coaster built around the outside of the building, which on a regular basis would come hurtling round the corner amidst the screams of its occupants. "Treasure Island" with its pirates and wonderful regular pirate fight shows. "Excalibur" with its medieval theme of knights, dragons and fair maidens. To name but a few! The time went very quickly and gratefully we took ourselves back to the hotel to claim our room, knowing that we had four days and five nights to explore further.

The MGM Grand is based on the "Wizard of Oz" theme, although why there is a glass enclosure with lions in it I don't know, maybe because of its huge golden lion symbol on the outside of the building, or the cowardly, lion from the story. Our room was fairly basic but comfortable, with a large king-size bed and a view from the 25th floor out towards the airport and distant rocky landscape. The only disappointment to us was that there were no tea and coffee facilities available in our room, so we had to always go downstairs and buy a tea or coffee when we wanted one. We got into the habit of getting ourselves some bottled water to keep in the room but not having tea making facilities was a small irritation during our stay.

After resting for a while we went downstairs to further explore our hotel. The casino floor seemed to stretch for miles and there is a constant sound of pokies pinging, handles being pulled and the occasional jingle of "jackpots" being won and bells going off! During our stay we were amazed at the fact that whatever time we went into the casino area there were always people at the slot machines, no matter how early we went downstairs (to buy our morning cup of tea) or how late at night. We saw several families and I wondered how the parents managed to save enough money to take their children to Vegas as cheap it is not! We surmised they must save for several years for a "big" holiday at the "Vegas".

As part of our prize we had three excursions planned for us. The first was a day's riding on canyon trikes. We were duly picked up outside our hotel and driven for about an hour out to Red Rock Canyon. There we were "schooled" in the intricacies of riding three wheeler dune bikes. There were about 8 of us in all and we were each supplied with our helmets and goggles (and gloves if we wanted them). I had never driven a motor bike before only ever having ridden pillion a couple of times with my brother and Michael, so this was a little daunting to me. However, after being guided over the "nursery run" to enable us to familiarise ourselves with our bikes, we all began to really enjoy the experience and I surprised myself by managing to handle my bike very well as we bumped, skidded and leapt over the landscape! At lunch time we stopped and were supplied with chicken and salad for lunch, which we all devoured hungrily. During the afternoon we were taken on the more advanced runs and this is where the group seemed to spread out. At one stage I seemed to lose sight of the bikes up front and felt very isolated as I followed what I hoped was the trail they had taken. All too soon, however, we were heading back to our vehicle for the return trip. It was a great day and I have the photographs to prove that I did it!

Although Keith and I were getting on really well, I found that Vegas only seemed to make me miss Conrad and the love I felt cheated of with him. Vegas is a city for lovers to wander arm in arm in the evening through the fantasy world built there. I found myself feeling very irritated by poor Keith and annoyed with myself because of the unfairness of my feelings towards him. Needless to say we did not "re-avow" ourselves to each other and in actual fact I don't think I would have utilised the Vegas "chapels" in any case as they all struck me as terribly tacky with their "Elvis" celebrants and "cowboy" themes.

We decided to call Samantha and Dan to let them know we had arrived safely and to briefly describe our surroundings. Fortunately, we did keep the conversation short because as it turned out the telephone rate in the hotel was incredibly high.

The next prize excursion we were to have was an helicopter ride at night over the city. However, this was postponed a day due to the high winds over the city. We did eventually go, however, and I have to admit to feeling a little apprehensive at the thought of riding around in a helicopter. We were picked up by the courtesy car for the airline and taken to the city field. There in the office we were offered a glass of champagne and sorted into groups of four. The champagne was a great idea, as it really calmed the nerves and got us all into the spirit of things. There were two or three helicopters and we were ferried out to the strip in our groups. As the helicopter took off I admit to having a quiet little prayer, but as the trip progressed I quickly relaxed and let myself enjoy the full vista of Vegas at night, which is an incredible experience. As far as the eye could see to the horizon was a mass of coloured lights and spires with towers reaching up to the sky. The "Luxor" casino is built in the shape of an Egyptian pyramid and from the highpoint and centre of this pyramid a light shines way up into the sky and is said to be the most powerful "searchlight" in the northern hemisphere, this was truly a high point in our trip. There was the magical lighting of the castle at "Excalibur" and the pirate ship shining into the night from "Treasure Island" and our own hotel glowing in luminescent green. I hope I shall be able to conjure up the memory of those views for the rest of my life. All too soon, we were banking round to land and our ride was over, but never to be forgotten.

Our days were spent exploring the different hotels. The only differences were really on the outside, on the inside the casinos all looked the same, some smelled smokier than others. The exception to this was "New York, New York" which Keith and I both liked. The interior area had been decked out to resemble what I supposed to be typical New York side streets, complete with sidewalk cafes and pubs. We did have a go at the pokies and managed to win and lose about $20.00 (the last of the big spenders!) Obviously, we had to keep an eye on our finances and indeed twelve months later I was still trying to pay off the little money I spent and put on my credit card! One of the most beautiful was the "Venetian" casino based on, of course, Venice incorporating a canal running through the middle of it complete with gondolas, and the most exquisite Venetian glass, but so expensive. The ceiling had been decorated so that it resembled a beautiful blue sky and clouds, so you would swear you were actually outside on the canal banks of Venice.

One memorable visit we made was to the "Liberace Museum". This was unexpectedly interesting as we perused his numerous (and colourful) cadillacs and his rhinestone encrusted pianos! Some of his famous, bejewelled costumes were also on show and his numerous, huge rings were displayed, including gifts from royalty and celebrity alike. The museum was in the process of being re-developed as the exhibits were outgrowing the premises, so a lot of his belongings were actually packed away but the display as it was held our interest for a good couple of hours.

The final prize we had were tickets to a show called the EFX Show – with Rick Springfield. This was truly an incredible show incorporating lighting, sound, 3-D glasses, humour and special effects at their best. I remember Rick Springfield from my early years and to me he looked just as gorgeous in his 40s (or 50s?) when we saw him, as he did as a young heart throb of 30 years ago. The theme of the show was men of history who had believed in themselves, with a section on "Merlin", "Houdini", "Barnum, Barnum" "H G Wells and his Time Machine". It was a wonderful show and a great finish to our stay in Las Vegas.

When it came to checking out we called to find out what we had run up in the form of costs, etc and found to our horror that our phone call to Samantha initially and one we made (very briefly to Alex) had been charged at US$177.00! We protested at this charge and they took off the call to Hawaii which by itself was nearly US$100.00 Never use a hotel phone to call long distance if you are the one footing the bill!

So once again we grabbed a cab and made our way to the airport and home to Aus!!

2003 – AT HOME

$\mathcal{W}$ hen we returned from the USA early in 2003 it was mutually accepted between Keith and I that things weren't right to go any further so we settled into everyday lives again with Keith living at his place in Karrinyup and me in Ellenbrook. However, out of interest Keith had his place valued and was pleasantly surprised to find it was worth more than he expected. Added to this his next door neighbours were interested in buying his half of the duplex, so he decided to sell.

At the time there was a lot of advertising for Lifestyle villages for "young-minded pre-retirees and retirees" to lease a block of land and have a preformed house built on it. One such complex was the Joondalup Lifestyle village, based in Wanneroo (not far from Joondalup). We made a few enquiries and after considerable thought Keith decided to buy into this village. It was really well set up with a central community centre with heaps of activities, its own pool and gym, etc. I secretly hoped he would find someone there to settle down with. After he sold his unit he came to stay with me – in separate rooms – which suited me just fine. In fact it suited us both (although not entirely to Keith's satisfaction I am sure) as he had somewhere rent free to stay and I had someone at home for Alex to come home to from school each day. He stayed with me in all about 4 months whilst his new house was being built.

At the same time, I had come to the conclusion that Alex had to have a bigger room in which to "veg". Her own room was woefully too small so whilst perusing the paper one day I noticed an advertisement for house and land packages in Coolamon in Ellenbrook. Out of curiosity I rang one company and got some information. The lady I spoke to was, like me, on her own and about the same age and she had used the equity in her existing house to help finance another being built. After looking around for a while I looked at some display homes and quite liked the finish of Dale Alcock homes so began to look for a house and land package. The finance advice I got made it clear that I couldn't borrow as much as I needed on my own income. As it happened Brad was looking for an investment property and decided to go halves with me in the finance arrangement by buying half of Beaufortia Crescent. I checked with Conrad first and asked him if he still wanted to be involved in our house or be bought out – he said he wanted to be bought out as he could not afford to help with the running costs of Beaufortia, so it was agreed; I would have the house valued, would borrow enough to pay him out, and Brad would take his place on the house Title.

The contracts were signed. We chose what I thought was a smaller block, but in actual fact turned out to be approximately the same size as the current house and block, although the new house was going to have a very large bedroom for Alex, which we had managed to get by converting a 4 bedroom home into a 3 bedroom one.

At the same time, however, Keith and I had both decided that we wanted to have a family Christmas with Samantha, Dan and the girls for the 2003-2004 Christmas/New Year, but this would be around the time the new house was to be built. I made sure things could be delayed with completion of the new house until after we returned to Australia early in 2004 and we set about saving for our big trip. Unbeknown to me, Brad had also decided he was going over to spend Christmas with Samantha and Dan this year, so we were really going to have a "family" Christmas.

Nothing was started on the new house until around July. I had chosen a corner block (so I would only have neighbours on one side) in Coolamon, another village in Ellenbrook. It turned out to be a good choice as in less than twelve months Ellenbrook had opened their "prestigious" land area – Charlotte's Vineyard – just down from where I was intending to build my new place, which could only push up the value of all the land around, including mine!

Keith's house was completed in April and he duly moved into it. It was small but functional for what he required. It was fun helping him choose the furniture, and colour scheme for his place but he seemed to be spending less and less time there and was with us more often than not. I had mixed feelings about this. Alex seemed to need him at home and admittedly it was nice having things done around the place and of course, the company is good, but I am one of these people that can actually quite happily be on their own!

Keith had been saying for a while that he was very aware that his father dying of cancer and Martha contracting bladder cancer, heightened the risk of him suffering some kind of cancer. He had been having bowel problems for a while and after having investigative procedures was informed that his bowels were home to around 60-odd polyps and they had to be taken out. So one Monday in July he went into hospital for an operation which resulted in a large amount of intestine being removed due to the number of polyps in situ. The polyps had been tested and one had begun to turn cancerous but had not spread, so his caution was well founded. The first week of his post-operative stay in hospital was very traumatic. The stomach valve which automatically closes following any kind of surgery refused to start functioning again so he had tubes in and out over the first few days, which was not pleasant. He was very, very weak and to add to his woes his drug shunt site became infected and he was running a very high temperature the Sunday following the operation. This particular day I was taking Alex to see a dance show at the Burswood and we called in to see him on the way. He looked and was very, very sick. For the first time since his operation I thought he really might die. Brad came down to visit his father during this time and it shook him pretty badly to see his father, who had always appeared strong and in charge to him, in such a sorry state. My thoughts whilst at the show were very sad as I envisaged a life without my "best friend" around. Fortunately, this was the lowest point of his stay in hospital and over the next few days he grew stronger and after about two weeks in total he was released into my care, because of course there was no way he could stay in his new house alone to convalesce. The ensuing six to eight weeks were very frustrating for Keith, as it took him a long time to re-gain his health and strength. However, with continuous effort and trial and error with his diet and dietary aids, he eventually recovered.

There were very few hitches to the building of my house. We had to choose bricks a second time also the paving bricks because the "boom" in the housing industry had caused widespread shortages to brick supply, etc. We watched with growing excitement as first the slab went down then the bricks were placed around the perimeter of our new home. By the time we got close to leaving for the US (in December) the outside bricks were almost finished and the window and door frames were in place.

Conrad's brother and his wife (and daughter, June,) were moving to Melbourne. They had decided to become Salvation Army officers and this necessitated their studying in Melbourne for a couple of years. They were selling their house and would need somewhere to live for a couple of weeks between selling and leaving, my house was going to be looked after by a friend from our church, Shauna, but as she normally lived at home there was no problem with her staying at my house for a couple of weeks, then letting Nick and Lacey stay there for another couple of weeks, then Shauna would return for the remaining week prior to our return from the US. This was the only economical way of looking after the four cats I had acquired, as I had priced their being placed in a cattery for the five weeks and the cost was prohibitive to say the least.

In order to finance their studies the Salvation Army and friends and relatives pitched in to put on a Fund Raising Concert for Nick and Lacey. One of Conrad's groups, would be the main performers, but June was going to play the piano and Alex and Sam (her friend from Stagecoach Theatre School) and then Alex and June were going to perform also. Alex was, of course, very excited at the prospect of performing. She absolutely thrives on "being up there" in front of an audience. She and Sam performed a dance routine formulated for their Stagecoach end of year presentation, which was an excerpt from "Chicago". I was very proud of Alex as she strutted her stuff. Then June played the piano and sang, which she did very well, the only difficulty being she did not have a microphone, so could not be heard as well as she might have but she still did well.

When Alex and June began their routine, which they had planned, choreographed and rehearsed by themselves, I had to fight to hold back my tears of pride. They did very well and I had to stop myself from feeling it would be a shame that they would be living so far apart in the immediate future – they really get on very well. The evening was a huge success and Nick and Lacey scored a good financial start to their studies in Melbourne.

The time duly arrived for us to leave for the USA – we flew out around the 17th December. Brad had previously flown in from Kununurra so we all caught the plane together. It was a very long trip! We eventually arrived stressed and tired to the bone 30 hours later! There was only one hitch, at Los Angeles, when we presented our tickets for boarding we discovered the check in clerk who had initially designated our seating had taken too many parts from Brad's ticket and they were demurring about letting him board. Eventually, however, they did let him board with us but for a few moments there we all panicked and in our state of tiredness this was really difficult to cope with.

Samantha and Dan's house was lovely. It was a two-storey home, which they had decorated with lights for Christmas. It was on an estate of very similar houses, with basic differences to distinguish them but all with the same tiling and roughly the same colouring. Unlike the houses in Australia there was a dearth of lawn in the back and no trees around the place. However, they had decorated it beautifully and it was a very welcome sight to us all.

It was lovely to be with them and the days leading up to Christmas were a real joy as we waited with anticipation for Christmas Day and our first "family together" Christmas for nearly ten years. Dan's sister, Marjory, and her husband, PC, joined us for Christmas dinner, which Dan took delight in cooking. The table was decorated with festive runners, centre ornaments and an incredible amount of Christmas paraphernalia done by Marjory with help from Alex. After the opening of presents in the morning, and clearing up the absolute mountain of Christmas wrapping paper, etc., the Christmas lunch was hugely enjoyed by us all and I basked in the joy of having all of my children and grandchildren in the same place, together for Christmas for the first time in over ten years.

It was strange to experience a cold Christmas after thirty years of hot Christmas holidays for Keith and I, and a first time for both Alex and Brad. It didn't snow immediately but waited until the start of January when it snowed very heavily, the heaviest falls in the Washington State area for many years – especially for us! I have never really felt a hot Christmas as being "legitimate", so cold and snow was lovely. Samantha confided to me that she thought she might be pregnant again and was terrified about it. Her main fear was that she had experienced two horrendous miscarriages earlier in the year, one being particularly harrowing in that she had had no idea anything was wrong until she went for a check-up and they told her the baby had died in the womb and they had to give her something to induce a miscarriage! One day when we were out snowboarding Samantha slipped on the ice and landed heavily on her bottom. I told her that if that did not dislodge this baby, then nothing would and she would be just fine. It was going to be hard, however, leaving her to cope with her worries on her own when we left.

Unfortunately, not long into the New Year we all became ill, one after the other, with Alex starting the chain by constantly vomiting for about 12 hours. In sequence we all went down with the gastric bug, which debilitated us all for approximately nine days. This was doubly unfortunate as Brad had less time than we did before he had to fly back to Australia and resume work, so his holiday was grossly cut back because of illness and the subsequent heavy falls of snow, which made driving anywhere particularly hazardous.

Our first trip out in the snow was to Mount Rainier, not far from where Samantha and Dan lived. We could not go very far up the mountain because of the heavy snow falls, but we managed to have our first snowball fight! We stopped to eat at a chalet-like inn that evening and watched as snowflakes fell slowly and silently outside, whilst we drank warm, tasty drinks and ate large meals inside! Lovely!!!

We could not go very far with the two girls in tow and they too had been very sick with the stomach bug. Holly, in particular, seemed to pick up every bug going so Dan and Samantha were somewhat protective of taking her into "crowds"! There were quite a few days when we were stuck in the house because either Samantha was at work or Dan was at work, so we would go for a walk down to the centre of the town. Eatonville wasn't a very big place but it had a few shops to look around and the walk at least got us out of the house. One thing Keith and I noticed very early on was the lack of play areas in the town, for small children. Australia seems to factor in a small play area, with climbing apparatus and swings, etc., into all of its new suburbs, so to find an established town with no park and play areas at all, was to us, most odd!

We took a trip into Seattle one day, which was not particularly successful with the two girls in tow. We managed to go up the Seattle Needle and visit the local markets, but that was about as much as we could manage in the one day. A feeling I got whilst walking around Seattle and looking at its buildings was the similarity I saw to the big department stores and office buildings in London – they seemed very familiar in that way.

Despite the frustrations it was all too soon time to leave and the dreaded farewells at the airport loomed high on the horizon. The inevitable leave-taking whenever we have visited Samantha and Dan has always been hard to forget and this time seemed even worse, as we all struggled to control our emotions at the airport. This time we had two to make as Brad was leaving a couple of weeks before Keith, Alex and I and there was no plan of when he and Samantha would see each other again in the foreseeable future. The lead up to these departures is always the worst, and it is almost a relief to get on the plane and get it over with. I hated leaving "the family" as sharing the load with us enabled Samantha and Dan to get at least some time together when we babysat the girls for them. Marjory and PC lived too far away for convenient babysitting, so they were essentially on their own.

The trip home was just as long as coming out. We had a couple of longer stopovers, one of which was in Singapore so we took a short tour around the town. Unfortunately it was raining heavily so we could not go on the ferry ride component of the tour, but it was enough of an excursion to rouse our interest in and desire to visit Singapore again at some stage in the future. It struck us as a very clean, lush and colourful city and we wished we had had more time to explore further.

2004

*W*e flew back into Australia in mid-January to find my house not that much further ahead than when we had left. There had been a little progress while we were away but as the building industry in Australia mostly closes down during late December through January not a lot had been done. Progress from the beginning of February, however, was very swift. When the house got to lock up stage in late March/early April Keith went up and painted the walls with basecoat to at least start to prepare them for painting, although this wouldn't be done in the immediate future. In the meantime, the clean out of Beaufortia Crescent had to be started and there was an accumulation of stuff spanning the last 8 years. Alex's room, in particular took ages to clear out and sort through. We threw out lots and gave away even more! Eventually, however, we were able to pack up stuff and on the 2nd April 2004, moved into our new home (145). I arranged for an agent to look after the letting of the house for me, but this took time and in the ensuing month I had to find two mortgage payments; one for Beaufortia and the other for 145.

In the previous few weeks prior to moving into the new house Keith had hardly spent any time at all in his house at Joondalup Retirement Village and we had decided to try again to be together, so consequently, we shared a bedroom for the first time the night we moved into 145. It was very disconcerting for both of us. In the time since we had been separated (and subsequently divorced) Keith had begun to snore! I had become extremely sensitive to noise in the bedroom when I was trying to get to sleep so consequently I got up and slept on the lounge at 2.00 am that morning and Keith had a dreadful anxiety attack about the whole situation. He had moved all his things in with us and was in the process of selling his house at the Joondalup Village. Had we made a dreadful mistake? Over time, however, we re-adapted to each other and things settled into a semblance of routine.

Not long after we had moved into 145, we received a call from Samantha and Dan to say that they had decided to migrate back to Australia to live. I could not believe what I was hearing! They said that after the experience of having family around they could not stand those awful airport farewells and were going to put an end to them. We were so happy. They estimated it would take about 12 months to settle things over there. Samantha's pregnancy had progressed normally so she was now four months pregnant, but it was going to be a difficult year for them. In June of that year they made the decision to try and get Samantha over to Australia with the girls, as soon as possible so Keith decided to go over and give her a hand packing and looking after the girls and flew out for the USA on 26th August 2004.

We had decided to put in a pool, so duly got quotes etc., from pool manufacturers and installers. Paul, the father of one of Alex's friends, wanted to get into pool installation and asked if he could co-ordinate and install our pool – at a reduced price – using a concrete outline and pool liner. His estimated costings were very favourable compared with the quotes we had received so we decided to let him do it. He seemed to know what he was doing. Keith was looking forward to seeing some progress on the pool when he returned later in the year. Paul had said he would get it in by Christmas.

Samantha's baby was due in September but as it turned out Jake was in no hurry to arrive and because they had decided that Samantha and the children would return with Keith at the end of November, there was a time element to his arrival. He was due on the 12th September, but it would take at least six weeks to obtain a passport for him so Samantha requested that she be induced, which procedure was duly started on the 7th September. Jake, however, did not arrive until the 9th September. Fortunately, both mother and baby were well through it all if worn out by the waiting.

While Keith was away Alex and I settled into a routine, which primarily consisted of me rushing home Monday, Tuesday and Wednesday to get her to whichever activity was on the cards for that day! I gave up trying to get home, prepare and eat a meal as it was not possible because most of her activities required her leaving home at 6.30. So Alex would get herself something to eat when she got home from school, then I would prepare a meal after I had returned from taking her to her destination, eating mine in relative peace and saving hers for when she came home. I looked forward to Thursday and Friday and usually did not arrange to do anything on those days. On some Fridays Alex would go over and spend the night with her father, which allowed me the luxury of peace and solitude in the midst of my busy week. Towards December however, Conrad became very busy with rehearsals or performances which seemed to fall on Friday evenings, negating

Alex going over there. However, we enjoyed our evenings together, sometimes getting out a movie to watch. One night in particular Alex decided we should "dine alfresco" *viz*: in our garden so we set the table complete with a couple of candles – fortunately the night was very still so there was no problem keeping them alight and we proceeded to eat, laugh and dance in the open air watched by an incredulous moon and smiling stars. We had tremendous fun and I hope my fading memory never loses the ability to re-capture that night.

I enjoyed being on my own – with Alex. I am sorry to say I did not miss Keith at all during that time. There was extra work for me but I quickly got into a routine at the weekends and in fact felt more energized than I had felt for a while. We looked forward to Samantha coming home but I was under no illusion as to what was in store! Alex had become besotted with a boy at school, Leigh, who was in her school musical production. She also quite liked a local boy, Terry. One day Terry's sister, called to ask if Alex would like to go to the Show with them, so for the first time Alex went to the Show by herself. She spotted Leigh in the crowd whilst riding on the overhead chairs with Terry. Later that week she told Terry she could not go out with him, as she had chosen to go out with Leigh – a decision she came to regret!

Progress on the pool was practically non-existent after the initial hole had been bulldozed out. Paul was a one-man operation so came to do work on our pool when his other work commitments allowed, consequently by the time Keith and Samantha and family got back to Perth on 27th November nothing much had been done and instead of an almost completed pool, ready to receive copious gigalitres of water, there was an enormous hole around which we had to build some kind of barricade to stop the girls falling in! I had worried about the logistics of getting them all back from the airport, knowing full well there would be a lot of luggage and there were five of them to convey! Samantha's friend, Jane and Ken came to my rescue because they both came to the airport in separate cars and then Alan and Joan arrived, so we had four cars, but we only just managed to get them and their luggage all home!

It became apparent very early that my house really was woefully inadequate to comfortably accommodate the four extra bodies! Samantha and the baby took over the lounge leaving no spare area of space. The girls moved into Alex's room and their toys and activities took over the family area! Both Samantha and Keith were quite traumatized by the journey home with the three children and also not very well as everyone had taken it in turns to get sick back in the US and it was Samantha and Keith's turn to come down with the bug when they returned to Australia. The first few days back, consequently, were very, very trying as we all tried to come to terms with the cramped conditions, ill health and the noise of two toddlers in constant, close proximity! Keith had had enough, as he had been in the midst of everything for the previous three months and Alex and I had really enjoyed our peace and tranquility prior to everyone returning. Samantha was stressed to the max about the financial situation she was in as she had to rely on their joint bank account and Dan had told her not to spend anymore than was necessary, in order for him to save up the airfare to get to Australia. It was a really difficult period for everyone.

The first thing to do was try and get Samantha registered with Centrelink so she could begin drawing some family allowances on which to live. Dan was using his salary to pay off left over debts in the US and was paying his sister board, so there was no money for Samantha to actually live on! As it was coming into Christmas this was a heart breaking predicament to be in and the fact that Samantha was regarded as a "new immigrant" in spite of her Australian Citizen status, made her registration a long, drawn out matter of documents, documents and more documents. Even to open a bank account was impossible because she had insufficient documentation to add up to the obligatory "100 point" identification requirement. Add to the general frustrations the fact that everywhere we went we took the children then the whole process of gaining "identification" took on marathon proportions and drained us of any energy and enthusiasm for Christmas and the pool certainly was not going to be there!

The one encouraging factor at this time was the discovery that as Samantha was still an Australian Citizen and as Jake was less than six months old, she was entitled to the $3,000 once-off payment from the Government after having a baby, but of course, the paperwork required to ensure she really was entitled to it and that she was who she said she was, was exceedingly tedious, especially as some papers had to be signed by Dan over in the US. The run up to and over Christmas was very, very frustrating for all concerned.

My finances were drained to rock bottom as the income from the house was nowhere near the expenditure it incurred after agent fees, etc. were taken off the already too low rent! Add to this the occasional helping hand to Samantha whilst she was waiting for her money to come through and by the end of the Christmas period I was in dire straits financially.

CHRISTMAS!

*P*rior to knowing that Samantha and the children would be returning to WA with Keith in November, I had agreed to have Michael, Helen and their son, Tarshi to stay for Christmas! After hearing that Samantha and family would be with us, I still felt obligated not to reneg on my offer of accommodation for Michael and Helen, however, I have to admit that I was not looking forward to the added numbers in my already bulging at the seams little house! Brad was also coming to stay for a while and the interesting question of where everyone was going to sleep became paramount in my mind.

My English upbringing required that "guests" be given the master bedroom – and in any case I would be getting up to go to work part of the time Michael and Helen were over, so it made sense for Keith and I to sleep in the family/dining area in close proximity to the kitchen facilities. I say "it made sense" but in all honesty I wasn't that enthusiastic about the idea. However, we borrowed a "blow up" mattress from friends and regularly every night we would set up our bed on the floor by the back sliding door where we could get a lovely view of the "black hole of Calcutta" which should have been our pool! By day the mattress would be stored outside as it was too much of a chore to let it down and blow it up every day. By night we would battle to get comfortable on the thing as there was a dip in the middle caused by our not inflating it too much, if it was too hard, instead of us sliding into the middle we would slide off the end! Until Brad's arrival Tarshi slept in the bed in the office. The office was a small room to begin with and the addition of the bed and existing paraphernalia, for which we had not as yet found room, meant that once his case was in situ there was no room to do anything else but get into bed!

The girls, of course, were sharing Alex's room. I have to say Alex coped really well with the invasion of her space but did lament the loss of the office bed when she needed time to herself.

When Brad arrived, complete with dog, Tarshi moved on to yet another spare mattress in with Michael and Helen in our bedroom. Our cats, overwhelmed with the sudden influx of people (after the comparative peace and quiet of just Alex and me) had to cope with, not only Samantha, a baby and two toddlers but two weeks into their arrival the addition of two kittens which, in a moment of weakness, I allowed Samantha to get in preparation of her moving into her own place eventually. They had barely recovered from this onslaught when there was a further invasion of people and worst of all! A Dog!!! Licorice virtually left home and would appear from time to time – usually after about three days – to eat, sleep and then would be off again, we think into the bush. Misty got crankier and would hiss at anything that moved, Teddy Bear got a wild, trapped look into his eyes and Pippa proceeded to comfort eat and as a result became (and still is) the original "fat cat on a mat"!

During all this we were trying to get our pool up and running! We were promised it would be in by the end of November, Christmas, the New Year and then nothing... for about six weeks. On Boxing Day we all mournfully stared at the hole that was supposed to have been our swimming pool and steamed both physically and emotionally in the uncomfortable heat of Summer, seething with anger and frustration, whilst we swiped viciously at the hundreds of flies which had invaded the place. We needed to swim! So we packed up the children and went first to Swan Aquatic, they had closed at 12.30 (it was 2.00 when we arrived there), then on to Altone Road – they also closed at 12.30! We finished up at the paddling pool at Whiteman Park! Well, at least it was wet and comparatively cool – but we should not have had to do this, we had planned to have our own pool for Christmas – wasn't that why, back in August, I had magnanimously invited everyone to Christmas dinner!!?

Christmas 2004 will have to go down as one of the most unrelaxed, chaotic, frustrating Christmases on record. In fact, in retrospect our family now calls Christmas 2004, the "Christmas from Hell". Michael and Helen took themselves off to spend time with Michael's daughter in Albany, staying away a little longer than they had planned, I suspect to give everyone some breathing space. I am sure, however, they had some vast misgivings at their decision to still spend Christmas back in Western Australia as their constant remarks of comparison between their (home) State and their (adopted) new State were testament to their discomfort due to the heat, the overcrowding and the 'pace' of life in the West! Tasmania never got as hot as this, Tasmania does not have this number of flies, the choice of healthy fresh food was so much better in Tasmania. I exploded a couple of times and told Michael to desist from comparing WA with Tasmania on threat of imminent danger - me!!

I think we all learned a lot about our level of tolerance over that particular Christmas. Mine was not high and Keith's was non-existent. Despite all the trauma and irritation, however, it was SO good to have Samantha and the children on hand instead of thousands of miles away. The only sad note was that Dan was still thousands of miles away and getting increasingly despondent by the day. It seemed to be taking so long to finalise his application for Australian Residency, but in actual fact it took a lot less time than it could have done and eventually, on the 11th February 2005, he surprised us all by arriving on the doorstep, unannounced and beaming from ear to ear!!

Things started to get better all-round from the time Dan arrived. The children were better, Samantha was happier and we had someone else to share the constant care of our extended family. He brought with him a little money and with this he and Samantha went out shopping for household things in preparation for them moving into my old home in Beaufortia. They were going to be my new tenants.

The change over from the tenants to Samantha and Dan went very well. Dan arrived on the 11th February and they were ensconced in Beaufortia on the 19th February. It was wonderful to have space again – for Alex to have her room back, but at the same time, not have that terrible feeling of loss because Samantha and Dan and family had either been left behind in the USA or gone back there, they were here with us at last!

2005

By February, the pool had progressed as far as having the liner inserted into it. Internal measurements had been taken by a representative from the company supplying the liner and the guys duly came to put it in the pool. All went well until they reached the edges and found the liner was too large; it did not fit! They whipped it away and it was another week before they came back. When they had come to fit the liner that first time they had covered the steps with white cushioning. When they took away the ill-fitting liner they left the cushioning surface on the stairs but what they did not tell us was that this surface is very, very slippery when wet! A couple of days after they had been and gone the first time, Keith noticed some newspaper had blown into the pool area and went down the steps to retrieve it, the white surface was wet and his feet went out from under him, and we think his right foot hit the wall of the pool on the side. I did not know anything about it until he came hobbling in from the back garden area and told me he had sprained/twisted his ankle.

As we thought it was just a sprain, and as he had been able to walk back to the house after the accident, it was considered best that he just rest and elevate the ankle and I duly stayed home to be 'his feet' for the day.

His ankle swelled appropriately and after about two days we decided it would be better to let the doctor take a look at it. So Keith took himself off to see the local doctor, who confirmed our thoughts that the ankle was sprained and referred him for some physiotherapy. I thought at the time it might have been a good idea to get the ankle x-rayed but the doctor did not suggest this on that first visit. However, after about a week of physio treatment the physiotherapist was not happy with Keith's progress and suggested he get the ankle x-rayed. It was when checking the x-ray we discovered that Keith had not sprained his ankle but had in actual fact fractured his lower bone about an inch from the ankle joint itself! The doctor then arranged for Keith to see an orthopaedic surgeon for further review. A little late in the day!

By the time Keith and I went to see the surgeon Keith had been hobbling about on his ankle for about ten days. The surgeon was very, very surprised that Keith had been able to walk on it at all, and put it down to the fact that the fracture was an inch away from the ankle joint thus the ankle was still bearing weight. If he had fractured the bone any closer to the ankle he would not have been able to walk on the foot and this would have alerted the doctor initially that all was not well. Still, the surgeon was pleased with the way Keith's bone was healing and as Keith did not want a caste on the ankle, allowed him to avoid surgery but he had to wear a support bandage for a further month or so until the bone had healed itself. Which it did in due course. We did think about suing but really could not be bothered with all that entailed. We were just relieved Keith did not have to lumber around in a caste (and thus be unable to drive) for weeks!

Progress on our pool continued, slowly, but by the end of March it at last had water in it and on the coldest day in WA for something like 20 years, we all stood around shivering, but nonetheless, admiring, our pool full of (cold) water. In spite of the incredibly long time it took to complete, it really looked a picture and Paul had done a good job on it.

Samantha obtained a job very quickly after Dan arrived. She had more freedom to get out and do what was necessary to find a job; hand out resumes, call and see hospital HR departments, etc. Dan, meanwhile was checking out the requirements for him to join the police service and in their travels they went to Joondalup. Samantha immediately loved the Joondalup Hospital and duly left her resume there and within a day received a phone call to go and see them about possible employment. She was offered a position nursing, utilising whatever hours she wished to have. Initially, it was only about 4 or 5 days a fortnight then subsequently she accepted 9 days per fortnight, as hers was the only income coming in. If only it had been as easy for Dan to get into the Police service! In the meantime, there had been advertisements for the Prisons Service so Dan also applied for work with the Prisons.

As Samantha was working Dan became 'Mr Mom'. He did very well too! Fortunately, he loves cooking so utilised the opportunity to try out different recipes. He got the girls into a good routine and things settled down into some semblance of order for them. However, in the June Samantha found out she was pregnant again! So now there was a time factor for Dan to get employment somewhere.

In the February of 2005, the Ellenbrook Cultural Foundation arranged for Ceroc Classes to be carried on locally. Ceroc dance is a cross between Latin American style and Jive. I decided I would like to give the classes a go and duly dragged Keith and Alex with me. There was a good turnout, but with the usual lack of male numbers to match female, even though I enjoyed the classes for me, there was too much standing around. Keith hated it. He could not coordinate his limbs in time to the music at all, but Alex took to it like a duck to water. She loved it! More importantly though, she was (and still is) very good and her dancing continued to go from strength to strength. So much so that in May she and her partner (Shaun from her Johnny Young Classes) entered the State Ceroc Championships and came third both individually and as a couple, after only three months of dancing! Followed by winning no less than four first places and one second place for events they entered in the Championships held in November of the same year.

Alex also tried out for the school production – "Singin' in the Rain" and got a principal part, so she was ecstatic! It was a lot of work and rehearsals but she enjoyed every moment of it. Academically, it had been a very good year for Alex, having been awarded several achievement awards during the year.

In the July we went up to Kununurra to stay with Brad for a week. When you are used to the city, country living takes a little getting used to, particularly the further North you travel. It struck us as odd seeing the aboriginal population lying around the streets, usually drunk, or seeing them under the trees during the day, flaked out. Brad gave us a great holiday though. We toured a couple of natural bush areas with hidden billabongs and ancient aboriginal artwork gouged into the rock faces. We had a trip up the Ord River to Lake Argyle in one of Brad's work boats. We did not see many crocodiles on that particular day, but you knew they were there! We visited the Wyndham Crocodile Farm – that was very interesting. One particular crocodile was estimated to be about 80 years old. They grow teeth every year and this particular crocodile had almost exhausted his supply of teeth, so was not really expected to be around for a great deal longer.

Just before we left for Kununurra Alex began "going out" with a boy from the Salvation Army Youth Group, Chris. She still quite fancied "Carey" at school and was also still lamenting her treatment of "Terry". She had realized she still liked Terrry and apologized to him but he was not interested now in a relationship with her. She quite liked Chris, however, so decided that she would be his girlfriend. It was the beginning of a six month relationship which brought joy to them both, and towards the end, a closeness between the families. However, while we were in Kununurra Chris sadly informed her that his family had decided to move to Melbourne at the beginning of 2006.

In the meantime, rehearsals for "Singin' in the Rain" were nearing completion with the production due to be performed in August/September. The week of the show duly arrived and the continuous round of performances began. Alex was in her element and the friendship and love amongst the kids (and staff) in the production was obvious as it drew to a very successful conclusion. We avidly studied the old film version of the musical with Debbie Reynolds and Gene Kelly, and searched the stores for clothes which remotely resembled the day wear of the time. Alex played her part very well and as always, we were very proud of her performance.

Dan continued to try and get things rolling to enter the Police Service. His academic record had at last arrived from the USA so he filed his application in April, however, nothing was forthcoming for weeks and even then, in order to find out what progress was being made on his application, he would have to constantly ring them to find out. In the meantime, he had been accepted to go for the various tests for the Prison Dept and was given a time to begin training – at the beginning of September. It had been a very frustrating year for Samantha and Dan with delays at every turn and with her due date drawing inexorably closer all the time.

My job at the Commission was beginning to get me down. The Chief Commissioner had retired, virtually putting me out of a position. I had a brief sojourn in "Records" but did not like it, so when a new Commissioner was appointed I put my hand up for the CLO in that Chamber, and got it. I had been in my new chamber for a few months but was not enjoying it. I did not like my Commissioner and was feeling quite trapped, with nowhere to go career wise, so I applied for another position in the July and after an interview was told I was successful so at the beginning of August I left my comfort zone at the Commission and commenced with the Department for Consumer and Employment Protection (DOCEP).

At the beginning of September Dan started the Prisons Dept training and so was on their payroll so Samantha could stop working virtually full time and Dan took over the main role of breadwinner. It was very timely for them as Dan had had enough of his "Mr Mom" role and Samantha was getting very stressed and tired being the main breadwinner. September 2005, however, was not a good month for me.

For the past five years I had been able to avoid any illnesses as such, apart from the odd cold, but time off, if any, was usually due to Alex not being well – for me to have sick leave was relatively unheard of; until the beginning of September. What began as a niggling sore throat was a virus which caused me to take a full working week off work and lose my voice for several days. This was very frustrating and embarrassing having just begun my new position with the DOCEP, in the Legal Unit. The ensuing weeks weren't much better in that the cough persisted together with the "glugginess" associated with coughs and colds. Keith also came down with the virus and we were still troubled with an irritating cough – particularly at night – for weeks afterwards.

On the 20th September my singing group the Ellenbrook Singers was cutting a CD at a local studio in Burswood. It was hard work, after which I acquired a new respect for recording artists! We finished about 10.00pm and when I went to my car I discovered it had been broken into via the rear passenger (nearside) window. It was a shock to the system and I was worried they might have incapacitated my car in some way in their search for items to steal. I hadn't left much in my car, but when I toted up what I was missing it came to roughly $400.00! The insurance company, however, was very prompt when, the next day, I rang them to report the damage. They had a repairman round to the house the same afternoon, with no charge on my insurance.

Two days following the break in to my car, on Thursday, 22 September 2005, at approximately 3.10pm I was returning to my office after delivering two envelopes to the Francis Burt Chambers at 77 St George's Terrace. I had walked down to the Chambers and in order to save a little time (and energy) I decided to catch a bus back up the Terrace to the Dept. A number 103 bus came along and I boarded it. It stopped outside of "Reveleys" in the Terrace, as usual, and as it pulled away from the stop I pressed the button for the next stop. I waited until the bus was nearing the intersection of Mill Street and the Terrace, the lights were green so I rose in preparation for exiting the bus.

As I was standing and holding on to a pole, the bus braked suddenly and sharply to avoid hitting a pedestrian and I was unable to keep a grip on the pole, due to the momentum of the sudden stop, and found myself being propelled down the bus, only coming to a stop when I hit my head on the front of the bus (I think) and landed first on my left side/back and rolling on to my back. I was extremely shocked and not too keen to move for fear of what damage I may have done to myself. I was aware of Thu Truong (a fellow passenger on the bus) leaning over me, asking if she could help me up. I remember telling her I would "just lie here for a minute" and after a few seconds very cautiously moved my arms, then my back in an effort to get up off the floor. I remember wondering whether this was the beginning of life in a wheelchair, as I was coming into land on the floor!

My lower back was very sore and I was aware of a sore spot on the top, right hand side of my head. I was helped to the front (right hand) passenger seat where I perched on my right buttock and held on to the pole in front of the seat. Thu asked me where I was going and I told her I was returning to my office. At first I said I would just go back there, when it was suggested that an ambulance be called, however, at this point I noticed sight interference occurring in my eyes and I became alarmed at what damage may have been caused to my spine, so consented to them calling an ambulance. Thu, very kindly offered to go up to my office and let them know what had happened, and in a few minutes I was aware of two of my colleagues, Ayshin and Lesley's, worried faces peering at me from outside the bus. By this time the Swan Transit Supervisor had arrived on the scene. I realised that a couple of other passengers had also been slightly hurt in the accident.

After approximately 20 minutes the ambulance arrived and a surgical collar was placed around my neck to avoid any further movement in case of damage. I was given some sort of inhalant medication to help me relax and with the pain, as I was going to have to move from the bus on to the ambulance trolley and this caused some extensive discomfort. I was then placed in the ambulance and my pulse and blood pressure were checked. My blood pressure, of course, was very high. Lesley came in the ambulance with me and Ayshin made efforts to contact Keith and tell him what had happened.

When I arrived at the hospital I was extremely uncomfortable as I was told I had to lie flat on my back and avoid any movement until a neck examination had been done and had x-rays taken of my back. I found it most uncomfortable to lie on my back and not move and it seemed an age before a doctor could see to me. My blood pressure was taken again – even higher – but eventually a doctor checked my neck and responses and gave me the all clear to remove the collar and slightly raise the couch on which I was lying.

By this stage I really wanted to pass urine and was told I would have to use a bedpan! Yuk! However needs must and I was duly perched upon said pan. It was really hard to make my bladder work. It felt like a dream and in dreams you stop yourself from urinating and I had to concentrate to tell my brain this was not a dream, it was okay to urinate! It was a very strange experience. My urine was checked and there were no signs of blood in it, which was good. I was then taken to X-ray – Keith had by this time arrived – and they x-rayed my lower back to make sure nothing was broken.

The doctor informed me that there were no breaks – which was a relief – but there was substantial soft tissue damage, which only time and anti-inflammatory drugs could help. I was told I could go home. By this time it was nearly 8.00pm. I had been at the hospital for approximately 3 to 4 hours although it had not seemed that long. I was told to rest and when I could see my own GP about getting medication to bring down my blood pressure as it was very, very high. I was given a 'head injuries' leaflet and told what to watch out for over the next 36 hours and if I noticed any of the symptoms quoted I was to return to the hospital.

Unfortunately, the far reaching effects of this experience would not materialize for about 4 months.

I stayed in bed the following day and apart from feeling very uncomfortable sitting, it wasn't as bad as I thought it might be considering the force with which I had hit the floor, however, by the end of Friday I was noticing a very bad pain in my left side at the back particularly when I coughed and I tried very hard not to sneeze as this really, really hurt!

I took my own blood pressure over the weekend and it was still horribly high. Keith suggested I go to a local lady, Sheila, who is a remedial masseuse and knew about natural remedies. I did not want to be taking anti-inflammatory medication at all as this interferes with the body's natural healing capabilities. Monday – the 26th – was a bank holiday so I had to wait until Thursday (the 29th) to see Sheila.

I got up a couple of times in time to go to work during the week beginning 26th September, but found the effort required to get up, dress and have breakfast left me physically exhausted and my back was very, very sore, so stayed away from work the whole week.

Although the whole of my back was sore during that week, the area on my side/back was the most troublesome and I went to see the doctor on the Tuesday for advice. I was concerned there might have been some internal injury missed in the original examination, because at that time the area was not so sore. I went to my own medical practice and saw a doctor there who gave me a cursory check up and could not find anything, took my blood pressure – which was still very high and told me to monitor it myself for a couple of weeks – no suggestion of medication!!

REMEDIAL MASSAGE THERAPY

I went to my first remedial massage session with Sheila on Thursday, 29th September. She also took my BP and told me to go straight away to my doctor, which I did the following day.

I saw another doctor at the Medical Centre this time, and she put me back on to Zestril for my BP and told me to make a further appointment for the following Wednesday afternoon, mainly to check up on my accident injuries as this was now a workers' compensation matter.

I returned to work on Monday the 3rd October 2005. It was rather hard to stay all day as my back was really sore by lunch time. In retrospect I probably should have gone home after the half day and gradually eased myself back into full time work. I had a massage on Monday night with Sheila, which eased it for a while but the following day was probably worse for a while, necessitating me lying down all evening on the Tuesday, after I returned from work.

Wednesday night was not too bad, Thursday was uncomfortable again but not as bad as Tuesday night. The sore area on my side had begun to dissipate somewhat, to the extent that at least I could cough without too much discomfort, however the lower back pain began elevating in its place!

I hoped that would be the end of my ongoing health woes and indeed October was not too bad, until I started getting toothache! What now!! It was the weirdest toothache, a throbbing, hurting pain that seem to spread across the side bottom teeth and gums, so much so I could not pick out which tooth was the aching one! Then it would subside – it came in waves. I made an appointment with my dentist after a particularly uncomfortable weekend, very unwillingly as I do not like going to the dentist, and the receptionist said she had had so many people ring with toothache this last week, I couldn't be fitted in until the following Thursday. Her words started me wondering about my toothache and the fact that I had said it did not feel like any toothache I had had in the past. I happened to be speaking to Sheila later that morning and mentioned my toothache and described how it felt and she said she had experienced identical toothache over the weekend and we wondered whether it was, in fact a virus.

The 'toothache' problem continued for about two weeks. It started to go so I helped it along by beginning the use of 'Sensodyne' toothpaste, which really helped but best of all, I didn't have to go to the dentist!

This was the beginning of my trying to stabilize my hormone system with "natural remedies" instead of manufactured creams, which I had been using. It also ushered in the battle to find out what was causing my immune system to be practically non-existent! Sheila put me on "Femeran" to try and stabilize my hormone system and when my hot flushes began returning, she then put me on "Liverclens".

After about a week of the two treatments, and after gradually cutting back on my hormone cream, one day I actually forgot to use my creams until I was driving to work and thought I would probably have a bad day from the 'flushes' point of view, but surprisingly it wasn't, so the "Femeran" appeared to be working.

My sessions with Sheila began to extend from remedial massage therapy to trying to work out why my immune system was virtually at a standstill. It was Sheila's opinion that all the stress of the preceding years were eventually catching up with me, particularly as my finances had taken a dangerous downturn, trying to maintain two houses with a rental payment which did not even cover the mortgage payments, let alone any other expenses! I had to sell Beaufortia to get solvent again, but, this would mean Samantha and Dan had to find alternative accommodation, which they could not afford until Dan had qualified as a Prison Officer and his pay increased. All sorts of past reasons for being continuously sick began to surface under Sheila's manipulations!

Alex found herself a job at Video Ezy in Ellenbrook then suffered a few moments of panic as her previous commitments encroached on her availability to work! She continued to see Chris and both of them would refuse to talk about his impending departure for Melbourne. She was involved in the School Cheerleading Championships, necessitating 7.30am starts at school on Mondays and odd rehearsal times throughout the week, plus two appearances at the Superdome at the Wildcats Games to actually perform. They got through to the last four and ultimately came third. They deserved a better placing as they were very good. She was also involved with the Ellenbrook Salvation Army youth activities, practices for the Year 12 Graduation evening, for which she had been chosen along with a Year 9, Ben, to perform and assist, and rehearsals for her modelling school graduation in December. During November and December Keith and I were losing track of where she had to be, for what and at what time!

Gradually, however, the countdown towards Christmas began. This year we were having people to our place for Christmas dinner as the pool was in and we had shade sails up – ripe for entertaining. Nick, Lacey and June were coming over from Melbourne as well. For Alex, however, there is always the "choice" of where to have Christmas lunch and she hated it. She wants to be with everyone! This year, it was the turn of her father's family to have the pleasure of her company and particularly as June was going to be here. I did suggest to Mary, before speaking to Joan about it, that maybe they would all like to come to us, but she was less than enthusiastic, in fact her attitude really irked me, so I resolved not to say anything to Joan.

The only blot on my horizon came the Sunday before Christmas (the 18th) when, whilst at church at the Salvation Army, my purse was stolen from my bag. It was my own fault, I put down my bag, which was open, and left it on a chair whilst I handed out morning tea to the partaking congregation. I looked at it and this little voice in my head said "should you really leave that there, it could be stolen?" but I pooh-poohed any prospect of my bag being stolen by anyone at the church. However, I did not reckon on outsiders coming into the church, which is what happened, and I discovered it was missing when we got home. Despite going straight back down to the hall and all of us having a quick look around to see if the purse had been discarded in the bushes we never found it that day. My credit cards and the other contents of the purse were found around the shopping centre sometime after Christmas, but by this stage I had cancelled all my cards etc but at least I got back the little picture of my family, which I usually carried in my purse.

In hindsight, it was a good idea just to cater for the Renton Clan on Christmas day as great fun though it was, it was a lot of work. As it happened December 2005 turned out to be the coldest on record! We did not get into the pool until well after Christmas, but the setting was great and we all said it was the best Christmas for a while, particularly as last year's had been so disastrous! Having Brad down with us was a special enjoyment and we got to know his girlfriend, Anne, a little better. Although he seemed to be flitting between us and his friends' places the week or so he was with us it was still good to see him.

Brad had obtained a position with CALM in Jurien Bay and was starting in February, so we took the opportunity to go with them and have a look around Jurien Bay after Christmas, as while they were down from Kununurra, they wanted to see where they were moving to firsthand and also, if possible, arrange rental accommodation to go to upon arrival in February. It took longer than I thought it would to get there; the better part of three hours, but it was a pleasant trip. I have only been to Jurien a couple of times and that was a long time ago, so we were pleasantly surprised by how much it had grown. It is quite a township now and their rental charges reflect this! It was hard for Brad to swallow rentals of upwards of $180.00 per week as for the past two years he had been paying less than that per fortnight in a GEHA home in Kununurra! Anyway, we looked at a couple of places, one of which was really nice and they expressed their interest in taking up a tenancy. One of the homes was a fibro and tile building – a very simple three bed, one bath structure but because of its proximity to the beach it was valued at $525,000 to buy! I could not believe that price for what it was.

We had lunch at the local watering hole, then Brad and Anne decided to go for a walk along the beach with their dogs. As it was now 3.00pm we decided to head home as we knew we would not get back much before 6.00pm even leaving now. We left Jurien with pleasant impressions of the place and looked forward to numerous weekends spent with Brad and Anne in the ensuing year or so.

We had a BBQ with the Chris' family on the 28th December. It was not a warm night so not much bathing was done – although the young folk did go into the pool. Dan, Brad and Steven seemed to hit it off really well and it was with mingled enjoyment and sadness I reflected on the way it happens that you only really get to know people when they are about to leave, as in this case.

Normally, I don't do very much for the New Year celebration, but this year Chris' family was going to Edgecombe Brothers for a "Night of Nostalgia". The programme consisted of a BBQ, followed by a special outdoor screening of "Casablanca" then entertaining oneself until the countdown. Alex of course wanted to go so we duly rolled up, set up our picnic area and proceeded to eat. It was a lovely evening. I had never seen "Casablanca" and enjoyed the sheer professionalism of the vintage actors. It was a cold evening though, particularly for the time of year, and by the end of the movie I have to admit all Keith and I wanted to do was to go home, have a hot drink and go to bed!! Alex was having none of that, however, so bolstered by brewed cups of coffee, dancing and generally "hanging around" we managed to stay put until the countdown, staggering home at about 12.30am- 2006 had arrived.

2006

2006 started off gently enough. Did not do much on the 1st – just recovered from having a late night!

Dan's induction to the WA Police Academy took place at the Joondalup Academy on the 2nd. His was in a special (inaugural) class of previously experienced police officers who had joined and in some cases re-joined, the WA Police Service, so they did not have to do the full Academy course as they were presumed to know the basics of policing, and their training would be completed in ten weeks. It was reassuring to know that a couple of the new intake were actually WA policemen before and had left the service to pursue other avenues. They were back having decided that the Police Service was where they wanted to be and in some cases were prepared to take a demotion to begin again. There were policemen from England, the USA and a couple of Scotsmen.

Joondalup Police Academy is a very picturesque facility and after the ceremony, which was pretty brief and to the point, the new "recruits" and their families were treated to a lovely morning tea in the canteen. After this Dan gave us a guided tour of the training "village" which consists of mock takeaway, petrol station, house, bus-stop establishments where the officers carry out planned action in the case of robberies or attacks at any of these venues. They were very lifelike even to the point of clothes in the wardrobe of the "house". The only action at the time, however, was a kangaroo lazily munching away on the "village green". Judging by the kangaroo droppings around the place we were definitely intruding on his turf!

After we left the Academy Samantha, the children, Keith and myself went to the local park to allow the children a bit of a run, then went home. As we had all been up very early to get to the 8.00 ceremony we were all a little tired and did not do much for the rest of the day.

The first week in January was a difficult one for me and Alex particularly. I was surprised by how "down" I was feeling about the impending separation of Alex and Chris. They crammed in as much time as possible together, saw a couple of sunrises and sunsets but the day of leaving was drawing inexorably closer. It stirred so many memories of my own heartache with leaving Conrad and then eventually his leaving me for good, to the point that I could not separate my empathy for Alex from my own sad feelings!

I decided to indulge myself on the Friday before I was due to return to work by doing just what I wanted, with no one else around to encroach on "my time". Not that I was particularly adventurous! It was just nice to get on the train to Perth knowing that if I wanted to I could stay on it until I got to the end of the line – Fremantle – or not. I decided to have morning tea in Perth, so after collecting my new National card from the branch where I had asked them to send it, I meandered down to Myers then the Mall, window shopping. It was such a sense of freedom knowing I did not need to be anywhere at any special time and there was no one else to consider but myself. I spent the voucher Samantha had given me for my Christmas, so did not spend "my own" money (which was in particularly short supply) then happily sauntered home.

On the 5th we went to "Jimmy Dean's Restaurant" in Midland for a meal with Chris' family. It was there that I really got a chance to talk to Jodie, Chris' mother. She was naturally apprehensive about the move and hoped she and Steven had made the right decision. Of course, those of us in the West who didn't want them to go, didn't think it was the right decision, but for their sake, I hoped we were wrong. If we were right, however, they would be back in a year, so only time would tell.

Alex spent most of her non-working time with Chris. Either he was at our place or she was around there but eventually the dreaded day arrived and it was time to say "goodbye". Chris' family were with the Salvation Army Captains' family as their last stop in Ellenbrook so I picked up Alex from work and we went around there to take our farewells. It really was as difficult as we had all feared, with not a dry eye in the place. However, as we drove off I had to say to Alex that despite the upset it was with a sense of "relief" we eventually parted; the dreaded anticipation of the event was over, now all we had to do was pick up the pieces and heal. Alex was quite good really, but I was not surprised when she woke me at 12.45am later that night and asked me to sleep with her, which I did. Work was a Godsend over the ensuing days for Alex. She did not have much time to brood and also Ceroc started up again, and she was very excited about that because the WA Competitions were happening in March. The following Sunday was the worst for her, however, as she wanted to go to church and Chris and his sisters were a large contingent of the youth of the church. I could not go with her because it was the weekend we were moving Samantha and Dan into the new house. I have to admit to being a little cross with her for putting herself in such a position, but she explained to me that she needed to go there to get that first week without Chris over and done with, and as she was working the following weekend, this would have to be the weekend she went. It was upsetting for her and she cried on her sister's shoulder later that day, but at least she had faced a sad situation and coped. I was proud of her.

A bright spot in this rather sad time was the fact that the house Samantha (and Alex) had gone to see in Ellenbrook was just what Samantha and Dan were looking for to rent and they heard a couple of days later that they could have it. Samantha was so thrilled (and relieved) and I must admit to feeling a huge weight lift from my shoulders, knowing they had somewhere to go. We moved them into the new house over the weekend, which was sheer hard work. They settled in so well, however, we knew it was meant for them. All that was left now was to clean the old place and then sell it.

Beaufortia really was very grubby and I was glad we had decided to get it professionally cleaned, even though it cost a packet to do so. There was no time (nor the energy) in the ensuing week to do the job ourselves as it was having its first "home open" the following Sunday. The cleaners did not disappoint and we were pleased with the way it had cleaned up. There were just a few minor touches needed, which we attended to during the week and it was ready for the inaugural "home open". We were guardedly optimistic because the real estate market in Ellenbrook had been very buoyant and our house was probably one of the cheapest homes available in the area. I thought the price was fairly set at between $270,000 and $290,000. I was hoping to get approximately $280,000 for it.

Craig, the real estate representative, called on the Sunday evening after the inspection, to say the house had attracted about 15 lots of people through it. Four of these had expressed interest in the house and another had actually put in an offer for $275,000, $5,000 less than I was hoping for but it was a young couple with pre-approved finance, so was virtually a "cash" deal. I then had to make the decision whether to accept the money and have a quick settlement, thus sorting out my finances that much quicker or hanging out for the additional $5,000. I opted to accept the offer and felt very happy about it. I just wanted to clear my debts and get on with a relatively debt-free life. There followed, for me, an anxious two weeks as we waited for confirmation of their finance (in writing) and also the hurdle of the girl's father going through the house giving his seal of approval! Eventually, however, the father was happy and the finance was approved and we settled down to await finalisation of the sale.

Over the next five weeks we had to go down and water on a weekly basis to keep it looking good and we were paying two mortgages. I say "we" but actually Keith had to pay the Beaufortia house mortgage because I could not negotiate suspending mortgage payments with ING (the bank behind Homeswell). While all of this was going on we waited patiently for Samantha's baby to arrive. He was due "somewhere" between the 8th and 13th February! Alex of course wanted him to be born on her birthday, and as I had booked to begin my holidays on the 8th February, it would be convenient for him to make his appearance then.

During the December Alex had periodically complained of a sore throat, for which the doctor had prescribed anti-biotics. The soreness would clear up for a while then recur. She was also rather tired, but as she was heavily involved in so many activities, we were hardly surprised. At the end of January, however, Alex once again developed a sore throat and additionally a pain under her left, front rib when she breathed and coupled with her on-going tiredness I knew something was not right and had long suspected that her recurrent sore throats were more than 'viruses' as the doctor always liked to dismiss them. I organised a doctor's appointment for her and as Keith was taking her, told him not to let Alex leave the surgery without the doctor ordering a blood test for Glandular Fever. It was an anxious wait for the result but I knew in my heart this was what ailed her. We found out she did have GF and although Alex was devastated at least we knew what we were dealing with now. The only problem was there is no treatment and one of the main symptoms of the virus is a crippling and on-going lethargy and Alex's Ceroc dance competitions were just five weeks away.

The following week was horrendous for us all. Alex suffered enormously with a very, very bad sore throat and I struggled with the sheer frustration of not being able to do anything to help her, except give her painkillers every four hours. This in itself was a trauma because Alex's throat was so sore swallowing was agony for her. The mornings were the worst because as she was a mouth breather when she awoke, the pain from her throat being dry as well as sore was agony. We both dreaded the mornings, to the point that I set my alarm to wake her during the night so she had a painkiller at the four hourly interval, hoping it would lessen the pain in the morning. After about a week to ten days Alex began to suffer less with her throat, which was her main symptom, but she was still very tired.

Whilst all this was going on with Alex, Samantha went into labour with Leo and he was actually born on Alex's birthday – the 8th February. Alex wanted to visit Samantha in the hospital and as GF is not contagious other than by passing via saliva – e.g. drinking from the same cup or sharing utensils, or kissing of course, she could not harm Samantha or the baby so we went to the hospital. During the visit Alex asked if she could go and get a drink from the vending machine. When she came back she said she had had problems getting out the bottle of water for which she had paid. Later that night she said she felt very unwell, which was really worrying because I did not know what to expect from GF. She became very distressed and then vomited three or four times during the night. I had no idea whether she had picked up a stomach bug at the hospital because of her practically non-existent immune system, or this was yet again another facet of the GF. Of further concern was the fact that I had read the liver can be very adversely affected by GF. The following day she was understandably exhausted but did not vomit anymore. So we will never really know what that particular segment was all about!

We were never allowed to verbalise to Alex that she would not be able to take part in the Ceroc competitions. She would not even think about not taking part. We were being told continually, however, by those who had actually had GF or knew of someone who had suffered with it, that it would take weeks and months to recover from it and we had less than five weeks.

I plied Alex with Mangosteen three times a day. It had worked for my brother-in-law and his Chronic Fatigue Syndrome (CFS) so we hoped it would work for her. I also obtained homeopathic remedies from my remedial massage friend, Sheila. Something worked! By the end of the third week Alex wanted to return to school and Ceroc – of course. Very cautiously we allowed her to gradually increase her activities, including her work at Video Ezy, watching all the time for signs of fatigue.

Eventually the day of the competitions arrived and as Alex's energy level was apparently normal she did manage to enter them– much to everyone's surprise and pleasure. Alex and Shaun not only managed to "dance all night" – entering four events – but they won them all and were named Western Australian Female and Male Champions. It was a very emotional moment when they went up for their awards, again and again, knowing the drama that had been played out over the preceding five weeks. They looked a picture of joy in their specially made lime green and black costumes – and everyone was thrilled for them.

On the 13th February Brad commenced work at CALM in Jurien Bay. They had travelled down the previous week and moved into the house the local agent had located for them. Because there were papers to be signed for the house settlement Keith and I decided to drive up to Jurien to see them and their new home. The trip to Jurien is between two and three hours. Not a bad distance and after having to travel by plane in order to visit Brad in the past it was lovely just knowing he and Anne were two or three hours away.

We were pleasantly surprised by their rental house: It was fairly new in design with a lovely big open area for living, dining, office, and kitchen and three good sized bedrooms. The storage areas were good too. The house was on a large block with a shed and plenty of room for the dogs to run around. Jurien itself does not have a large contingent of shops but there was enough for immediate requirements. We did not stay long on that first trip as it was mid-afternoon by the time we had finished sightseeing and we did not want to be too late getting back as I had work the next day.

On 7th March Beaufortia "settled" so by the end of that week I was at last in a position where financially my torment had come to an end! It was with the greatest pleasure I paid back debts owed, including paying back Keith some money, although by no means all I owed him, clearing credit cards and bills. Granted there was not a great deal left by the time I had done this but the feeling of at last being free of my crippling debt was wonderful. The settlement agent did not perform particularly well, however, following the settlement and it took another 4 to 5 weeks before they had fully returned all that was due to me, with much prompting from me!! For several weeks I would drive past my old house just to see what the new occupants had done with it and to my horror I learned they had removed my "step down" into the lounge! I loved that feature! Oh well, it was their house now.

When I look back on 2006, in the future, it will be forever etched on my mind that it was the year I spent an absolute fortune trying remedies to overcome my menopause symptoms and in particular, those wretched hot flushes!

I continued to see Sheila, my masseuse, to receive treatment for my injured lower back, but she was more than a masseuse in that she wanted my hormonal problem sorted too! Since starting to go to her, she had persuaded me to try getting my hormonal system to work naturally and that by using my oestrogen and testosterone cream I was condemning myself to using them for the rest of my life, and that "herbal" was the way to go. I had followed her advice reluctantly, because at least I had been relatively "flush free" for 12 months and did not want to start that again. I duly began trying different combinations of herbal remedy. Each one was "guaranteed to work" on even the most stubborn cases! Well, my case proved to be the most stubborn she had come across. Nothing worked. For the first day or so after beginning each different remedy it would appear that my flushes were not so bad, but it was almost as if my body was tentatively trying this, then discarding the pill or potion as the wrong answer and I would be back to square one! So here we were several months on into 2006, no closer to finding the answer to my hormonal problems and a lot lighter in pocket. Two particular concoctions were so vile I was surprised my symptoms did not scurry away in terror!

The next attempt at a cure was via an Iridologist! He looked into my eyes and told me my circulatory system was "tired" (I could have told him that) and prescribed his tinctures. These seemed to work quite well on my energy levels at least – they did not touch my flushes, but at least I had the energy to cope with the rotten things. They also alleviated my need for sleep in the middle of the afternoon, which had been a problem for a while. It was particularly bad some days and my drive home after work was fraught with the danger of my driving off the road due to falling asleep at the wheel. At least good had come from something!

Sheila had been trying to get me to see her mentor, Austin, as she had run out of ideas for me, so I duly went to see him in the middle of the year, thinking to myself that I wished I had never started on this crusade for the natural answer, at least my creams worked. Anton's theory was that my adrenal glands were burned out and my liver was not functioning properly. This all made sense given my many years of emotional and financial stress, so I duly began his programme of treatment, including a liver test, which necessitated my weaning myself off caffeine for a few days. As I also could not take any analgesics whilst doing the test, I had to make sure I had weaned myself fully from caffeine sufficiently to avoid a caffeine withdrawal headache, as I had no access to painkillers.

I performed all the various chores of the test over one weekend and on the Sunday night I posted it off for the results. I saw Austin about three weeks later and it was as he had thought, the first filtering part of my liver was not working properly and any hormone I was manufacturing was not actually getting to the parts of my body where it was needed. My adrenal glands were also pretty well "burnt out" so they were not manufacturing anything either. Austin duly put me on to a regime of about 12 tablets a day, in an effort to calm and heal my adrenals and to kick start my malfunctioning liver. It was a matter of waiting for a couple of months to see if his remedies were going to work on me.

During this time I continued to see Sheila, who still preached gloom and doom about my immune system and blood pressure! I would go to her for a massage feeling "quite good" for me, and by the time I left, following her dire warnings of my failing systems, would slink away feeling I was at death's door. The Workers' Compensation insurers were also calling for a check-up with their own doctor to see where I was with healing of my back injury.

I went to see the insurance doctor, and once again this ability I have of having people open up to me about themselves, came into play. I had been in his consulting room for about 15 minutes and during that time I learned lots about his past career path, likes, dislikes and current state of contentment with his working lot in life! Almost as an afterthought he gave me a cursory check-up, asked me what symptoms I was still experiencing and what I currently wanted to do. I told him I wanted off the workers' compensation merry-go-round and he agreed that it would probably be best to sign me off with a compensation payment for my partial disability. I was quite happy with that but Sheila was not and there ensued a war of words between us, ending with me demanding to be left to sort out my life in my way without everybody telling me what to do.

Whilst all this was going on I had managed to get myself rear-ended in my car whilst standing at the lights, on my way home, early in May. I did not think much about it at the time, except that it felt like an almighty hit and I was surprised to see so little damage to the back of my car in comparison to the strength of the impact that I felt. Once again I was off to the doctor to try and avoid problems with whiplash and at first it did not appear that I had sustained too much damage at all. However, by the beginning of August I was starting to realise that my back aches and pains were in a different place and in actual fact my neck and shoulders were feeling very sore. So after hopefully signing off with worker's comp. for my accident on the bus, I was now back on the merry go round with the Third Party Insurance Claims with regard to my neck and shoulders! Meanwhile, the flushes marched merrily on.

From the beginning of the year we had been hearing about the purported trip to Italy that Alex's Italian teacher, was hoping to organise for her Italian students class, later in the year. We had several meetings for the parents and students that were interested in the trip and then in June it was finally accepted and approved by both the school and the Education Minister. It is amazing how things work out, if I had sold my house two years earlier when I had tried to do so, I could not have afforded to send Alex on the trip. Because, however, I managed to sell the house this year there was money available to finance her trip and she was able to go with the group.

As Alex had had several setbacks caused by her GF during the year, as the time for departure got closer I began to pray vehemently that Alex would maintain her good recovery from GF and be able to go, so it was with a sigh of relief that on the 22 September we saw her and 10 of her classmates, plus staff, off to Italy for just over three weeks. We had decided to also get away for a week, and I had booked accommodation for Keith and I in Albany, so the day after we saw Alex off to Italy we drove down to Albany for the week.

Our accommodation in Albany was basic but very comfortable, being a self-contained unit comprising of a lounge, kitchen, two bedrooms and bathroom.

The back of the units faced on to a small lake on which numerous ducks of all types swam and quacked their way through the day. Two particularly large ducks, obviously well used to being fed titbits from the holiday makers, regularly came to the back door each morning looking for crumbs. We were about a 20 minute walk from the nearest beach and about a 3 minute drive into Albany town centre.

We quickly got into a routine of getting up about 7.00am, having breakfast then going for a walk somewhere. Sometimes to the beach, a walk up to Mt Clarence, or driving first and walking once we got to our destination. We visited the Sandalwood Factory, Denmark, the old fort in Albany, the usual tourist places *viz*: the Blow Holes, Salmon Holes and Jimmy Newell's Harbour, to name a few. It was a good exercise in pre-checking places, which would be good for the family to visit when we all came down to Albany in the January of 2007, as we were planning a family holiday at the beginning of that year.

We really liked Albany and were struck by how well maintained the old buildings had been kept, so there was a real sense of history in the town. The undulations of the terrain, with its houses all facing out to the King Sound, all added to a sense of spaciousness and fresh air and further enforced our anticipated enjoyment of the family holiday there.

Healthwise 2006 had been a terrible year. Alex with her glandular fever, and me having on-going problems with the bus accident and then the whiplash. The only bright events to look back on have been the birth of my fourth grandson, Leo and Alex and Shaun's successes with their CEROC; first in March, here in Perth and in June, when they travelled to Sydney and took part in the NSW CEROC Championships there. Once again, they won their Intermediate event, but added to this was a successful entry into the "Showcase" part of the competitions, when despite being up against dancers with longer experience in CEROC, they managed a very compendable third placing in that event. However, with the sale of Beaufortia and an end to my financial miseries a feeling of optimism is the prevailing emotion and I at last look forward to a fresh start to the second half of my life.

2007

One morning in 2007 I got up and prepared to go to work as normal. My tinnitus was particularly loud and as I was getting dressed, I was assailed by the most awful, gut wrenching dizzy spell. I slid to the floor in the bathroom and was violently and constantly sick! The experience was a nightmare, made worse because Keith had gone to work and Alex was staying over with a friend. I was unable to stand and could not open my eyes as the constantly spinning made me vomit again. I thought I was having a stroke.

I managed to call an ambulance then realised they would not be able to get in when they got here so I crawled, feeling my way through the bedroom door and into the passage, down to the front door and with great difficulty managed to unlock and open it. After which I just lay in the hall, continuing to dry retch.

The ambulance crew duly arrived and compassionately dealt with me, stretchering me to the ambulance. I had to keep my eyes closed because I could not bear to experience the vertigo with them open. I was transported to hospital where they proceeded to check for heart attack, stroke, x-ray (for brain tumour) then injected me with an anti-emetic to stop me from continuing to dry retch. I was held in emergency for 5 hours until the vertigo finally stopped, leaving me feeling very nauseous and totally drained, achey and feeling as though I had been run over by a Mack truck. Of course, I have never actually experienced being run over by a Mack truck but I am sure I would have felt that way! I had not, however, had a stroke, heart attack and appeared not to have a tumour, at least.

The following days showed a temporary lessening of my tinnitus but I felt very seedy – like a prolonged hangover but without the enjoyment initially experienced in the getting said condition.

There followed many appointments with ENT specialists, who ultimately diagnosed Meniere's Disease. No one really knows what brings on Meniere's it can be caused by a heavy knock to the head or even a virus. Both of which I had experienced in 2004 – the tinnitus started in 2004 – 2005.

2007 was shaping up to be not much better than 2006 – only this time it was me that was having health problems. I seemed to fall down a lot! I was advised to go on a salt free diet. I had no idea it was so difficult to stay free of salt. Everything has salt in it apparently, but this was the first stage of treatment in Meniere's Disease. Going out at lunch time was fraught with danger! I was now working at the Family Court of WA and one day I was coming back with lunch for myself and my Magistrate when I actually fell up the steps to the Courts. I tried valiantly to save the Magistrate's hamburger but this left no hands to break my fall so landed squarely on my forehead! I sat there for a while, stunned, then gradually stood up and wobbled back to my office. I walked into my boss's office where she recoiled in horror at the huge "egg" now forming on my forehead! I would trip without apparent cause and finished up with bumps and bruises. My worst injury, however, was when I forgot there were two more steps to go down when leaving the post office and putting out my hands to protect myself, landed on my right wrist. Once again I stood up, feeling very shaky and surveying my arm thought it pertinent to take myself to hospital. Fortunately, I was in Victoria Avenue so only had to walk up the hill to Royal Perth. I must have looked dreadful when I arrived in Emergency and they took me straight through. It transpired that I had both dislocated and broken my wrist. So they had to first fix the dislocation then transferred me to another hospital to have surgery on my broken wrist.

After I eventually got back to work, my workmates tried to dissuade me from going out at lunchtimes, because they couldn't be sure I would get back in one piece.

My vertigo attacks continued through 2007 and 2008, some I could contain by sitting totally motionless for a couple of hours (very embarrassing in the workplace) but others I could not stop and would end up sitting in the toilet for ages vomiting and waiting to be picked up by Keith (if I was at work).

During 2009 my condition really deteriorated. One day in particular I will always remember. We had just finished a court hearing and I felt the now dreaded onset of an attack. My Court Officer, Peter, literally had to help me from the court room, through the packed area outside and into my office, after which I rushed off to the ladies. My hearing had also deteriorated to the point that I now wore a hearing aid and the catch phrase from me was "Come round to my left side" and friends knew not to whisper their secrets into my right ear – although they would have been safe – I had not heard a word.

Meniere's Disease is not a life threatening disease but it makes you wish you could die sometimes! I had half a dozen trips by ambulance to hospital to obtain intravenous fluids after prolonged days of sickness and vertigo.

Having trodden upon the primary rungs of treatment, no salt, no alcohol, no sweet stuff, no caffeine – no life really – I was told about the Meniett Device (MD).

The MD works on the principle of stabilising the pressure build up in the offending ear – you know, that feeling you get on a plane when you need to clear your ears – unfortunately with Meniere's there is not the luxury of being able to get rid of that pressure but the MD works by artificially releasing the pressure for you.

Before you can use an MD you have to have a grommit put into your ear to facilitate the air entering directly into the eardrum. So in 2010 I entered hospital to have this done under local anaesthetic. The days running up to the operation were fraught with anxiety, as I felt I had to be well enough to undergo the procedure in order to use the MD – upon which I was pinning a lot of hope of a more normal life. The vertigo attacks are so sudden. Sometimes you can feel an impending attack looming over days, usually by the ever increasing tinnitus, and at other times you can be feeling relatively okay and wham! your head suddenly begins to spin. It is caused by conflicting messages from your ears to your brain – from the balance organs within the ear – It's like trying to make sense of scrambled eggs. One ear – the faulty one is sending one message – and the other the okay ear, is sending another, whereupon the poor old brain throws up its metaphorical hands and says "Enough! Can't make sense of any of this, let's have a vertigo attack"!

The attack passes after 4 – 5 hours when the brain eventually manages to make sense from the good ear and the dizziness stops, leaving chaos, debris and misery in its wake.

Thus I really wanted this operation, and I prayed that on the day I would be okay to have it. I was okay and the grommit was input mid-2010.

My vertigo attacks were becoming very frequent, to the point that in May 2010 I had to make the hard decision to leave the Family Courts as I could not guarantee I could turn up the next day for work which of course, is a hopeless situation for everyone. I was really sad to leave my job as I loved it. I also thought maybe working closer to home, would cut down on my stress levels, travelling to and from Perth from Ellenbrook (an hour each time).

Around the time I was waiting for my operation, my son's daughter, Sophie Rose was born. So after I finished work on the 29th May 2010, I drove into Perth after work and because I was a bit tired I bought myself a coffee at the hospital and proceeded to their room. Bad mistake – caffeine!

Unfortunately, Anne had needed a caesarean operation to produce Sophie so both she and Brad looked the worse for wear when I got there. However, Sophie was gorgeous and I was very much enjoying seeing her for the first time. Half hour into my visit I felt those awful first signs of an impending vertigo attack and poor Brad had to drive me home to Ellenbrook in my car. That was a stressful journey in itself, as being from Jurien he wasn't sure of the route to Ellenbrook from Subiaco, I had to try and visualise the route and guide him home, peering out periodically from almost closed eyes to see where we were! Clutching my (always present these days) vomit bag! We eventually made it home, and fortunately, a friend of Alex's was at the house and he lived in Mt Lawley, so he offered to drive Brad to the hospital to finish his visit and get his car.

So the next phase of dealing with Meniere's began. Three times a day I would insert the lead from the MD into my ear and feel the familiar puffs of pressure into the eardrum. My MD became my full time companion. I took it everywhere with me and tried it for six months, however, after this time I wasn't at all sure it was working. Were my attacks any less frequent? I couldn't really tell. So I stopped using it and reluctantly decided I needed the more drastic treatment, as the disease was sapping my energy, health and above all my self-confidence to go anywhere without someone with me, and indeed, hold down a job. I did have a position closer to home for about three months, but this did not work out so I left and had to rely upon my superannuation income insurance payments to augment our house income.

The next phase of treatment was to have Gentamicin injections directly into the eardrum, to kill off the balance mechanism in that ear, thus stopping the confused balance messages reaching my brain, it would then "listen" to the okay ear and keep me upright. The downside to this is that it can also affect the hearing organ on that side and make one's deafness worse. Well, I had already lost 70% of the hearing in that ear anyway so there wasn't much of a decision to make, if it meant I might stop having these vertigo attacks.

So I had two treatments at Sir Charles Gairdner Hospital ENT Department, with my dear friend, Wendy, driving me there and back home again. Wendy was a wonderful friend to me during this time and would often drive me to places because it was too dangerous to drive alone as the attacks would come on so suddenly and could cause an accident.

The treatments themselves weren't too bad, but the two or three days afterwards left me feeling quite sick and incapacitated. After the treatments, however, even though I still had a dizzy spell, that's what they were "dizzy spells" and not all out vertigo attacks. I had to continue with my fairly strict diet however, and still do watch what I eat.

Whilst at the hospital on one of my visits, the doctor told me about Clonazepam. He told me that in the USA, from where he hailed, they had been using this drug to treat the symptoms of Meniere's. The idea being that when I feel an attack coming on, I take one of these pills and the attack, will usually pass – but only after the Gentamicin treatment. So I took his advice and still use it to this day when I feel a little wobbly.

2007

$\mathcal{B}$efore all my drama began with Meniere's Samantha and Dan decided they would like to try a country stint in an effort to save a little money. So Dan put in an application for the police job in Geraldton and got it. Samantha had obtained a job she liked and was working at Joondalup hospital so it was quite a wrench for her to move, but rentals in Perth were really expensive and they had no hope of saving if they stayed there. Brad and Anne were also up that way, in Jurien Bay, so it was quite convenient for us to visit both of them in one go, with just a slight detour up to or on the way back from Geraldton.

We spent most Christmases in Geraldton with the exception of one year when Brad set up a huge tent in his back garden and we all went there for Christmas. Apart from being eaten alive by mosquitoes it went very well and we enjoyed our time together. The sea breezes were a welcome relief from the heat of Ellenbrook.

The house they rented in Geraldton, seemed, on first viewing to be great for them, with a huge family dining area and cover patio. The wind there however, was a nightmare inasmuch as the dust being blown over everything. They lived on a comparatively new estate so there were a lot of empty blocks and also next to a big open bush area. So dust and sand was a big problem. After three years the conditions became unbearable though as they started preparing the open space next to them for building. The noise and dirt blowing in became really bad and when the compound machines were used the vibrations in the house were such that sitting on a settee or chair transformed into a vibrating machine!

Alex, too had her drama during 2007. I returned home from a country circuit stint with the Courts, to find Alex with an apparent tummy bug. Stomach pains, and vomiting. We put up with it for the weekend. We did go to Swan Districts Hospital on the Saturday night, but after waiting for nearly four hours – with Alex in acute discomfort – we went home. On the Monday, I decided she had to see a doctor, which was just as well because he sent her straight away for an

223

ultrasound and it was seen that her appendix was very inflamed. They rang ahead to Joondalup Hospital emergency and we drove straight there. The staff put her through triage straight away. To help with the pain she was given a morphine injection, and it was then we discovered she inherited her grandmother's allergy to the drug and began to feel really unwell. Fortunately she did not have an anaphylactic shock, but the doctor advised that she never have it again.

She was taken for surgery and was in a lot of pain when she came round, as unfortunately she couldn't have the usual painkiller after the operation but was given pethidine instead, which caused her to be really sick for the next couple of days. So instead of being released home after an overnight stay, she was kept in hospital for four or five days, until she stopped vomiting.

We spent Christmas in Geraldton/Jurien Bay as Dan and Samantha had not long ago had their fifth child, Lincoln. He was born in October so travelling down to Perth was out of the question.

After Christmas Keith, Alex and I travelled over to Tasmania at the end of December for a visit with the Michael and Helen and some sightseeing. Michael and Helen have completely revamped an older home to suit their needs for Helen's music school teaching. They have a lovely view from their balcony over the sports oval behind them and they are a short walk to the beach.

Tasmania is a lovely place to visit. So many beautiful little towns and surrounded by the mountains – it reminded me a lot of Hawaii, apart from the climate of course. We drove up to Launceston from Hobart going up the East coast, visiting Bicheno, Coles Bay and saw Wineglass Bay with its breathtaking views of the crystal clear sea on white, fine sand beaches. We spent New Year's Eve in Launceston, in a motel, Alex and I went out in search of appropriate party attire and came back with ridiculous, sequin covered red and blue top hats. We bought some lemon, lime and bitters for Alex and some champagne for us and proceeded to pass the evening playing games, then watched a movie and later we were treated to a firework display being set off at the park opposite our motel. Alex was very merry and after looking at her bottle of lemon, lime and bitters we realised we had inadvertently bought her the alcoholic version! Getting our 14 year old daughter tipsy!

We took in all the beauty spots around Launceston, including a village called Grindewald, modelled on a Swiss Chalet complex, we visited a seahorse farm and then began the return to Hobart via the inland Heritage Highway. From there we drove down to Port Arthur and stayed in a small, but nicely modernised cottage, just outside the main town. We decided to take the Ghost Tour through Port Arthur that night, but considering its harrowing past, it wasn't as eerie as I expected it to be however, it was very interesting. It had its effect on Alex though and I slept with her that night!

Simon wasn't staying as long as Alex and I, and also her boyfriend at the time, Tim, was joining us from Melbourne. So we duly delivered Keith to the airport to take his flight back to Perth and picked up Tim the following day. I collected a hire car as there were too many of us to fit into Michael and Helen's car.

We travelled to Mt Field and walked to Russell Falls and picnicked for lunch, finishing the day back at Bellerive Beach eating fish and chips on the beach – very spectacular as we watched the sun go down over the horizon.

We had a scary drive up the side of Mt Wellington, very near the edge! The views were wonderful from the top but I was glad to get back down to lower ground.

Alex and Tim flew back to Perth before me. I stayed on for a few more days to spend them with Michael and Helen and then I returned to WA on the 12 January 2008.

I loved Tasmania. I would love to live there but the rest of my family is in WA so unless we all up stakes and go – highly unlikely – there isn't much chance of that.

2008/2009/2010

*B*y this time I was fully ensconced in and enjoying my work at the Family Court of Western Australia (FCWA). I had been offered the job at the end of April 2007 and in the middle of July I had my first taste of going on a country circuit.

We travelled down to Bunbury to spend the week there hearing cases and conferences. To say the General Lists in Bunbury are hectic is to make a massive understatement! The court room is about two thirds the size of the Perth courtroom and everybody and their dog who has anything to do with a case being heard manages to cram into the court. Add to that sometimes, that the internet connection to the appointments section back in Perth sometimes doesn't work properly, and the job of making forward hearing dates becomes rather difficult. There are always a massive amount of files, affidavits and correspondence to transport to Bunbury that keeping a track on it all and looking as businesslike as possible can sometimes become a challenge!

On one of these circuits, when we arrived to take the files, etc up to the Court room, we found the lift from the basement to the second floor was out of action and no one had warned us. We had, therefore, not allowed the extra time to physically carry all these files and paraphernalia up two flights of stairs and consequently by the time Peter and I had finished doing this we were both exhausted and the hearing start had been delayed by about 15 minutes. The ensuing chaos, due to our not being able to set up things as we normally did provided our Magistrate (as she later informed us) with a performance no less amusing than a Keystone Cops film with one or both of us scrabbling around trying to locate the appropriate Affidavit for the file and still look as though we knew what we were doing. Despite all this, we all enjoyed the country circuits as in the evenings we had a chance to socialise a little between ourselves and the local barristers.

Alex's dancing successes continued as she and her partner Shaun, won nearly every competition category they entered. I look back on this period and view it as a whirlwind of trying to keep working through the vertigo attacks, trying various methods of controlling the symptoms and in between many trips up to Geraldton to see Samantha and Dan when possible. We also found ourselves going for a short stay at Denham, as Brad and Anne moved up there for a while, during the time their house in Jurien Bay was being extended and renovated.

By the beginning of 2010, however, my vertigo attacks were becoming so frequent I was missing a great deal of work and had to seriously consider leaving. I really did not want to leave FCWA but my lack of reliability due to ill health was becoming a problem to myself and to my employers. So much so that in May 2010 I decided to resign and try and obtain a position closer to home, which I did but even this did not help the attacks and their frequency.

In the midst of my problems Samantha found she was pregnant again in 2010. I knew she desperately wanted another girl, but they really had not planned on a sixth child and the whole situation caused problems between Samantha and Dan. She came down to Perth for an amniocentesis test and it was ultimately confirmed in the July that she was expecting a perfectly healthy baby girl. I couldn't help comparing her experience to mine all those years ago, when I was undergoing the self-same test and being told I was expecting a perfectly healthy baby girl. History repeating itself. She was well but tired right up to the last few weeks, but began having health problems, to the point that she was flown down to King Edward Hospital to wait out the last few weeks, on complete bed rest, and so began an almost daily trek from Ellenbrook to Subiaco to visit Samantha, in an effort to stop her going mad with the inactivity.

Eventually, on the 29th November baby Angela was born. Samantha continued to have a few problems after the birth, but after about a week we once again travelled up to Geraldton to escort mother and new baby home.

At the end of 2010, Dan applied for a position in Albany so in January 2011 we travelled up to Geraldton again to help clean and pack for their move down South.

2011/2012

*A*t the beginning of January we drove down from Geraldton with Samantha, the children and two of their four cats to Perth. Dan stayed behind to finish up the cleaning and to bring down the remaining two cats a couple of days later.

The children were camped en masse in our lounge, Samantha and Angela had our bedroom, I slept in with Alex and Keith slept in the office! Added to this we had two cats camped in our laundry in an effort to avoid a feline war with our own five cats and a dog. Chaos! Fortunately, the pool was a saving grace, keeping the children happy during the day. Dan followed a couple of days later with the other two cats but mercifully he left the following day to go on down to Albany with the cats.

Conrad and Wendy joined our little band of travellers, both two legged and four, and on the 7th our caravan travelled down to Albany. It took us six hours and was somewhat excruciating.

Keith stayed back at Ellenbrook to work and housesit. Alex, Conrad and I stayed at the Albany Holiday Park – Wendy was going to join us but opted to stay with her son. Our cabin was basic but comfortable, but in any case we were only there to sleep, spending all day at Samantha and Dan's new house unpacking seemingly endless boxes! However, by the Sunday we had made good headway and decided to have a little look around at Emu Point. It was such a relief to be away from the oppressive heat of Perth. Conrad left the following day and Wendy and I drove back on the 10th.

The night after I got back, Alex's beloved cat Timmi, did not come back at his usual time for his evening meal. At about 9.00pm I noticed a "streak of white" out of the corner of my eye fly past the window outside. A few moments later there was a knock at the front door and a lady was standing there asking if I had "a white coloured cat". I said yes and much to my alarm she informed me it had just run under her car and headed in this direction. I rapidly thanked her and rushed outside to see if I could find Timmi. I found him cowering on the bathroom windowsill, looking very shaken, but outwardly uninjured apart from a slight graze on his ear and the top of one of his legs. He had passed right under her car, narrowly missing being squash ed. I never told Alex about this (she was thankfully at work at the time) for a couple of years. Needless to say, I was very careful about getting him inside by dusk after that.

At least the Gentamicin treatment had lessened my vertigo attacks, and together with the extra pills suggested by the ENT specialist I was managing to keep going relatively well.

In February 2011 Big W opened in Ellenbrook and much to my surprise was obtained a position at that store – in the Fitting Rooms. I was also in charge of incoming calls and enquiries and the loudspeaker. It wouldn't have been too bad if the actual desk of the fitting room had been open with just the fitting rooms themselves enclosed, that way I could keep an eye on the mens' and womens' apparel sections. The amount of shoplifting that went on and does go on, in large stores is a real eye opener.

The pilfering of underwear is the hardest to detect, especially as the thieves usually wait until there are a few people waiting for tags before they come out and quickly hand in their tags and disappear. As soon as possible I would check the fitting rooms and sometimes find tags ripped off new bras and undies, where they had kept them on, re-dressed and quickly exited, by which time it was too late the get them stopped at the shop exit! Although, even then it is difficult to check if someone's underwear is their own! I did ask a couple of times to be moved from the fitting rooms and out on to the floor, but they wanted me to stay put, so in the interests of avoiding my brain going to train oil through lack of use, I reluctantly resigned after six months.

I continued to travel back and forth to Albany as and when the need arose. With Samantha and Dan in jobs with sometimes conflicting shifts it was sometimes necessary for a third person to be there to help out with the children.

We had been notified earlier in 2011 that Jessica, Alex's cousin, was getting married in Melbourne and we had decided we would all go over. Keith did not go but Alex, Conrad, and his family and I all booked our airfares for the 19th November. However, a couple of months beforehand we were told the wedding was off. We all wondered whether or not to go anyway and decided we would to give them all a bit of moral support.

Conrad and Erin had gone over with the rest of the family before Alex and I so they met us at the airport and after a quick visit to Nick, Lacey and June, we went to our hotel. It was basic but comfortable and centrally situated in Melbourne. We visited the Melbourne Museum because there was an Egyptian exhibition being held there and spent an interesting and absorbing couple of hours perusing ancient Egyptian relics, including the tomb of TutanKhamen. After a few days in Melbourne Alex and I flew over to Hobart to catch up with Michael, Helen and Tarshi again. It was a visit that was all too short as we had a lot of fun and Alex and Tarshi got on really well.

By 2013 Alex had changed dance partners and was now dancing with Jessup. They were doing really well and travelling to as many interstate and overseas competitions as they could afford. She also had a new boyfriend, Carson, and when at the end of January I brought the girls up from Albany for a short stay, mainly so they could see the Sky show on the 26th, Alex and Carson had a great time in the pool with them. They also took them to the movies one night, which was a bit of a break for me, even though Holly and Sandra really are quite self-sufficient.

I continued to apply for both full time and part time jobs and had a fair few "oh so close" disappointments but in hindsight it was just as well as I spent a great deal of time travelling to and from Albany during 2013, so it would have been a problem with a job! I did manage a couple of temporary assignments.

We also began making arrangements for Alex's 21st birthday. She wanted it to be at the Wembley Hotel White Room – just a fairly small affair with family and friends. One of the rare occasions when both Brad and Anne and Samantha were at a social function together. It was a good evening with lots of her dance friends. It went on until 1.00am then Alex and her friends were going on elsewhere to continue the night.

Late in 2011 Alex and Jessup started organising the WCS group, as they are the most advanced in that dance genre in WA. However, after about a year things started to go a little sour, as quite often happens when money and business enter a friendship. So together with her part time work at Video Ezy and running these evenings two and three times per week she was kept really busy. In between all this she was travelling interstate and overseas to earn the extra points needed from competition to gain their "Advanced" status. In April 2012 a group of them from the WCS travelled over to the USA for a stay of up to five weeks. They toured around the various competitions from place to place, as WCS is much more active over there with big monetary prizes. It was also the only way to advance their dance status. They did extremely well and came back by far one of the most experienced and credentialed dancers in the genre in Australia.

In May I travelled down to Albany to spend some time with Samantha and Co. and whilst I was there I received a phone call from one of my job applications, wanting me to come for an interview. As I was still in Albany when I received the call I arranged to leave early on the Friday morning and call in to see him on the way home. It was an enjoyable visit for a change, with none of the children sick, and we also got to have coffee with Wendy who had moved down to Albany earlier in the year.

It was around this time that Keith started talking about eventually retiring and maybe moving down to live in Albany, to be near Samantha and Dan for the long haul. I was in two minds about this as I still enjoyed having Alex at home and it would mean we would have to sell the Ellenbrook house in order to do it. We would, of course, make sure Alex had somewhere to go but still I was very torn by the whole idea, closer to Samantha but further away from Alex and Brad.

My job interview went well – it was five days a week, but just six hour days and only 30 minutes from home, so after a weekend to think about it I accepted the position as Administrative Assistant for Australian Seniors, based in Swan View and started there on 28th May.

The job was as secretary to the State Manager, but also I did the administrative work for the five rental villages in the State and also two residential estates. It was a difficult job to settle into though, because the lady that had been there was not available and the only other person in the office, Samantha the Accountant, didn't know anything about her job! My boss spent a lot of time travelling around visiting the villages. I have always believed, however, that the first six weeks in any job are not very pleasant; learning the ropes and becoming familiar with the work. Out head office was in Brisbane so every Monday there was a telephone "meeting" of the State Managers with me taking the Minutes. There were also five or six reports to complete for this meeting, so I tried to prepare as much as possible on the Friday, with only the last minutes details to be added on the Monday morning.

Around this time Alan, Alex's grandfather, suffered a slight heart attack and developed pneumonia and low blood pressure. Joan was not doing too well either, with her immediate memory facility deteriorating quite alarmingly. He was in hospital for a week then was sent home for bed rest. Because Joan was also a little unsteady on her legs, it was decided that they would have separate rooms to allow for the hospital bed for Alan. Neither of them were very happy with the arrangement – they had been married over 60 years and never slept apart.

With working practically full time and Keith also working his unsocial hours, we decided we needed a cleaner for a couple of hours. We arranged for Leanne to come and clean during the week.

We also tried to get down to Albany as much as possible at the weekends and when possible we took Alex with us because the children loved seeing her and she them, but inevitably if there was any kind of virus to be had the children seemed to get it and then Alex!

One day on my way home from work my car just stopped! I was waiting at a busy intersection lights when a light I had not seen before lit up on my dash board. When I tried to drive off there was no acceleration and I literally trickled across the intersection praying I would get to the other side. I managed to glide in neutral over to the shoulder of the road and it just stopped. I waited for the RAC who told me that there was a hole in my radiator and the failsafe system had closed down the engine because of the loss of fluid. When it was investigated the remains of a small bird were discovered in the radiator. We must have picked it up during one of our trips to Albany and it had stayed in place for a while then began to drop out causing a leakage. So lucky it was in the metropolitan area and not en route to or from Albany.

Things more or less flowed through 2012 including the fluctuating hearing in my right ear. Every so often for some unknown reason the hearing capacity would increase in my "deaf" ear, necessitating my hearing aid being adjusted occasionally. We travelled back and forth from Perth to Albany when we could. We told Samantha and Dan we would ultimately move down to Albany to be near them, but I don't think they really believed us.

I continued the search for a remedy to my menopause symptoms to no avail. I needed to stop using the patches I had been using because the oestrogen was causing fibroids in my uterus. The answer being use oestrogen and have fibroids, have an hysterectomy and use oestrogen but risk breast cancer! I pursued natural remedies and began a series of pills recommended by a chemist who specialised in natural therapy. I gave it a good go for four months but even he gave up on me after that.

The months rolls inexorably on towards Christmas and once again we were going down to Albany to spend it with Samantha and Dan. The children finished our Christmas stay with a nice bout of gastro, which only just stopped in time for us to leave to return to Perth with a clear conscience. We had a quiet start to 2013, which was very welcome after the turmoil of Christmas.

2013/2014

*T*he start to 2013 was rather sad in that Alan's condition had deteriorated and he was back in hospital with the doctors not really knowing what was wrong with him, but that he was getting weaker. He tried several times to get himself out of bed but only proceeded in falling and fluctuated between being awake and aware to being practically unconscious. It was awful to see him wasting away like this and was very hard on the family. Alex found it hard to visit him because seeing her dear Bampa like this really upset her.

Alex, Keith, Conrad and I decided to take another trip to Tasmania mainly because it was Michael's 70th birthday on the 3rd February, and we decided to leave WA at the end of January. Things were a little unsettled at work. There appeared to be a problem between Brisbane and my boss (and that in turn meant me), so it would be interesting to see if I had a job when I came back, as they were talking about taking all the administrative side of WA over to Brisbane. However, much to my surprise just before I went on leave I received a letter from our new owners saying I had earned a bonus of $728.00! I was still not sure though how things would be when I got back though.

We went to visit Alan for his 88th birthday. By this time he was in a nursing home as St David's where both he and Joan had been living, could not care for him enough as he was now high dependency and Joan, herself, was now quite dependent also. He was semi with us but not quite. We all sang "Happy Birthday" and cut his cake but he wasn't really with us.

We flew out on 31st January and arrived at a wet Melbourne, followed by an equally wet Hobart. A bit of a shock after +40deg heat in Perth! Because there were so many of us and we had the corresponding amount of luggage we hired a car for the weekend at the airport. After a bit of a delay picking up the car, as there was a long queue waiting, we followed Michael to their place, where we stayed up chatting until really late.

The next day we decided to go for a ride to the top of Mt Wellington. It was so cold it actually snowed – in February – it snowed! That night we were entertained by Tarshi and his two Chinese friends, who were also staying with Michael and Helen. It was truly a houseful. We four were sleeping, dormitory style, in beds in the music studio downstairs, whilst the two girls were sleeping in the spare bedroom. On The Saturday we had the obligatory trip to Salamanca Markets for breakfast followed by a quick re-visit to Port Arthur – Conrad had not been there before. That evening we went to dinner with a few of Michael's friends to celebrate his birthday and a good time was had by all.

The Monday was our pick up day for the Maui Camper van we were hiring for our trip around Tasmania, so we were up bright and early to pack, clear out our beds and be on our way by 10.00am. We got lost once trying to find the camper hire company but after a while found it and after having been shown around our home for the next two weeks, we settled down to watch a DVD about the unit. We then returned the hire car and set out on our travels. Alex was our navigator.

Our first port of call was the Lake St Clair campsite. Our camp plot was a little isolated from the ablutions block, but nonetheless picturesque with the lake within viewing distance of our van. We managed to get a meal at the local eatery and made our way back, in the dark – without torches – to the van, whereupon we set about putting together the various beds. It was at this point that we realised how little of the introductory DVD we had actually absorbed, part of which was the bed setting up process! We tied ourselves in knots trying to set up the three beds, and laughed ourselves silly. So much so that the couple in the next door van enquired as to whether we needed any help to do the task. We did eventually get them set up, however, and settled down to sleep. We used the on board toilet facilities but soon realised the capacity was somewhat limited. Our destination for the next day was Cradle Mountain and an overnight stop at a place called Waratah. None of us were experienced in camper vanning so the search for a "dumping site" for the sewerage was done by looking on a map we had on board showing where all the various sites for this could be found.

In Tasmania the roads are very twisty and bendy so it takes a while to get from A to B. We soon realised we were not going to get to our Wednesday destination and booked cruise in time, so Alex quickly changed our reservation to the following day, Thursday.

We eventually got to Cradle Mountain, although by this time the trip was somewhat spoiled by the ever increasing smell creeping through the cab from the sewerage tank! I wasn't sure if these "dumping stations" were manned and was beginning to panic in case we got there only to find they had closed and the idea of trying to sleep in the van with the ever increasing pong was not a pleasant one. We soon learned that these stations were just places alongside the road with a special pump for the purpose of emptying one's tank. So with much relief we did the deed quickly, although the disappearance of the smell took a bit longer.

We were pleasantly surprised by our first view of Waratah, which is a picturesque little town, built on a hill at the centre of which is a working waterfall/mill. We picked up our key (again as arranged by Alex, because we were hopelessly running late by this stage) and found to our delight that the ablutions block was quite close (we were to learn to appreciate this fact throughout out trip), with heated showers and a free laundry facility. This time we were more organised and had bought a quiche for our evening meal, and ate this with a salad and settled down to an enjoyable evening playing cards.

Our destination the next day was to Stanley, via Burnie. Keith realised we were running low on diesel and made our way to the only petrol station in Waratah, before we even stopped the van, however, a man came d Andrew ing out of the office madly waving his arms at us to stop. Keith was in the process of doing so and asked him what all the flap was about. The garage owner (for that's who it was) went on to tell us, in a non-too friendly manner, that his overhead canopy outside the office had been knocked off several times by people driving vans such as ours and forgetting how tall they were! Keith had been fully aware of the height of our van, but this man was now obviously paranoid about vans like ours. He then went on to inform us he had no diesel! Now this was serious as Keith had no idea how much fuel was in the tank and it was showing "empty". We had no alternative but to drive towards our ultimate destination and pray we hit a petrol station before we ran out of fuel. To say it was nerve wracking is an understatement. Keith crawled along to conserve what fuel we had and it was with the greatest relief that about 40 kms into our trip we trickled into a Shell station, but only just. The tank had nearly emptied.

We weren't overly impressed by Burnie. It seemed a rather uninspiring town. We called into the local Visitors' Centre and picked up some brochures depicting places of interest. One of them outlined an eatery called "Annsleigh" not far out of the town, so we went there for lunch. It was a lovely little olde worlde restaurant set in the most beautiful gardens, still bright with summer flowering plants. We had a tasty meal but didn't linger too long as we knew it would take us a while to get to Stanley and wanted to get there before dark.

Once again, Alex had called ahead to a caravan site which we found was literally beside the sea harbour. So after parking for the night we wandered down towards the town and found a fish and chip shop right near the beach and settled down for a very welcome meal of fish and chips. Once again, we played cards until about 10.30 and went to bed.

We drove into Arthur River early the next morning to catch our boat for the river cruise along the river. We were escorted on our trip by a family of sea eagles, obviously well known by the boat owner, as he proceeded to feed them fish from the side of the boat. The boat then docked by a small clearing with a hut in it, for a picnic lunch, after which we were taken for a lovely walk through the rain forest further inland. We were out until about 4.00 and drove back to Stanley. We decided to eat at the Stanley hotel that night and thoroughly enjoyed the meal. There was certainly plenty of it. We waddled back to the van.

We spent the morning in Stanley. Alex wanted to go up by cable car to the local tourist spot called "The Nut", which as the name implied, was a very large mountain shaped like a nut. I was very apprehensive mainly because I don't really like heights but also, because of my Meniere's. Everything revolved around how my head would cope with new experiences because of my vertigo. The last year or so, however, the attacks had been much less distressing and I was beginning to get back my confidence, so I decided I would try out the cable car and with shaking legs I clambered aboard and waited to feel terrified. It was a lovely surprise therefore to find that a minute into the trip I was feeling not only fine, but exhilarated by the view and the whole experience. Conrad hadn't come because he really cannot stand heights, and opted to take a wander around the town instead. The cable car ride only lasted about five minutes and the view from the top of "The Nut" was breathtaking. I was so glad I had taken the chance and found I could cope okay.

Alex was intent on having strawberry pancakes for her birthday breakfast and we had pre-booked at the Strawberry Farm for this. The pancakes were truly spectacular and she had a lovely start to her birthday with a plate piled high with strawberries and cream. We all had the cooked breakfast, which was also available.

We were making for Launceston where the annual Wine and Food Festival was happening so after wandering around the festival, taking in the sights, sounds and smells, we took a walk around Launceston. This was our second trip to that city, and Conrad's first. Alex wanted some Ugg boots for her birthday, so we bought those at one of the tourist shops in the Mall. An hour into wearing them, however, and the soles were beginning to hang off, so when we ultimately returned to Hobart I packed them up with an accompanying letter of discontent as to the quality of their products and ultimately received another pair back with a letter of apology.

We made for a town called Longford to stay that night and ultimately drove back down to Hobart, calling in at a lovely little town called Richmond on the way. There are so many lovely, picturesque little towns in Tasmania and it makes travelling there so interesting as you do not have miles and miles of road and dust, as in WA, but small towns and villages to call in and look around.

We had thoroughly enjoyed our drive around and felt very much at home in the Maui but these things have to end and we arrived back in Hobart on the 10th February. We hadn't been back long when Alex, whilst perusing the website, came across an item about her WCS group back in Perth which did not mention her at all, just Jessup and his fiancée, Lina Alex did not know what was going on and was very upset when she left the room. I followed her and asked her what was wrong. She said she had just phoned Jessup - her dance and business partner – and he had told her he wanted Lina to have a more active role in the business and thus he was dissolving Alex's and his partnership to this end. Alex was understandably terribly surprised and upset by this sudden turn of events and both Conrad and I were livid with Jessup because of it. I rang Jessup after Alex left the room in tears and gave him a piece of my mind as did Conrad! We were so angry. Alex was even angrier with us for interfering but it was just so wrong. He had not said anything to Alex before she left and had just gone ahead and done it while she was away! She was still cross with us when, after an emotional farewell to Michael and Helen, we flew back to Melbourne that night, but we were not remorseful at all, it was a rotten thing for Jessup to do without telling Alex anything beforehand, apart from the hurt, she was humiliated as well and she did not deserve that.

We arrived back in Perth on the 11th to 39 deg heat! Such a contrast after the temperate climate of Tasmania. I was not due back to work until the following Thursday – Valentine's Day – and I was not sure whether there would be a job there or not, as things had been very uncertain before we left. The Operations Manager for WA had rung me before we left for Tasmania to tell me he was no longer working for Australian Seniors and I very much doubted that they would keep me on if they had removed the Operations Manager already.

On the Thursday I duly arrived at work to find an Eastern States official of the company waiting to hand me my letter of redundancy and informing me I could finish up that day. They did not want me to finish up the jobs I had in hand before I left even though I was quite happy to do so. In a way it was a relief to know at last but once again I was unemployed, so I decided to go down and spend a week with Samantha in Albany the following week.

We called in to see Alan, Alex and I, and he looked dreadful. His condition had deteriorated badly and it seemed it was just a matter of time before we lost him.

Before we left for Tasmania, Alex had applied for a position with Flight Centre as a travel consultant, an idea she had picked up earlier in the year when we went to a Trades Fair in Perth. Not long after we got back she heard she had got through to the second stage of recruitment for the job. I was still in Albany when I heard she had got a job with Flight Centre and they were just waiting to place her in an appropriate store. She ultimately was notified she had got a spot in the new Ellenbrook Flight Centre store. Couldn't be better timing as her interest with WCS had been sorely hit with the situation with her and Jessup's betrayal.

It was during 2013 we really started thinking seriously about moving down to Albany to live. I was truly torn, wanting to be there for Samantha and Dan and yet not wanting to leave Alex, as we would have to sell the house to fund our move down there. I had very mixed feelings about it, but also Keith was planning to retire next year also, so everything was pointing at 2014. In the meantime, however, I was till endeavouring to find a part time job. I had a few interviews but they were all full time and in Perth.

Alan was also sinking fast and ultimately passed away on the 12th March. We were all so sad and Joan couldn't quite understand what had happened to "her Alan" as her dementia had also escalated and she was very confused most of the time. His funeral was held a week later. It was held at the Perth Salvation Army Citadel and was a celebration of his life rather than mourning his passing. Alex took his passing very badly and I also felt really sad inside. He was a lovely man and his death left a hole in all our hearts.

I continued to drive up and down to Albany but now, we started having a look around at houses in the area. We looked at houses by themselves for Samantha and Dan and then thought about larger blocks with maybe a granny flat on the property for Keith and I, but it was always "in the future".

The boys particularly wanted to go to the Anzac Parade this year so I brought them back to stay with me for a few days and to give Samantha and Dan a bit of a break. After the Parade Alex and Carson said they would take them to see "Iron Man 3" to give Keith and I in turn, a welcome break. They stayed the five days then we drove back to Albany to swap the boys for the two girls, Holly and Sandra, as we were taking them with us to visit Brad and Anne in Jurien Bay. Then back to Albany to return them and spend my 65th birthday with Samantha and Brad. I was now officially a pensioner!

Before I left for Perth I had been looking through the real estate area of the local paper and spotted a lovely double storey house on an almost 3 acre property, with a granny flat there also. I was curious to see the property so showed it to Samantha and we decided that on the way back to Perth, and as it was "open for inspection" she would come with me to look at the house in a place called Elleker, just 14 kms outside of Albany on the Denmark road.

As we turned the corner into Wright Street, we spotted the house and loved it on sight. It sat amid a manicured lawn, surrounded by trees and open space and we could see what I assumed was the granny flat just behind it. We followed other people into the house, together with the children, and it felt so roomy and "right". The children ran up the stairs and found there were two bedrooms, a common area and another huge room – ideal for three little boys to share. Downstairs consisted of a theatre room, large family/dining area and country kitchen, office, laundry and three other bedrooms – six bedrooms in all. It was perfect for Samantha and Dan. We spent some time looking around the house, with Samantha getting ever more excited by the place. Almost as an afterthought, we went to look at the granny flat and were brought down to earth with a wump! My immediate reaction was "oh what a hovel"! It had what I thought was a grey concrete floor, but later found out was grey coloured lino. The kitchen was old and there were 2 minute bedrooms, only one of which was a separate room, the other was a partitioned off room from the main living area. Such was our enchantment about the big house, however, that I just thought "well, this can be renovated" and we quickly returned to the other house. There was a lot of interest in the property and we hardly dared hope that we might be able to get it. I went on up to Perth and Samantha returned to her place full of hopes to get the house. I told Keith about it when I got home and we called Samantha and Dan later that night. They had decided to put in an offer on the property. They found out when they did, that there had also been another offer on the property, but this offer was dependent upon the sale of their home whereas our offer was virtually a cash offer with finance. Our offer was accepted and Dan applied for finance and we worked out our side of the finances. By this time I was beginning to panic as we had since found out the only source of water to the property was a (very large) water tank; there was no mains water out there. There was, however, a very prolific bore with very good water, but still. Brad had his misgivings about the deal and had done some investigating of his own and found the land was good but, like me, was concerned about the water supply. There was also some confusion as to the status of the granny flat. The original owner had built the flat for his family to live in whilst he built the main house. It was then going to be the garage. He had got a temporary dwelling agreement from the Shire but this had since lapsed and it was now not considered suitable as a dwelling. There was, therefore, a lot of legal work to get through before the settlement could take place. The next couple of months were an emotional seesaw for us all; waiting for finance to be approved, waiting for the Shire to approve dwelling approval for the granny flat, and a few hiccoughs with the paperwork with spelling errors, etc.

I continued to travel back and forth to Albany, as there were problems with the childrens' health, en masse, and Dan was going away for work in the July so there was no way Samantha could cope with the children, and stay sane, by herself so I spent most of July in Albany. Alex, too, was having her fair share of health problems, as had been the case ever since she had her Glandular Fever all those years ago. Keith was beginning to become very tired with his work and the unsociable hours it entailed and was now seriously planning his retirement. He couldn't wait to get to Elleker, I was much more apprehensive. I've never been a country girl and living virtually in the country did not appeal to me very much and I still did not want to leave Alex, so between us July was not a particularly healthy month for any of us.

At the end of one of our multi colds I took myself off to the doctor because I had an irritating cough that would not go away. Whilst checking my throat the doctor noticed that the left side of my thyroid was swollen and she asked me how long I had had that swelling. It must have been there for ages as I had always been aware of it. She did not like it, however, and arranged for me to have an ultra sound, which subsequently disclosed that I had a very large node on the left side that needed to be investigated. So I was told to have a Fine Needle Biopsy (FNB) to ascertain whether or not the nodule was cancerous. Great! Not being a person who copes too well with any "medical procedure" at all this was not good news. So in the midst of waiting for settlement on the new house I was faced with this new stressor.

Settlement happened on the 29th August, so after weeks of cleaning and packing at their rental place, Samantha, Dan, Keith and I, together with a couple of Dan's work colleagues packed up a moving van and moved the Family von Kent out to Elleker. It was a relief to finally get them there, but there was still a lot of work to do unpacking and sorting out the absolute mountain of stuff accumulated by them over the years. The first night they stayed in the house there was a howling gale and noise in the upstairs area was so loud Jake came downstairs to sleep. I must admit I did sleep up there from time to time and it really is very loud. We still had to do the final clean-up of the rental house, before handing in the keys. Eventually, after an exhausting two weeks Keith and I returned to Perth, we hoped, for a well-earned rest. Because we knew we would have to sell the house, we moved some things down to "the hovel", including two of our cats, in order to start clearing the Perth house and prepare it for sale. I still had very mixed feelings about this but really we had no alternative, we were now in debt up to our neck in order to buy the Elleker property and we had to sell sooner or later. We hadn't been in the hovel a week when the hot water system packed up and we had to buy a new one. We also needed to buy a washing machine, but not a fridge, we used the little fridge from the Perth house as a stop gap in the hovel. We also discovered the transition from suburban living to urban was not without its problems when you have pets. Samantha and Dan had two small dogs and we had no gates. They were also very yappy dogs so anyone who had the audacity to walk past the gate would get an onslaught of dogs yapping at their heels, which of course was ultimately going to cause a problem. We tied them up. There was also the problem of the blending of two households of cats. Samantha and Dan had four and we had four – only two of which I brought with me. Another unforeseen problem was that of the bandicoots which inhabited our neighbour's property. Two of Samantha's cats were ardent hunters and we were always worried about their hunting and killing the bandicoots, which unfortunately they did from time to time. It was awful, they hunted birds, bandicoots and later on baby rabbits. Samantha tried to keep them in at night but when you have a household of children running in and out it is impossible to keep track of where your cats are! It became a nightmare for me. I felt so bad bringing all this destruction to the local wildlife.

This was not a good time for any of us, Alex's future was uncertain. She was talking of maybe spending some in the USA with her dancing, she had offers to move in with friends but this could not happen until November and in any case, she could not take her cat and dog with her. Her father said he might consider moving in with her but he couldn't do that until the New Year anyway. Alex and I felt like displaced persons. Keith was happy in Elleker. He had bought a ride on mower and was in his element sitting aboard mowing the vast lawns, but he was also pushing for Alex to pay rent in the Perth house, which I did not agree with as I had bought the house for her and me all those years ago, why should she pay rent to stay there?

In the midst of all this turmoil I was informed I had to have a Para thyroidectomy to remove the left side of my thyroid gland. The initial findings of the FNB had shown the nodule was benign, but the only way to be sure was to remove it and physically have it checked. It was also very large and in time would impinge on my windpipe and cause problems for my breathing. So in either case it had to go. I made an appointment to see an ENT surgeon recommended to me by my doctor, but by now my trips to Perth became an oasis away from the turmoil going on in Elleker, added to which we now had a cockerel as well as five chickens, two rats, and three budgies.

Because of everything that was going on between now and Christmas, when I spoke to my surgeon I asked her whether surgery could be postponed until the New Year and she said that should be okay, but if I felt any tightening in my breathing I was to let her know as soon as possible as things could get "very ugly" very quickly in these cases. So surgery was set for January 2014.

Alex went over to Melbourne for a competition at the end of October, so while she was away I "house-sat" my own house. Looking after my two remaining cats and Timmi. I was due to drive down to Albany again on the Tuesday, after she returned. When she came home she was happy but I could tell there was something on her mind. I had a job interview on the Wednesday, in Albany, but tried to change it so I could spend the extra day with Alex. I lost out on the job because they would not hold my interview time, but I found out that whilst in Melbourne this visit, she had met and "fallen for" another man – she was still going out with Carson, but I knew there had been problems for a while with them. As he lived on the Gold Coast, I knew at that moment I was going to lose her to the eastern states. Since her break up with Jessup I was aware she had not been happy with the dance scene in Perth, it was no longer a happy or challenging place for her, the only answer was to move over east and now, it appeared that place would be the Gold Coast. I was devastated. Once again I was losing another daughter to distant shores. Even before that she was flying out to the USA for a competition, on the 26th November and would be away for a few weeks.

October and early November were really difficult for Alex. Even though she did not wish to go out with Carson anymore, she still valued him highly as a dear friend and missed the fun they had, especially as her new love interest, Jed, was so far away. He was going to the USA competition as well but that was still a while away. There was also the fact that we had to break the news to Conrad that his only daughter was thinking of moving to Queensland next year, so all their plans of maybe moving in together would not now come to fruition. It was about this time, I started experiencing a few panic attacks. I think all the stress and upset of the preceding years, and particularly the new problems we seemed to be facing with the Kents, were catching up with me and I became a very anxious, unhappy person.

We were also in the throes of getting an architect draw up some renovation plans for the hovel, to ensure they would comply with the City of Albany's sometimes pedantic bylaws. Our architect, Roslyn, had drawn up plans to maximise the internal space we had because the City of Albany would not approve utilising more than 72sq m. of internal space for an unattached granny flat. So to overcome this, she had designed a front verandah which could be enclosed if we wanted it but it would not be deemed part of the internal structure.

In November the on-going dramas with our animals continued, with Samantha's three rabbits all dying within 3 days of each other from Calicivirus. It was awful. We were both upset and I took her into Albany to get away from the house and have a spot of lunch. Inevitably we went to the pet shop and bought two "boy" rabbits but said we would pick them up later that week after we had had a chance to disinfect the cage and arrange to have them immunised for the Calicivirus. Didn't want to go through that again. So a few days later, newly immunised bunnies, George and Wilbur, were installed in the cage. Later we fixed up a run for them outside.

Late in November I drove up to Perth again to house-sit whilst Alex was in the USA. She flew out on the 26th and I was staying in the house until she returned in December.

Whilst I was there Dan called to ask if I would pick up an 8-seater van he had bought, sight unseen, from John Hughes Motors. They drove up with Angela on the Wednesday, with Samantha driving as Dan had literally come home from nightshift and after changing they had jumped in the car and set off for Perth. They were also having a night out whilst they were here, so I looked after Angela in order for them to do that.

I was due to return to Albany on the 7th December but decided to stay up the extra day and go to Carols by Candlelight with Alex in the Ellenbrook Amphitheatre. I am glad I did as it proved to be the last time I could do that for a while.

It was about this time that our water tank ran out of water, so we had to change over to the bore. Ugh! The sulphur smell was awful. The water looked clear enough after a while and after the existing sludge had cleared but it smelled terrible. I am was now drinking from bottled water and even cleaning my teeth with bottled water poured into a cup. We knew that when we had the renovations done we were going to have to organise some sort of filtering system, as obviously the capacity of the water tank was not going to be enough to sustain the demands upon it.

We spent Christmas that year in Perth, as Alex was flying out to the Gold Coast for New Year. Brad, Anne and Sophie came down and Conrad came over. It was a lovely day and we called Samantha and Dan and they seemed to be having a good time. Sophie enjoyed the pool. Brad and Anne were cleaning up their house in Guildford, ready to sell it so we did some babysitting, and we were quite glad to leave the heat of Perth to return to Albany.

The year drew inexorably to an end and Wendy, friends of Samantha and Dan and we had a New Year BBQ. Just to mark the end of the year, Samantha and Dan's water heater died that day and we had to get an emergency plumber in to replace it. It was just fortunate it happened on the 31st, when the shops were still open and not on the public holiday on the 1st!

The first days of 2014 passed quietly enough. Alex had returned from the Gold Coast but was decidedly unforthcoming about her relationship with Jed.

The plans for the hovel renovation have gone into the City of Albany and we are hoping there won't be any more demands to comply with further, unforeseen bylaws. We have to get an extra leach drain put in for the septic tank so got quotes for those. The search for kitchen, bathroom and general plumbing fittings started in earnest. Picking colours for the walls, floorcoverings, and so on. I had forgotten this part of building or renovating houses. In the midst of all this was the usual turmoil of six children on school holidays and finding things for them to do and when Dan was sleeping, keeping them quiet! Samantha and I took them to the beach a few times and as many outings as we could afford, but generally, they seemed happy to stay around the house and computer.

Our Perth house officially went up for sale at the end of January and we opted to try auctioning it. The auction date was set for late March which would allow time for settlement. Alex was planning to move over to the Gold Coast in May, just after my birthday. I had five precious months with her and endeavoured to spend as much time as I could up in Perth. In the meantime of course, I had my thyroid operation to look forward to on the 29th January.

I duly booked into the hospital and the operation was done at about midday. I was expecting to feel sore and sorry when I woke up but I felt really quite good and despite Keith, Alex and Conrad calling in to see me I just kept falling asleep. I felt quite nauseated for a couple of days and was told this was probably the anaesthetic and because I could not take my tinnitus medication prior to the operation, my ear was really noisy. The main cause of my discomfort, I think was that the operation affected my Meniere's condition somewhat. I was in hospital in all three days. I had an appointment to see the surgeon in her rooms on the 6th February, so stayed on in Perth for a while. I couldn't have faced the trip back yet anyway. I called Samantha and Dan and the usual dramas were unfolding with the dogs being reported to the rangers and they had to pay a fine and re-licensed in three days. So nothing had changed.

My surgeon told me my nodule was benign and the operation had gone very well. I apparently had a lovely long neck to operate on and she could work really well. That was something I suppose.

For Alex's birthday we went out for a family dinner on the 7th and on the 8th we went to her favourite eatery, "Elixir" in Wanneroo for brunch with a bunch of her friends. She was then going out for the afternoon and evening with her friends.

The race to get the house ready for viewing was on in earnest now and we took a heap of stuff to the tip and arranged for some of our stuff to go into storage. We got a lot done, went back to Albany for the weekend but I had to return to Perth a few days later into the following week and I travelled up by bus and Keith stayed in Albany to help with some conflicting shifts between Samantha and Dan's job. I was also going to finish the packing up of stuff to go into storage at the end of the week. It was a difficult time as I ploughed through our belongings, which to keep, store, throw out?? Alex was also having to go through her stuff because most of her belongings were going into storage as she couldn't take them with her to the Gold Coast.

The real estate agent, Matt, came on the Monday with a photographer to take photos and make a video of the property, ready to put on the net. We were very pleased with the photos and video, and our property appeared very appealing.

I was very torn between Samantha and Alex at this time. The stress of the ongoing dramas in Albany were taking their toll on Samantha but I had to be in Perth to keep it ready for inspections and home opens. One surprise, however, "George" the rabbit turned out to be "Georgina" and she had given birth to five babies. She must have given birth to them at least three or four weeks ago, judging by their size. Our menagerie was growing!

Alex and I made the most of our time together by going out for a brunch whenever she had a day off from work. The house actually looked really good with the minimalist effect, and we had quite a few people through looking at it. Each time I returned to our hovel in Elleker the oldness, dust and spider webs seemed even more noticeable because I had left a spotless house back in Perth. In my absence Keith had bought electronic collars for Samantha and Dan's dogs and they had laid out the electronic barrier. Felt cruel training the dogs, as we had to let them get 'zapped' to feel the consequences of going over the line. However, they seem to be learning rather quickly, thank goodness. We also started losing our baby bunnies. They had got large enough to climb and were climbing through the wire and the cats were waiting for them. The only baby left was one who was born with a slightly crooked leg and so could not climb. This ultimately straightened out, but at the time it was what saved it from the same fate as its siblings. By this time, Georgina had had another litter of babies, so we got Wilbur fixed to avoid any more litters.

Alex had applied to transfer her job from WA to the Gold Coast and was told she had been given a job in the Surfers' Paradise branch of Flight Centre.

So, she had a job and somewhere to live. Everything was falling into place for her. My dread at our parting was growing. All the travelling to and fro to Albany was also having its toll on my back and thighs, so I had to go to a physio to get those problems sorted. However, things were progressing well and we had chosen our builder, Warren Bennett, to do our renovations. I also discovered that my painful back was actually shingles! All the stress of the past couple of years was manifesting itself physically in me now.

About this time, we were discussing where we were going to live whilst the renovations were taking place. We toyed with buying a caravan but discounted that for the sheer inconvenience of having to go into Samantha and Dan's house to the toilet during the night. So then we decided we would live off site, by renting.

It was also getting close to auction day, on the 29th March. We were disappointed to hear from Matt that we only had one registered bidder for the auction. The day of the auction dawned and there were a lot of people there but a few were our family, giving moral support, and curious neighbours. No one bid! It was so embarrassing. The one bidder we had registered didn't front up. The only light on the horizon was that we had received an offer prior to the auction but it was too low, and this person turned up to the auction and afterwards, negotiated with Matt to buy the house. Not quite as much as we were hoping to get but at least we had sold the house to someone who had finance all lined up. After all the build up of the past couple of months, we all felt very deflated for the rest of the weekend.

Brad and Anne were also pretty stressed at this time, as their house in Guildford had not sold and Brad was having to keep driving back and forth from Jurien to do maintenance work on it.

Having sold the house we drove back to Albany with the last of our cats, Pippa. We now had all four cats living with us in the hovel. I have to admit to wondering a few times as to whether we had made the right decision in buying an urban property that had to be renovated, but there really wasn't a lot of choice in the matter. We continued to find the various items needed for the house and the renovations were due to begin in May so we started looking in earnest for somewhere to rent. We had been told that the Visitors' Tourist Centre dealt with short term accommodation, so we went in to see them and were told about a unit in Middleton Road which was available for the time we wanted it and what was more, the owners were quite happy for us to take the dog. We had would have Minkie staying with us because Alex couldn't take him with her straight away to the Gold Coast.

Every parent, with a part of themselves, wants their child to strike out confidently on their own but not too far away! Keith and I broke our hearts when Brad, our youngest decided to go jackerooing up North – hundreds of kms away. Then another heart rending time when we lost Samantha to the USA, thousands of kms away. Now Alex my 'youngest cub' was leaving and I had been dreading it for months, probably years, because I knew her future did not lie in Perth.

We had planned to have a family farewell dinner combined with my birthday on the 9th May and she was flying out in the early hours of the 10th. When we got back from the dinner, which was a bitter/sweet occasion, it was not really worth going to bed as we had to be up by 5.00am to get to the airport. Alex and I just cuddled in my bed until it was time to get up and wake the others. It was terribly hard on all of us, not least of all Alex, she had to leave her dog and everything familiar to start afresh, even though she had good friends and a special love interest to go to, she still was taking a huge step. Saying goodbye to her at the airport, was just awful. Even now the memory of it evokes tears. I was a basket case when we got home, and oh so thankful that Samantha and Brad were still around to give hugs. The unlikely saving grace to this weekend was the fact that we had to get everything ready and packed for the removalists on the Monday so the weekend was fraught with activity into which I threw myself in an effort not to think about Alex.

By the time Keith had departed for Albany with a trailer load of items, then the removalists had gone first to the storage unit to drop off stuff there and then on down to Albany, Samantha and I were left with still an unbelievable amount of stuff to sort through, pack and throw out. We finished up with at least five garbage bags of rubbish, some of which we managed to deposit around Ellenbrook bins, but we still had to leave a note of apology to the next owner asking him to put a couple of bags out for the rubbish the following week. We worked solidly all day and it became apparent that it would be most unwise to try and drive down to Albany on the Monday night. So Samantha and I decided to book into the Pioneer Motel at the base of Bedfordale Hill ready for an early start down the Albany Highway the next day.

We had a really nice double room and a great meal at the adjoining restaurant and relaxed for the first time in months. The evening was an oasis of peace amid the turmoil of the last few days. Even the journey from Ellenbrook to Armadale had been unbelievable. We had so much stuff packed into the back of Samantha's car – not the least of which was a huge teddy bear belonging to Alex, which Samantha refused to leave behind, but jammed it in the back seat and packed things around it. The front passenger foot well was chokabloc so I sat hunched with my feet placed wherever we could find room.

I dragged myself through the next few months, putting my sadness to the back of my mind as much as I could, but sometimes it would well up and I would be unable to do anything but cry. Fortunately, we were busy with doing things to help the renovations on the hovel, which were going really well to plan. Each night we had to come over to Elleker to feed our cats, who had been removed – with great difficulty – from the hovel and based in the large shed on the property. We could not take them to our rental accommodation, and having them looked after would have been too expensive besides, four months is a long time to be in cat cages, no matter how good the facilities.

The previous year Alex had reminded us that we had always said we would like to have a river cruise along the Rhein and Danube. So she booked it for us and this trip was looming up at the end of September. The race would be on to be back in the hovel before we were due to fly out on the 24th. As it happened we were able to move into our brand new (on the inside anyway) home the weekend before we were due to leave for Perth and our flight. During our stay at Middleton Road I experienced my first vertigo attack in nearly eighteen months. It was a real jar to my confidence as with the trip looming up I was afraid the whole, awful situation with Meniere's was starting again. Fortunately, it calmed down but I was still very aware, once again, of what I was eating as my diet was definitely something that contributed to attacks.

Alex had done a great job organising the trip even the start was a chauffeur–driven limousine to the airport. We were flying out to Amsterdam, staying overnight there before joining the cruise the next day.

When I look back on the trip the first thing that springs to mind is our experience with cyclists when we stepped outside of our hotel in Amsterdam for the first time. We were practically run over. In Europe bicycles are hugely used for transport. They even have their own lane. So pedestrians have to keep well over to the side as the cyclists have right of way. You have to be on the watch for traffic coming at you from a different side of the road, cyclists, scooters and the fact no one seems to obey the traffic lights. I nearly got wiped off by a tram which trundled through our crosswalk whilst the "pedestrian walk" green light was on.

We were only in Amsterdam for a short while admittedly, but my impressions of the place weren't particularly good, it seemed quite grubby with rubbish in the canals and on the streets. One funny incident springs to mind, we had gone over to the local Pancake Haus to have breakfast and as is our custom I asked for my decaf cappuccino coffee and Keith asked for a "flat white" (coffee). I got my cup of coffee but Keith got a bottle of plain water! After much confusion we managed to explain to an English-speaking waitress, that he wanted a flat white coffee. Over there, they serve flat water (or "Wasser") and sparkling water and they thought he wanted a flat water. We knew to be specific next time.

In retrospect I think we would have been better arranging the trip to go straight to our cruise ship, but the idea of an overnight rest was good in principle, but not as it turned out in practise. So we were glad to be picked up the next day and taken to the ship.

We were cruising on the MS Amalyra cruise ship. This was one of her last cruises before going into dry dock for refurbishments. She looked, however, really nice and we were pleasantly surprised by our cabin. It was a little smaller than we expected and our "balcony" was only six inches wide, but the rest of it was great! We had a welcome aboard bottle of champagne in our cabin and felt very much at home straight away.

Most of the passengers were middle age or older, with a spattering of younger people on board. The ship's crew could not have been more helpful, going out of their way to make the trip as pleasant and enjoyable as possible.

We travelled through several countries on our journey, Holland, Germany, Austria, Czech Republic and finishing in Hungary. The scenery along the Rhein and Danube was breathtaking with the colourful little towns dotted along the waterway, the mountains in the background and so many castles perched on the top of these mountains. I was glad I was not traversing the roads leading up to these structures, they were so steep. The lock system, in itself was very interesting as we travelled up the Rhein and then ultimately down the Danube, our ship would enter a lock, with very little room to spare as it 11.5m wide and the locks were 12m wide! (That's why we had six inch balconies), then come out the other side 12m higher than we went in whilst on the Rhein and 12m lower on the Danube. The meals were top class, with the chef interacting with the guests every night after the meal to ensure we were very happy with what was served. We always were.

The only unfortunate occurrence of the cruise was that several passengers, Keith included, became unwell with a flu like virus which laid them, and him, low for a few days so he missed out on a couple of the tours we had booked because he was just too tired to go. I managed to get to see everything, and fortunately he rallied enough to take the Vienna tour towards the end of the trip. We had uncharacteristically good, dry weather, which the Cruise Manager remarked on daily.

The last part of our cruise was in Budapest where I ran around buying my presents to take home. I had picked up some nic nacs on our tours but wanted to finalise a few things there. The last night of the cruise was magical as we had a farewell dinner followed by a night cruise up and back in the harbour. The lights of Budapest on both sides of the river were beautiful with buildings outlined in many coloured lights.

After we disembarked we stayed overnight again, in Budapest. This time we were not particularly impressed by the hotel accommodation, however, and the overwhelming feeling in Hungary – Budapest is still one of them getting out from under the communist regime they had for many years. Salaries were low and rentals high, the only thing going for them was that health, education and university courses were free. Just as well because generally people would not have been able to afford anything otherwise. I also discovered that black tea was still relatively unobtainable in the hotels. There were endless choices of herbal teas, and coffee sachets but ordinary tea, apart from Earl Grey, was not available. I discovered this when I asked reception for some ordinary teabags and she said she would try and get some! She then called back later to say they did not have any other tea but Earl Grey. Whilst later perusing the shelves of a grocery store I saw a box of Lipton's tea underneath a sign saying "New!! Just imported!! Lipton's tea". Now it all made sense.

We flew back to Australia on the 11th October having been away 17 days in all. We had enjoyed the experience but were glad to be heading home. If I was to do something like that again I think I would rather go with a readymade group of friends with whom to share the whole experience as at times, I felt a little lonely during the trip, particularly when Keith did not feel like doing anything. We enjoyed the company of several different people whilst on board, some from Perth, Melbourne and New Zealand. Most of them seemed to have joined the cruise in Paris a few days earlier, flying from there to join the ship in Amsterdam.

It was good to see everyone again. We were also pleased to hear Brad had decided to come down with Sophie to visit for a few days the following week. We continued to settle into the (new) hovel, with sojourns down to our large shed to pick out things to put into the house. Most of our smaller belongings, ornaments, etc were in storage in Perth but we had quite a bit in the shed, too much in fact because we were trying to fit in stuff that had been in a three bedroomed, larger house into a two bedroom granny flat! It took a while for Keith to get over his virus from the ship and in the end he had to go and get an antibiotic to fully clear his chest.

I now began to think about what I was going to do with my time, as up until this point, apart from time out for sickness (and redundancy) I had worked all my life and had no hobbies I could now follow. The Meniere's had left me with an inability to turn quickly, so a dance group was out. My thyroid gland had affected my voice to the extent that singing now was a very hit and miss activity, so a choir was out. I continued to just help out Samantha with the children and get my house in order and do my one day at Snowball auctions, during the months running up to Christmas. Alex was coming over for Christmas, thank goodness.

Prior to leaving for our cruise I had applied for a one day a week job, working at the local auction house, Snowballs. I had only gone in to train a couple of days prior to leaving for our cruise. I had applied for the position just before I left to go over and see Alex at the end of August. I was notified while I was in Queensland that I had got the job, so one day a week was taken care of at least!

My visit to Alex was really wonderful. She had organised a river dinner cruise on the Brisbane river paddle steamer, on the Saturday after I arrived and a visit to Mt Tamborine, for a fossick around up there, followed by going to her church on the Sunday. I can honestly say my time spent with her over the following week, both on the Gold Coast and later in Hobart, visiting Michael, were the happiest in years. I loved being with her, spending time with her and meeting her lovely friends, including Jed and his family. The townhouse she shared with Emily and another girl, who was away whilst I was visiting, was lovely and it was great to see Timmi, the cat, again. But like all good things they had to come to an end and once again I had to say goodbye to my girl and tearfully return to WA. The only bright thing on the horizon for me was at least I knew I would see her again in December for Christmas, however briefly, at least I would see her.

Sophie and Brad duly arrived and after an initial shyness on Sophie's part she was soon running around with her cousins and in particular Angela because they were much the same age. We took a few excursions out together but Sophie only really wanted to play with her cousins. They were only here about three or four days but it was lovely to see Sophie interacting with her cousins and once again I wished Brad and Anne lived closer.

I was very busy on the one day I was working at the auction house. It was nonstop from the time we got there until we left after 5.30. I experienced a few dizzy spells whilst at work but most I managed to curtail with my pills. There was one, however, which was really bad. I had gone to work that day with a very blocked left ear and did not realise how much this would impact on my Meniere's. I was okay right up until I walked up to the bank with the day's takings, but began to feel that awful familiar start to an attack and I prayed I would get back to the shop okay. I staggered down York Street, as close to the wall as I could for fear of falling. I must have looked drunk to passers-by. Crossing the road twice was really dangerous as I could not walk steadily at all and was afraid to turn my head to check for cars. Eventually, I got back to the auction house and proceeded to be violently sick in the toilets. It was so humiliating. There were customers in the shop at the time and I had to reel past them to escape to the toilet in time. Keith had to come and get me, leaving my car there to pick up the next day. Looking back, I know now it was at this point that my enjoyment of the job started to wane. The busyness I loved but I felt unreliable to myself and to my employer, added to which I was having trouble understanding the system with the limited time I had trained prior to starting.

I started knitting again. Two years ago I had started knitting a cardigan but had become so busy with the move and everything else that was happening, that I left it unfinished so I decided to finish the garment. I am not sure what happened, usually I knit really well. This time, however, when I started to sew it together I realised something was not right! The sleeves hung over the end of my hands by about 3 inches and the neckband was long on one side and short on the other. The sleeves did not quite fit into the appropriate place and the overall finish to the item was one that would grace the body of the hunchback of Notre Dame! I looked at myself in the mirror and laughed and laughed. I wish now I had gone over to Samantha's place that night and shown her my "cardigan" we would both have laughed ourselves silly instead of just me. The next day I took my creation to the Good Samaritan bins in the hope that whoever emptied them would look at my creation and have as good a laugh as I had.

I continued to have dizzy spells, which I found rather surprising as the whole time I was away I had not had any. It would not be until a lot later that I realised the only difference between the two occasions was, apart from being more relaxed of course, that I was having decaffeinated coffee all the time whilst away, but when I came home I had reverted back to having my mixed coffees with Keith, so I later realised that I could only afford to let myself have one coffee per day which had proper coffee in it and the rest had to be decaffeinated.

The months until Christmas went quite quickly thank goodness as we were all looking forward to seeing Alex again. She returned from the USA very pleased with her personal performance but also for the rest of the group, who had also done really well over there. We went to Sandra's Graduation from primary school and once again I was reminded of our own experiences with our three which evoked nostalgic memories of happier times.

We had a busy run up to Christmas and it was going to be a busy Christmas/ New Year break because my brother's stepsons, Ashley and Matthew plus a friend were coming down to visit and so were Brad and Anne, but not until the 27th, so unless Brad and Anne got here early they would miss Alex as she was leaving for

Perth to spend a couple of days with Conrad on the 27th. She did, however, catch up with Ashley and Matthew in Perth for a few hours.

Alex duly arrived in Albany on the 24th. I paid her fare to fly from Perth as it would have taken precious hours out of her visit to drive down. As soon as she hit Perth her hay fever erupted again, she'd always suffered badly with hay fever, even for the first couple of months living in Queensland. Wendy came over for Christmas lunch and the atmosphere was its usual chaos with paper flying everywhere and new toys being tried and played with. Dan and Keith mainly did the cooking, they were in their element. Since moving down to Albany Keith had virtually taken over the cooking and was discovering that he really enjoyed it. All too soon, however, it was time to take Alex to the airport to return to Perth. Such a short but sweet time with her, but she had to spend time with her father and his family too, one of the downsides of living so far away from the rest of the family, you lose a whole day virtually just travelling.

It was great to see Ashley and Matt and their friend Roberta when they came. They have turned into such great lads. They have done a load of travelling, but sadly never see their mother and of course never my brother. Indeed I had not seen nor heard from him for nearly ten years.

Samantha, Brad, Dan and Anne all went out on the 27th to celebrate Samantha and Dan's 20 years of marriage. I was glad they were all together as Brad and Dan get on very well and they had a great evening together. Brad and Anne stayed a further day then left to return to Perth then ultimately Jurien Bay.

So, 2014 trickled to a halt and I pondered over the past few years, with happenings both good and bad. Health had been a battle, settling into rural living and adjusting to living somewhere completely different had been a battle and of course, Alex leaving home for the first time had been heart breaking. Now, however, I had to start putting together a new life with new activities and goals and hopefully better health. A tale of three lives? I wonder?